Kiplinger's
Practical
Guide to
Investing

Kiplinger's
Practical
Guide to
Investing

HOW TO MAKE MONEY WITH
✦ STOCKS   ✦ BONDS
✦ MUTUAL FUNDS   ✦ REAL ESTATE

TED MILLER
Editor, *Kiplinger's Personal Finance Magazine*

KIPLINGER BOOKS
Washington, D.C.

Published by
The Kiplinger Washington Editors, Inc.
1729 H Street, N.W.
Washington, DC 20006

Kiplinger publishes books and videos on a wide variety of personal-finance and business- management subjects. Check our Web site (www.kiplinger.com) for a complete list of titles, additional information and excerpts. Or write:
Cindy Greene
Kiplinger Books & Tapes
1729 H Street, N.W.
Washington, DC 20006
email: cgreene@kiplinger.com
To order, call 800-280-7165; for information about volume discounts, call 202-887-6431.

Library of Congress Cataloging-in-Publication Data

Kiplinger's practical guide to investing: how to make money with stocks, bonds, mutual funds, real estate / Ted Miller.-- 1st ed.
    p. cm.
Includes index.
ISBN 0-93872-168-2 (hardcover)
    1. Investments. 2. Finance, Personal. I. Title: Practical guide to investing. II. Miller, Ted.

HG4521 .K48 1999
332.6--dc21

99-046710

This publication is intended to provide guidance in regard to the subject matter covered. It is sold with the understanding that the author and publisher are not herein engaged in rendering legal, accounting, tax or other professional services. If such services are required, professional assistance should be sought.

First edition. Printed in the United States of America.
9 8 7 6 5 4 3 2 1

Acknowledgments

HE ADVICE IN THIS BOOK DID NOT SPRING SPONTA-
neously from the mind of its author, nor is it
based entirely on the author's own experience. It is, at its core, the result of the professional and personal intelligence-gathering and reporting of
writers and editors throughout the history of the Kiplinger
organization, which has been explaining the workings of the
investment markets to readers for most of the past 100 years.
These have been years of booms and busts, of scams and
scoundrels, of gimmicky promotions and genuine innova-
tions. The financial journalists at Kiplinger make their living
by sorting though these things and separating what works
from what doesn't. I have had the privilege of synthesizing
their observations and advice in this book. If there is any wisdom here, it is theirs, not mine.

 I gladly cite the contributions of the many people now on
the staff of *Kiplinger's Personal Finance Magazine,* with a grateful
nod to those too numerous to mention who have served the
magazine so well in the past. Of the current staff, none has
been more supportive of this project than Knight Kiplinger,
the magazine's publisher and editor-in-chief. In addition, he
contributed more than a few ideas for the book. Kevin
McCormally, executive editor of the magazine, bird-dogged
every tax fact in this book and wrote Chapter 12 himself. The
people responsible for most of the magazine's investment coverage of course did most to develop the advice reflected in
these pages. My thanks to Fred Frailey, Manuel Schiffres,
Steven Goldberg and Robert Frick. I also thank the other writers and editors who contribute so much to *Kiplinger's* magazine

and thus to any book that grows from it. They are Janet Bodnar, Jane Bennett Clark, Kristin Davis, Mary Beth Franklin, Ed Henry, Brian Knestout, Kimberly Lankford, Rosemary Beales Neff, Elizabeth Razzi, Ronaleen Roha, Catherine Siskos, Mark Solheim, Melynda Dovel Wilcox. Thanks also to Magali Rheault, who runs our research operation, and to Barbara Hoch Marcus, the magazine's chief copy editor, and to each and every member of their staffs. Accuracy and fairness are their benchmarks, and they keep us focused on them.

How to turn all the knowledge and energy of these people into a book? By following the lead of my editor, Patricia Mertz Esswein. Her professional calm and deft editorial touch kept a potentially unwieldy project on target and on time. Her organizational and editorial skills are considerable. Without them, this book could not have happened.

I am also grateful to Norma Shaw, who paved the way for the author in virtually every single chapter, relying on her own financial training and expertise to dig up the facts and make the preliminary judgments needed to cover the subjects at hand. Her contribution was crucial.

Many thanks to Priscilla Taylor, a first-rate copy editor, who, with the assistance of Allison Leopold, ensured that the text was as clear and easy to follow as possible.

Books done right can be beautiful physical objects, and I believe this one qualifies. That's thanks to Daniel Kohan, who designed the cover, and to Heather Waugh, who created the handsome and very readable pages.

My sincere thinks to all these people for their contributions to this book, and also to my wife, Carolyn Clark Miller, whose support and encouragement was so willingly given.

Contents

Introduction

HAT'S YOUR FINANCIAL DREAM? THE FINEST college and graduate education for your children? A business of your own? A retirement of unusual ease and fullness, free of financial worries? Accumulating enough wealth to make generous gifts to your favorite charities? Whatever your financial goals, you won't achieve them by accident. All will require planning—and the implementation of the plan through skilled investing.

It's the unusual person who loves investing as a hobby—the process of selecting investments, following their progress, changing them as needed. To most of us, investing is simply a means to an end, the way to accomplish our goals. But whether you're an avid money manager or a more passive investor, you've got to have enough knowledge of successful investment techniques to stay on course and keep out of trouble. That's how this book will help you.

At the beginning of the '90s, America was wracked with doubts about its economic prowess, and many small investors were nervous, too. The U.S. was just coming out of its first national recession since 1982, and several regions, including the Northeast and California, were still mired in recession. Real estate, a hot investment in the '80s, was falling in value in many areas. Stock investors, sobered by the Crash of '87, were hit again by a bear market in 1990. Some economic forecasters said the U.S. was in for a tough decade of lackluster growth and waning influence in the world economy, with only modest gains for investors in American companies.

They were wrong, and we at Kiplinger foretold it, disagreeing with their gloomy forecasts. We believed that America's best days were not behind us. From the pain and anxiety of corporate restructuring, technological productivity gains and global competition would come stronger, smarter American competitors in the world economy. And for the individual investor there would still be time to accumulate substantial wealth. After a rocky start, the '90s have proved to be just that—a decade of solid growth, filled with great opportunities for the savvy investor. And we believe that there's plenty of dynamic growth still ahead, as the U.S. enters a new century.

We at Kiplinger have been providing personal-finance advice and business forecasting information to our readers for more than 70 years, through years of modest growth and booms, recessions and depression. And through it all, those who have followed our advice have prospered.

We don't offer fast ways to vast riches, or secrets only we know. Quite the opposite. The Kiplinger way to wealth comes not from get-rich-quick schemes, playing the markets or speculating for fast profits. It consists instead of participating in the steady, long-term growth of carefully selected assets.

When it comes to smart investing, there's really nothing new under the sun. The fundamental key to creating wealth—buying a broad mix of quality assets and giving them time to grow—has never changed.

But some things have changed—and changed radically—in the past few decades. For one thing, there has been an explosion in the sheer number and kinds of assets that are readily available for the average investor to consider. There are vastly more small-company stocks, mutual funds, real estate trusts and even "securitized debts": mortgages, consumer installment loans, and short-term corporate debts that are bundled together to be bought and sold like bonds.

One of the best illustrations of this proliferation of investment choices is the mutual fund industry. In 1950 there were fewer than 100 funds selling shares to the public; today investors have more than 7,000 stock and bond funds to choose from.

Another big change in the investment climate has been the very pace of change itself. The fortunes of even the most solid companies can shift fundamentally in a short time. The rapidity of technological change has shortened the life cycle of high-tech products, making yesterday's leading-edge design tomorrow's unwanted dog.

Still another challenge comes from the globalization of business. While this adds new dimensions for investment opportunity, it also means that tough competition can come out of left field with little warning, not to mention the risk of changes in currency valuation, international trade laws, government regulation, and so on.

For decades we at Kiplinger have been tracking these changes—in fact, anticipating most of them—in the pages of our weekly *Kiplinger Washington Letter* and our monthly *Kiplinger's Personal Finance Magazine*. This book was written by the *Magazine's* editor, Ted Miller, to help you be a smart investor. It is designed to enable you to sort through these choices and understand the investment environment, so you can make intelligent decisions and be prepared to act when necessary to enhance your financial well-being—or to protect it.

But being prepared to act is not the same as being compelled to act. More often than not, what looks like a significant development really isn't, and it doesn't warrant a shift in investment strategy. The smart investor is not a financial dervish, responding frantically to the daily headlines. The hallmarks of competent investing are patience, informed calmness and skepticism of fad and fashion.

Smart investing does not involve lots of transactional activity—trading actively (or even everyday, all day, as in the phenomenon of day trading), selling short, switching frequently among mutual funds, using exotic hedging techniques. In fact, this kind of approach is pseudo-sophistication, at least as practiced by most individual investors. The truly smart investors, whatever their income, occupation and investment experience, are the ones who calmly make a plan, select the right investments to implement that plan and give it time to work. (Of course, some active traders make good money, but only those who are willing to make an enormous commitment to the daily tracking of all their investments. Most people are unwilling to do this, preoccupied as they are with family, career and hobbies.)

This book will help you make and implement your plan, whatever your investment goals. With it at your side, you'll be ready for the year 2000 and beyond—an exciting time for the investor, full of pitfalls for the impetuous and opportunities for the well informed. There will be substantial growth in the world economy, as trade barriers decline and nations jockey for position in emerging industries. The United States, as the world's most open economy and biggest exporter—open to foreign capital, immigration and products—will benefit enormously from the growing openness of other nations.

The self-education of the individual investor is a never-ending journey. We look forward to helping you along the way.

KNIGHT A. KIPLINGER
Editor, *The Kiplinger Letters*
Editor in Chief, *Kiplinger's Personal Finance Magazine*
Washington, D.C.

Kiplinger's Practical Guide to Investing

PART ONE

Get Ready

CHAPTER 1

Investing in the 21st Century

T THE DAWN OF THE 21ST CENTURY, WE CAN SAY with no danger of exaggeration that we are living at a time when more wealth is being created for more people than ever before in the history of the earth. There have been other great wealth-building eras in American history, but when Rockefeller, Carnegie and others grew rich a hundred years ago or so, there were no stock-option plans for the midlevel managers of Standard Oil Company, no profit-sharing plans for the furnace stokers at the Carnegie Steel Company in Pittsburgh. Today such corporate share-the-wealth arrangements are commonplace, to say nothing of tax-favored wealth-building mechanisms like 401(k) plans and individual retirement accounts. The computer empowers us with investment information, timely advice and instant execution once available only to well-moneyed customers of the toniest brokerage houses. It would be impossible to overstate the significance of this great democratization of wealth-building opportunity. What's more, the spread of market-based economies is taking the same kind of opportunities to virtually all parts of the world.

This book is full of ideas for finding investments that will help you build your own wealth. But when you invest money in a company, you're casting a vote of confidence not only in the prospects for the company itself, but also in the prospects for the economy in which it must sell its products or services. This chapter will attempt to describe why the American economy—and the global economy—of the early 21st century deserves that confidence, and why now, even after years of strong gains in both our stock market and economy, we still have a long way to go.

Let's begin with the unarguable. Surely everyone would agree on three overriding and inescapable facts about the current state of the world's economy and America's place in it:

FIRST, THE GLOBAL ECONOMY HAS CLEARLY ARRIVED. It is not on the horizon; it is already here. The U.S. economy depends on it: Exports account for 12% of our economy and imports account for another 13%. That means that one-fourth of America's economy—and all the incomes and jobs that go with it—depends on world trade. To put a dollar sign on it: That's more than $2 trillion in imports and exports of goods and services, with 12 million American jobs linked directly to American exports. On the other side of the coin, imports can sometimes cost jobs. But no nation can merely export and allow no imports. In the global economy, the competitor six time zones away is potentially as serious a threat as the competitor six blocks away, and the customer on the other side of the world often looms as large in a company's marketing plans as the customer around the corner from corporate headquarters. This is what high-speed communication and transportation have done to the world's commerce, and there's no turning back.

SECOND, THE U.S. WILL PROSPER IN THE YEARS AHEAD IF IT COMPETES SUCCESSFULLY IN THE GLOBAL ECONOMY. This is so obvious that it seems almost pointless to state it. Whether it's banks or burritos, chemicals or cosmetics, cars or computers, televisions or tractors, the companies that can do the job faster, cheaper and better will take markets away from those who lag, and national borders aren't going to stop them.

THIRD, THE U.S. IS SUPERBLY WELL-EQUIPPED TO COMPETE IN THE GLOBAL ECONOMY. Many Americans entered the last decade of the 1900s unsure of this, but as we enter the first decade of the 2000s, few doubt it anymore.

Global, Global, Toil and Trouble?

THE EFFECT OF THE GLOBAL ECONOMY HARDLY NEEDS DOCU-mentation for anyone who can read the nameplates on the cars on our highways and on the VCRs in our living rooms. In other nations, you can't miss the growing number of McDonald's outlets, Coca-Cola cans, IBM and Compaq computers—not to mention American movies and television shows dubbed or subtitled in the local language. And this con-sumer's-eye view of things is just the tip of the iceberg. The list of generic products traded around the world is almost end-less—electrical parts, plywood, finished metal shapes, fish, corn, pharmaceuticals, plastic materials, industrial machinery, newsprint—forming a vast commercial chain among nations that none wants or can afford to break. International trade has been a major factor in the growth of the world's economies for the past 50 years, and especially in the past 20 years.

The world economy of the future will increasingly come to be dominated by so-called transnational corporations. A trans-national combines several multinational firms from various coun-tries into one huge corporation. You can see this happening in automobiles—Daimler-Benz and Chrysler have become DaimlerChrysler—and in pharmaceuticals, where America's Upjohn has joined forces with Sweden's Pharmacia as Pharmacia & Upjohn. It's also happening in banking, with Deutsche Bank and Bankers Trust merging into a global powerhouse that oper-ates far beyond the borders of their native countries. The role of many small and medium-size enterprises will be to supply the multinationals with ideas, inventions, technology, raw materials, parts and business services.

As the world's largest economy, the U.S. stands at the center of all this and has much to gain from it. With less than 5% of the world's population, the U.S. accounts for 22% of its economic output. That share will almost certainly shrink in the new cen-tury. We will have a smaller share of a larger global pie, but at the same time, Americans' personal incomes will keep rising and our living standards will continue to improve. We will remain the world's largest economy for at least the next couple of decades or so. China, whose embryonic market economy could grow at a much faster rate than ours, may eventually overtake us in terms of total output. But person for person, we will remain the world's richest, most productive nation.

Meanwhile, new markets will be created around the world, driven by the spread of technology. Technology will help to boost the productivity of the world's labor force and that in turn will boost workers' incomes enabling hundreds of millions more people to afford more of the goods and services produced by their own economies and by the economies of other nations, including ours.

The global boom will be driven in part by global politics—specifically, the irresistible lure of economic development and untapped consumer markets. This lure is lowering trade barriers around the world—not always as fast as we'd like, not always with the kind of reciprocity we'd like, but it's happening. As trade barriers continue to decline, products will flow more freely across national borders.

The march to worldwide prosperity will not be uninterrupted. The laws of the business cycle haven't been repealed, either in the U.S. or the rest of the world. There will be recessions. But in general, globalization of trade will be a positive force for shorter, milder recessions because it will be harder for imbalances to develop and grow without someone somewhere spotting the situation and, by moving to take advantage of it, sparking the very changes needed to correct it.

The main beneficiary of globalization so far has been the U.S. As the 21st century arrives, nations and regions that account for more than a third of total global production—Japan, South Korea, Southeast Asia, Russia and parts of Latin America—are fighting their way out of recessions. They will be major beneficiaries of the world boom ahead, along with less-advanced nations, whose people account for 85% of world population but only 20% of world output. Their share will probably double in the next two decades.

America's Special Strengths

AFTER PROSPERING SO WELL FOR SO LONG, IS THERE ENOUGH life left in the U.S. economy? The answer is yes. Together with the streamlining of American business that has been taking place over the past couple of decades and noticed only recently, demographic forces will constitute a powerful and positive influence on the American economy well into the 21st century.

HOORAY FOR MIDDLE-AGED BOOMERS

Baby-boomers by the millions are arriving at middle age. They may not like the idea very much, but business economists are absolutely wild about it. The effects of the aging of this gigantic segment of the population can be expected to reverberate for the good throughout our economy for years to come. You'd have to assume a sea change in Americans' spending and saving habits to conclude otherwise.

Consider the stages of a person's economic life. In the early years you're completely dependent on your parents for support, a stage that ends when you finish school and start supporting yourself. You don't make much money at first, so you tend to spend it all on rent, car payments, food and clothes, probably relying on a lot of credit to get you through. As you move into your thirties, you're still in what might be called the acquisition phase of your life. Somehow all the money gets spent. Statistics say that you've gotten married along the way and it takes the income of both you and your spouse just to keep the household running. You're doing a lot of spending supported by a lot of borrowing. Multiply yourself by about 70 million and you'll have a pretty good idea of what was happening to the American economy for much of the past three decades.

Now, as you approach your mid to late thirties and contemplate your forties, your priorities begin to change. You're further along in your career and making more money, but the demands on it are different. You've become a parent, and as the kids grow, the reality of college expenses looms. The thought of retiring someday takes on real meaning. As a result, you look for ways to save and invest the money you once spent without a second thought. You have entered the nest-egg–building years.

Multiply yourself by about 70 million and you'll have a pretty good idea of what will be going on in the economy for some years to come. Consider:

The number of nest-egg-building households headed by people between 35 and 44 years old approaches 24 million, a spurt of some five million in ten years. What's more, the number of households headed by people between 45 and 54 is approaching 20 million, a growth of almost 50% in the same time period. These millions are living and spending and saving in their peak earning years.

Households headed by 35- to 54-year-olds—the combination of the two exploding cohorts just described—spend more on food, housing, clothes and practically every other category, including financial products and services (stocks and bonds, for instance) than households headed by any other age group.

The households closest to the 35- to 54-year-olds in terms of their volume of spending and saving are those that bracket both sides of that age group: They are headed by 55- to 64-year-olds, a group that is growing, and 25- to 34-year-olds, a group that has declined in numbers but is expected to resume growing after 2005. Both age groups will be contributing to America's spending and saving.

PLENTY OF JOBS

Clearly the demand will exist at home for the goods and services that American companies sell. Foreign demand also will feed the bottom line for companies prepared to compete. At the same time, demand can be expected to continue for the kinds of financial products and services people use to fund their college and retirement savings and investment plans. Americans will get the money to support all this spending and saving from the amazing American job machine, which has presented the new century with an economy sporting one of the lowest unemployment rates in anyone's memory.

One effect of the huge number of baby-boomers hitting the job market in the 1970s and '80s was a clumping of workers at and near the entry level. This influx of inexperienced workers was responsible in part for the relatively poor productivity gains America experienced during those decades. Workers were plentiful—too plentiful, really, for an economy characterized by downsizing corporations—contributing to the dual problems that developed in the late '80s: sluggish wage increases and high unemployment.

As boomers have grown older, the pressure on the economy to generate millions and millions of entry-level jobs year after year has subsided because the younger population groups following the boomers are smaller. This slower growth of the labor force has helped to hold down unemployment, despite continued corporate downsizing. Indeed, the American economy may be generating more jobs than there are American-born workers to fill them, creating a growing demand for immigrants.

The Investment Climate Ahead

W HEN YOU ASSESS THE FORCES THAT WILL CONVERGE IN the American economy in the years ahead, this is the picture that emerges:

INFLATION WILL BE TAME, THANKS TO A NUMBER OF FACTORS. For one thing, it's very difficult to raise prices in this global economy because somewhere in the world some other company is willing to do the job faster, cheaper and maybe even better. In many categories—especially apparel, home electronics and some other consumer goods—prices will actually decline. Another reason for the expectation of tame inflation: a plentiful supply of oil that will keep energy prices in check, not just for America but for the world. Even if OPEC succeeds at one of its periodic efforts to move prices to a significantly higher level, the effect will be dampened by the fact that they are supplying only half as much of our imported oil as they were a decade ago. As a result, figure on an average inflation rate of about 3% per year. That's something to be concerned about and to account for in your investment plans, but 3% is a manageable level. (For comparison, inflation averaged 7.4% per year in the 1970s, 5.2% in the '80s and a tad over 3% in the '90s.)

BUSINESS PRODUCTIVITY HAS ACHIEVED A HIGHER LEVEL. That's the payoff from more than a decade of reducing work forces and refocusing effort. The U.S. is the world's leader in manufacturing productivity, and we're not going to relinquish this lead anytime soon. One reason: The U.S. spends more than Britain, France, Germany, Italy and Japan combined on research and development. Business productivity growth in the U.S. seems to have reached a new plateau of about 2% per year, twice what it was in the 1980s. As economists figure these things, with the U.S. labor force growing only about 1% per year, a 2% growth in productivity allows a 3% growth in economic output without triggering upward pressure on payrolls and, thus, prices. And 3% economic growth per year is a nice, sustainable number.

INTEREST RATES WILL REMAIN MODERATE. They'll go up and down, but a surplus on the federal budget reduces the government's need to borrow money in competition with business. And saving and investment by boomers nearing retirement should infuse the financial markets with enough capital to finance business expansion without pushing rates up.

So we can look forward to seeing our living standards rise as the growing global economy creates a growing marketplace for the goods and services we want to buy and sell. This rise in living standards, in turn, will generate growing profits for companies that compete successfully—and for investors who can spot them in advance.

That's the big picture. As an investor, you need to decide on your goals and choose the investments that will help you achieve them. The rest of this book will help you do that.

CHAPTER 2

The Keys to Successful Investing

 NY DISCUSSION OF INVESTING MUST BEGIN WITH two simple truths. First, investing requires taking some risks. Your hope for investment success depends in part on your ability to control those risks without passing up reasonable rewards. And reasonable rewards, over time, should be enough to generate the wealth you seek.

Second, the best opportunities for building wealth occur in healthy, growing economies. Thus, your personal prosperity depends in part on the prosperity of the world's major economies—for we truly live, work, save and invest in a world economy, not just an American economy.

This book will show you how to minimize your risks without sacrificing a reasonable reward. It will argue that the years ahead offer more opportunities for more people to acquire meaningful wealth in their lifetimes than perhaps any other span of years in history. The chapters that follow will describe those opportunities and recommend ways to profit from them.

The experience of the Kiplinger organization in reporting, analyzing, interpreting and forecasting the ups and downs of the world's economies dates back to 1923—a period that spans the Roaring Twenties and the Great Depression, World War II and the Cold War that followed; the humiliation and shock of Sputnik and the triumph of landing men on the moon; the rise of Communism and its dramatic collapse; nerve-wracking conflicts in the Persian Gulf and the Balkans. We have experienced years of growth and years of recession, stock-market booms and stock-market busts. Those years of experience applied to the economic forces at work in the world today lead us to conclude that the next century has the potential to be a period of unprecedented economic boom.

It will be a worldwide boom; America will share in it and in many important ways will help to create it. The course won't be perfectly straight and uninterrupted, but the general direction will be clear. Chapter 1 laid out some of the reasons we believe this.

If you're in a hurry to get rich, this book won't help you. Buy a lottery ticket or enter a magazine-subscription sweepstakes instead. All you risk is the price of the ticket or the price of the stamp and the envelope, and you have a pretty good idea of your chances.

But if you're patient, the economic climate of the years ahead, coupled with a nearly inexhaustible supply of ways to get in on the action, can make the next decade or so uniquely profitable for people like you. This book will show you how to accumulate a six- or seven-figure chunk of money while you still have enough lifetime left to enjoy it. Building wealth this way takes you along a path that's short on thrills, but it's short on spills, too. And the nice green scenery along the way keeps you interested in the trip.

You can devise a plan to achieve this goal regardless of your current style of saving and investing. If you tend to neglect your finances, you should create a plan with neglect in mind. Lots of successful investors put their portfolios on autopilot, spending only a few hours each year monitoring performance. Others prefer to pay close attention to what's happening to their money.

Whichever description fits you, you can accumulate remarkable sums of money by applying the following five keys to investment success. Note that we call these keys, not secrets. There are no investment secrets. The methods employed by successful investors are well known to those who follow money matters closely, but they tend to get lost in the clutter and clamor of the day-to-day action. This chapter will present a bird's-eye view of the methods behind the apparent madness. Later chapters will show you how to apply them to your own investments.

You'll probably be familiar with most of the investment terms used in these pages. If you come across any that stump you, consult the glossary following the appendix.

Key #1: Make Investing a Habit
How to have $500,000 or more in 20 years or less

YOUR TASK IS NOT TO DEVISE THE MOST INGENIOUS INVESTment plan ever conceived. Rather, your task is to create a plan that suits you and stick with it. For most people who start with a small amount, the best chance to acquire measurable wealth lies in developing the habit of adding something to the pot regularly and putting the money where it can do the most for you.

The rewards can be considerable compared with a lackadaisical approach to saving and investing. Suppose you take $5,000 and stick it in the bank, where it earns a nice, safe, sedate 3% interest. Twenty years later you come in to claim your deposit and discover that it has grown to a not-very-impressive $9,000 and change.

Meanwhile, your brother-in-law socks $5,000 in one-year certificates of deposit (CDs) at the same bank, with instructions to roll over the proceeds into a new certificate every 12 months. In addition, every month he buys another CD for $100 and issues the same instructions. Over 20 years he earns an average of 5% interest. His nest egg: more than $54,000.

That's a lot better, but it's not going to finance a worry-free retirement. Suppose your goal is a lot loftier than that: You'd like to have a nest egg of a half-million dollars. You've got 20 years to get there and $5,000 to start. You're willing to investigate investment alternatives that should boost your return above what you'd earn in a bank account. What's a reasonable return to plan on, and how much will you have to contribute along the way?

For reasons you'll find described in Chapter 4, we think an average annual return of 12% to 15% over the long run is a reasonable expectation for individuals who apply the principles laid out in this book. At 15%, with $5,000 to start, you'll reach your $500,000 goal if you contribute $320 a month to your investment account. With a 12% return, $450 a month will get you your half-million in 20 years.

Less-ambitious plans can also work wonders. Starting from zero, putting just $50 a month into an investment that pays a compounded average annual total return of 15% for 20 years will get you a nest egg of better than $75,000. Stick to the plan for 30 years and you'll have more than $350,000. Double your contribution and you'll double the size of your nest egg. For a look at the results of a variety of regular investment amounts earning different rates of return, see the Appendix.

Another possibility is to start small and gradually increase your monthly investment amount as your income grows. For instance, you can start with nothing, put $100 a month into your investment account for five years, raise it to $200 a month for the next five, $300 a month for years 11 through 15 and $400 a month for years 16 through 20. At the end of the period you'll have more than $250,000. Boost your monthly amount to $500 for years 21 through 25 and your fund will grow to more than $500,000, assuming you earn an average of 15% per year.

These examples are simplified, of course, because they don't take taxes or commissions into account. But the point is this: Making investing a habit is a key to making investing a success.

Key #2: Set Exciting Goals
Why not a condo on the golf course?

INVESTMENT GOAL SETTING IS AN INTENSELY PERSONAL AFFAIR that will be guided by your own style and preferences. But if you set nebulous, generalized goals, such as "financial security" or "a comfortable retirement," you're going to have trouble measuring your progress along the way. You may even struggle to maintain interest in the project. Vaguely defined investment goals can lead to halfhearted efforts to achieve them.

Better to set goals you can grab onto, goals that excite you. Instead of "financial security," why not "a million-dollar net worth by age 60?" Instead of "a comfortable retirement," why not "a two-bedroom condo on a golf course on Hilton Head Island, plus an investment portfolio that will yield $3,000 a month to supplement my pension?" Now those are real goals. You can put a price tag on each and use that price tag as an incentive to keep up your investing discipline.

Setting investment goals is a lot like reading a map: Before you can get to where you want to go, you've got to figure out where you are. The easiest way is to fill out the personal balance sheet on page 16. (There's an online version of this worksheet on the Kiplinger Web site, at www.kiplinger.com. Use the search function. Type in "Managing Money Planning Center." Go to "Calculators" at the bottom of the screen. Click on "What's your net worth?") It's largely self-explanatory. You may have to do a little guesstimating about the value of your furniture, jewelry and so forth, but don't spend a lot of time trying to be precise about those numbers. It's the financial portion of your balance sheet that should concern you the most: money in savings accounts, stocks, bonds and mutual funds, real estate and the like, plus your equity in pension plans and other sources of current and future income.

Another approach is to pose a few basic questions: How much money could you raise if you were to liquidate everything you own and pay off all your debts? How difficult would it be to get your hands on that money? And where would that money come from? What you learn about where your money is will also influence your goal setting and the routes available to get to your goals.

There are no "right" or "wrong" investment goals. They can be whatever you want them to be, and naturally they will be influenced by your income and job security, your ability to take risks, your age and your financial prospects in general. In addition, the time you have to achieve your goals should influence the kinds of investments you might consider. Most people have several goals at once.

SHORT-TERM GOALS. Suppose that a vacation in Europe is one of your goals and that you want to go next summer. Such a short time horizon suggests that the stock market wouldn't be a good place to invest the money you're setting aside for the trip. The market is subject to wide swings, and you wouldn't want to be forced to sell your stocks in a downswing just because the time had come to buy your tickets. Don't put into the stock market any money you know you will need in the next two or three years. Certificates of deposit that mature about the time you'll need the cash or a money-market fund that allows you to withdraw your cash instantly by writing a check would be a better choice.

MEDIUM-TERM GOALS. Maybe you'd like to buy a larger house within three or four years. With more time, you have more flexibility. Safety is still important but you are in a better posi-

Where You Stand Now: Your Personal Balance Sheet

USE THIS WORKSHEET to calculate your current assets, liabilities and net worth. When you know where your current net worth comes from, you can see where your financial position is strong and where it is weak. This worksheet, along with the investment-mix worksheet on page 28, lays the necessary groundwork for setting your investment goals and making plans to reach them.

ASSETS

Cash in savings accounts	$_____
Cash in checking accounts	_____
Cash on hand	_____
Certificates of deposit	_____
Money-market funds	_____
U.S. savings bonds	_____
Market value of home	_____
Market value of other real estate	_____
Cash value of life insurance	_____
Surrender value of annuities	_____
Vested equity in pension plans	_____
Vested equity in profit sharing	_____
401(k) or 403(b) plans	_____
Individual retirement accounts	_____
Keogh plans	_____
Stocks	_____
Bonds	_____
Stock mutual funds	_____
Bond mutual funds	_____
Real estate investment trusts	_____

Other investments	_____
Collectibles	_____
Precious metals	_____
Estimated market value of:	
Household furnishings	_____
Automobiles and trucks	_____
Boats, recreational vehicles	_____
Furs and jewelry	_____
Loans owed to you	_____
Other assets	_____
TOTAL ASSETS	$_____ (A)

LIABILITIES

Balance owed on mortgages	$_____
Auto loans	_____
Student loans	_____
Home-equity credit line	_____
Other credit lines	_____
Credit card bills	_____
Other bills	_____
TOTAL LIABILITIES	$_____ (B)

CURRENT NET WORTH
(A minus B) $_____

tion to ride out bad times in the financial markets. For medium-term goals like these, you should consider longer-term CDs that pay more interest than the short-term certificates you would buy to help finance your vacation trip. You could even consider mutual funds that invest in stocks that pay good dividends but don't tend to fluctuate much in price (see Chapter 6). That would give you high income (for reinvesting in more fund shares), a chance to ride along if the stock market zooms, and pretty good protection against all but a catastrophic drop in stock prices.

LONG-TERM GOALS. A comfortable retirement is probably the most common of all financial goals—so common, in fact, that it gets its own chapter in this book. A college education for the kids is another common goal (it gets its own chapter, too). For long-term goals like these, consider a wide range of possibilities: stocks, corporate and government bonds, and long-term CDs for diversification. You should also take maximum advantage of tax-sheltered plans, such as individual retirement accounts. IRA earnings accumulate tax-deferred, and contributions may be tax-deductible; 401(k) plans offered by your employer provide many of the same advantages. These are described in detail in Chapter 14.

With several years and sometimes decades ahead of you, financial assets that aren't strictly investments also come into play: home equity, pension plans and social security, for example. Your goals and choices should be influenced by the size and the accessibility of those assets, as we'll discuss in later chapters.

Your goals are likely to change, so it's important to reassess them from time to time. For instance, the kinds of growth-oriented investments that might be perfectly appropriate while you are accumulating a retirement nest egg and have a long-term horizon could be inappropriate after you retire and need income to pay the bills. Luckily, the investment universe is so vast—not just stocks and bonds and certificates, but also hybrids too numerous to mention here—that you'll never be at a loss for choices.

Key #3: Don't Take Unnecessary Risks

There are two times in a man's life when he should not speculate: when he can't afford it, and when he can. —Mark Twain

MOST PEOPLE WOULD SAY THAT RISK IS THE CHANCE YOU take that you'll lose all or part of the money you put into an investment. That's true as far as it goes, but it doesn't go far enough. A more complete definition of risk acknowledges the availability of investments carrying virtually ironclad guarantees that you will get all your money back plus the interest promised you: savings accounts and certificates of deposit in federally insured banks, savings and loans, or credit unions, for instance. Also, with all investments, even government-guaranteed ones, you run the additional risk that your return will be less than the inflation rate.

In fact, savings accounts, certificates of deposit, Treasury bills, savings bonds and a handful of other government-backed investments establish a useful benchmark for measuring risk.

Risk is the chance you take that you will lose your money or that you will earn less from your investment than the rate of inflation or less than the interest available at the time from insured savings certificates or U.S. Treasury–backed obligations.

To put it another way, risk is the chance that you will earn less than 4% to 5% on your money. If you can't reasonably expect to do better than that for the risk you're taking, then there's no sense in taking the risk.

How Can You Control Your Risks?

It's difficult to pick up a book on investing without running into something called the pyramid of risk; this book is no exception. If the pyramid of risk is familiar to you, feel free to skip this section and go right to the next. If it isn't familiar, the following short discussion could be the most important part of the book for you.

The pyramid of risk is a useful visual image for a sensible risk-reducing strategy. It's built on a broad and solid base of financial security: a home; money salted away in insured savings accounts or certificates; plus insurance policies to cover expenses if something should happen to your health, your car, your home, your life or your ability to earn an income. As you move up from the pyramid's base, the levels get narrower and narrower, representing the space in your portfolio that is available for investments that involve risk. The greater the risk of an investment, the higher up the pyramid it goes and, thus, the less money you should put into it.

Real estate markets weaken from time to time, raising the question of whether homeownership belongs at the very base of the pyramid. We believe that it does, for security as much as for wealth. Others might place it up a notch. The image itself is more important than some of the specifics of what belongs on each level of the pyramid.

How much should you have in savings? Three to six months' living expenses should be your goal. Bank, savings and loan, or credit union accounts are good places to keep this money, but look for opportunities to earn more than the 2% to 4% these institutions tend to pay on their run-of-the-mill deposit accounts—by putting most of it in certificates, for example. Use a money-market fund for at least part of this rainy-day money. Such funds aren't federally insured, but they are prudent, conservative places to invest and they often pay a higher return than savings accounts. Chapter 3 describes them and recommends several other low-risk ways to step up the return from your savings.

Once you've built the base of your pyramid, you're ready to move up and become an investor. One level up from savings, insurance and homeownership is the appropriate place for mutual funds that invest in low-risk, dividend-oriented stocks and top-quality government and corporate bonds. Individual stocks and bonds that you pick yourself are on the same level. Most financial experts would put investment real estate on the next level up from stocks. At the very top of the pyramid go the investments that few people should try, such as penny or micro-cap stocks, commodity futures contracts and most limited partnerships. We recommend against these and several other risky ventures and explain why in Chapter 11.

Thus, the pyramid, which is broad and solid at the bottom and gets narrower and smaller as you move up, is the perfect image for the sensible deployment of your financial assets. As long as you remember that, you'll never stray too far out of your risk zone.

HOW MUCH RISK SHOULD YOU TAKE?

Controlling risk means more than being "comfortable" with an investment. Certainly you should never invest in something that makes you uncomfortable or in something you don't understand, but it is our frequent observation that too many investors seem perfectly comfortable with entirely too much risk—until the bottom falls out.

True story: Several years ago, investors gathered in a meeting room in Englewood, Colo., to hear their portfolio manager report on recent performance. This particular manager's specialty was buying and selling stock options, a technique that greatly magnifies the effect of movements in the price of the underlying stock (see Chapter 11). If you choose the right option, you can make more money than if you actually owned the stock. If you choose wrong...well, the adviser chose wrong, so wrong that he lost an estimated $100 million of his clients' money and didn't have the nerve to show up at the meeting. Instead he sent a videotape, on which he explained how his mistaken opinion about the direction the price would move on a single stock had resulted in massive losses to the people in the room. This man misjudged the stock, but he knew exactly how his clients would react to the news: He had hired security guards to patrol the room as his videotaped message was played.

More than 1,000 investors were thought to have been hurt by this single miscall. They had been drawn into participating in this risky—but perfectly legal—investment strategy by dreams of extraordinarily high returns, or by ignorance of what the adviser was doing, or both.

These luckless investors are a sad reminder of the most enduring truth about the risk-reward relationship:

The bigger the promised reward, the bigger the risk.

Put another way:

The bigger the risk of the investment you undertake, the bigger the potential reward should be.

This risk-reward relationship applies no matter what the investment, who the investment adviser, what the condition of the financial markets or the phase of the moon. The landscape is littered with the discarded portfolios of investors who forgot that basic fact.

Does this mean you should avoid all high-risk investments? No. It means you should confine them to the top of the pyramid—to the attic, where they can never occupy a very significant portion of your investment portfolio. Invest only as much as you can afford to lose because there is a good chance you will lose it. You should also learn to recognize the risks involved in every kind of investment.

RISKS IN STOCKS. A company's stock could decline in price because the company hits the skids or isn't being managed well. Shareholders lose faith and sell. Or a perfectly well-managed and prosperous company's stock could fall because lots of investors decide to move into bonds or cash on a particular day and sell millions of shares of stock of all kinds, or stocks of a certain kind. That happenstance would drive the entire market down, without bothering to differentiate the good stocks from the bad.

RISKS IN BONDS. Bond prices move in the direction opposite to that of interest rates, rising in price when rates fall and vice versa. But individual bond issues can be hurt even if interest rates in general are falling. All it takes is for one of the rating services— Standard & Poor's Corp. and Moody's Investors Service are the major ones—to downgrade its opinion of the company's financial stability. A bond issue that's paying an interest rate noticeably higher than that of other bonds with similar maturity dates is probably being forced to pay more to compensate investors for the higher risk inherent in a lower safety rating. That, in a nutshell, is the situation with "junk" bonds: low ratings, high interest, high risk of default.

RISKS EVERYWHERE. Real estate values go up and down in sync with supply and demand in local markets, regardless of the health of the national economy. Gold and silver, which are supposed to be stores of value in inflationary times, have been decidedly unrewarding in times of tolerable inflation. Even federally insured savings accounts carry risks—not that the government won't cover insured deposits, but that their low interest rate won't be enough to protect the value of your money from the combined effect of inflation and taxes.

What is a prudent risk? It depends on your goals, your age, your income and other resources, and your current and future financial obligations. A young single person who expects his or her pay to rise steadily over the years and who has few family responsibilities can afford to take more chances than, say, a couple approaching retirement age. The young person has time to recover from market reversals; the older couple may not. A more complete discussion of risk appears in each of the chapters devoted to specific investment alternatives.

Key #4: Keep Time on Your Side
$10,000 today, or $10,000 a year from today?

A PENNY SAVED IS A PENNY EARNED—OR SO THE SAYING GOES. In fact, a penny saved may be more or less than a penny earned, depending on when it is earned and how it is saved. The reason is rooted in a concept called the time value of money (and its close cousin, opportunity cost).

Which would you rather have, $10,000 today or $10,000 a year from today? Of course, you'd choose the take the money now—anyone would. Besides possessing the sure knowledge that a bird in the hand is worth two in the bush, you understand that the value of that $10,000 you have to wait a year for will be eroded by a year's worth of inflation and a year's worth of lost interest on the money. To put a dollar figure on it, if inflation is 4% and you could earn 5% interest in a year, the thrill of being handed $10,000 today is worth about 9%, or $900, more than the thrill of being handed $10,000 a year from today.

The time value of money works against you if you're the one waiting to collect the money, but it works in your favor if you're the one who has to pay. Success with your money often lies in being able to identify the winning side of the time-value equation.

Let's say you're a big winner in the local lottery. For your prize you are offered the choice of $50,000 in cash or an annuity worth $100,000. Which should you take?

The answer depends on how long you'd have to wait to collect the $100,000. Annuities are contracts that pay a certain amount of money in regular installments over a specified length of time, often ten or 20 years, rather than in a lump sum. Stretching out the payments creates a big benefit for the company that owes the money because it collects interest on the unpaid amount while the recipient waits to collect. For instance, if the $100,000 were paid out in annual installments stretched over 20 years, and the company earned 8% on the unpaid amount, all it would need to come up with today in order to meet that schedule of future payments would be about $50,000. Thus, your choice of prizes would really be no choice at all; you'd just be picking a collection schedule.

It is the time value of money that permits state governments and other sponsors of sweepstakes and lotteries to promise fabulous payouts that actually exceed the amount of money they take in by selling tickets. Consider two sweepstakes, both of which promise a million-dollar prize. One pays it right away and the other, which advertises an "annuity value" of a million dollars, pays you $50,000 a year for 20 years. That's a million dollars, all right, but it doesn't cost the sweepstakes sponsor nearly that much. In fact, the sponsor could probably purchase an annuity contract from an insurance company that will fulfill its obligation for about half the eventual payout. Clearly, the sweepstakes that pays right away offers a much more valuable prize. You could use it to purchase the same annuity, and waltz to the bank with more than a half-million dollars in change—not counting taxes, of course.

You don't have to win a lottery or a quiz show to contemplate whether you're headed for the winning or the losing side of the time-value equation. If you keep in mind one basic principle—that a dollar you pay or receive today is worth more than a dollar you pay or receive tomorrow—you'll wind up on the winning side more often than not. A couple of examples illustrate why:

PAYING THE KIDS' COLLEGE BILLS. Your future rocket scientist faces education costs of about $342,000 when he or she enters Stanford or MIT in 18 years. That's a huge sum, but because you're familiar with the time value of money, you know the smart thing to do is to find a way to pay those bills today, when your dollars are worth more than they will be in 18 years. Assuming a time value for the money of 10% per year—meaning you could earn that much on the money between now and the time you have to pay it—the value of the $342,000 you need 18 years from now is $61,568 today. Salt that away in an investment earning 10% a year and you've got the bills covered. If you haven't got that amount, gather as much of it as you can and get the time value of money working for you, easing at least some of the burden when the college bills come due. Or raise your sights a bit: If you could manage to earn 12% on the money, you'd need $44,515 today to have $342,000 by your child's freshman year. Chapter 13 describes some ways to achieve such a goal.

PAYING OFF THE MORTGAGE. Ignorance of the time value of money can cause you to think you're doing something smart when you're not. For instance, you have probably heard praises sung for the 15-year mortgage. Because you pay it off sooner than a 30-year loan, you pay less interest and thus save tens of thousands of dollars. But the homeowner with the 15-year mortgage parts with the money sooner than the 30-year buyer, and the time value of money suggests some caution may be in order before making extravagant claims of savings. You need the answers to two questions: What else might you do with the extra money you'd be spending on the higher monthly payments required by the 15-year mortgage? How much could it earn if you invested it in something other than mortgage payments?

Suppose it costs you an extra $200 a month to pay off the loan in 15 years instead of 30. That's $200 a month not available for something else—investing in a mutual fund, for example. Say the mortgage rate is 8% and the mutual fund earns 12%. You could benefit from that 4% difference by putting the money in the fund instead of paying off the mortgage. That $200 a month earning 4% compounded for 15 years grows to almost $50,000. That's your *opportunity cost* to pay off your mortgage early, and before you crow about how much you've saved over taking a 30-year mortgage, you need to subtract it from your savings.

Opportunity cost is the cost of doing one thing and not another. To make sure you don't overlook it, ask yourself before you make any investment or spending choice: "What else could I do with the money?"

Key #5: Diversify Your Investments

There's more to it than putting your eggs in different baskets.

THERE ARE AT LEAST THREE GOOD REASONS TO DIVERSIFY your investments. First, it's common sense not to put all your eggs in one basket. Second, no investment performs well all the time; as a rule, when one thing is down, another thing tends to be up. And third, some investment experts believe that you can actually increase your return with a sensible strategy of diversification.

RIDING THE UPS AND DOWNS

The wisdom of diversification is immediately apparent when you examine the ups and downs of various investments over the years. Here's a snapshot of selected recent years, with inflation figures thrown in for comparison. For the Dow Jones industrials, the figures assume that that all earnings were reinvested in the same stocks.

Stocks managed positive returns in four out of the five years selected. Gold soared in 1979 but hasn't been heard from since. Bonds and money-market yields ride highest in when inflation is up. Real estate investment trusts, which invest in commercial properties or mortgages, bounce around quite a bit. A different selection of years would have shown a different pattern. For instance, the Dow Jones industrials turned in a dismal performance in 1973, 1974 and 1977. Gold soared in each of those years and again in 1993, while real estate investment trusts fell so sharply in 1973 and 1974 that their survival as an investment vehicle was actually in doubt. They climbed strongly in 1991 and 1996.

The lesson here isn't hard to find: Invest in whatever you want, but invest in something else, too.

SPREADING THE RISK

One way to hedge your bets is to select a number of investment vehicles you like and divide your money equally among them. For instance, you might set up a portfolio consisting of equal parts cash (money-market funds, CDs, Treasury bills), bonds, U.S. stocks, foreign stocks, and real estate. Once a year, you could adjust the mix to maintain the dollar balance, taking the gains from the winners and spreading them out among the losers so that your asset distribution stays the same. Another formula, which is popular with many successful investors seeking to prosper while controlling their risks, is the 40-40-20 portfolio: 40% in stocks, 40% in bonds and 20% in cash equivalents.

Either mix creates a diversified portfolio, but thinking in such terms can lure you into a false sense of permanence about what is actually a very fluid situation. As stock prices and interest rates go up and down, the proportions in your portfolio will shift without your lifting a finger. In addition, there will be times when you want to shift more money into stocks or bonds or cash, for reasons described in Chapters 4 and 5. It is more realistic to think in terms of ranges rather than fixed percentages. Use the worksheet on page 28 to discover how your investments sort out today. The results will suggest moves you should make to get them more in line with the kind of mix you'd like.

This is the range of portfolio mixes Kiplinger recommends for investors seeking long-term growth, moderate risk and ease of access to their money:

Stocks: 50% to 80%
Bonds: 20% to 40%
Cash: 10% to 25%

This is the core portfolio designed to form the bedrock of your investment plan. That doesn't mean you should always be invested in stocks, bonds and cash to the exclusion of everything else, just that they should compose the bulk of your invested capital. You could keep 60% of your investments in stocks, 10% in bonds, 10% in cash and the remaining 20% in something else—real estate, for example. Real estate is left out of the core portfolio not because we don't think it can deliver solid gains but because achieving those gains requires specialized knowledge of local, not national, marketplaces. Real estate investing is the subject of Chapter 8.

Some investors consider their collectibles—antiques, automobiles, stamps, baseball cards—to be part of their investment portfolios. We disagree, for reasons set out in Chapter 10. If you have specialized knowledge of a particular field, enjoy collecting and have access to the kinds of information and markets that can make collecting a profitable venture, fine. But we wouldn't include collectibles in the core portfolio.

Gold is often cited as an inflation hedge that belongs in everyone's portfolio. We don't believe that the inflation outlook supports that position, and we address the subject in Chapter 10.

Another thing about the core portfolio: By "stocks," we don't necessarily mean individual shares. As later chapters will show, mutual funds are often the best way to own stocks, although knowing how to select a promising stock will make you a better picker of promising funds as well. By "bonds," we don't necessarily mean only corporate or municipal securities that are so labeled. Variations on the bond theme—mortgage-backed secu-

Investment Ups and Downs

	1979	1985	1990	1994	1998
Inflation rate	13.3%	3.8%	6.1%	2.7%	1.6%
Dow Jones industrials	10.6	33.6	−0.6	5.0	18.1
Corporate-bond yield	9.6	11.4	9.3	8.0	6.5
Money-market fund yield	11.0	7.7	7.8	3.8	5.0
Gold prices	126.6	6.9	−2.5	−2.4	0.6
Real estate investment trusts	30.5	5.9	−17.4	0.8	−18.8

Source: Investment Performance Digest, 1960 through 1998, by C. David Chase (Wiesenberger)

rities, for instance (see Chapter 9)—can perform the same function for your portfolio, often at a more attractive return. These investments are described in later chapters.

Keep these points in mind as you read through the chapters that follow. The core portfolio is intended not as a hard-and-fast formula but as guidance for constantly changing investment markets. Your exact mix should also take into account your age, income and investment goals. For instance, as you approach retirement it's natural to shift more of your assets into income-producing investments such as bonds or utility stocks and out of stocks that have long-term potential but are subject to market reversals.

DIVERSIFYING IN OTHER WAYS

Diversifying among different kinds of investments is a classic strategy that has served many people well. But it is only the beginning of investment wisdom. Alert investors perform at least two other kinds of diversification.

DIVERSIFY WITHIN INVESTMENT CATEGORIES. Stocks come in so many shapes and sizes that to say "put 60% of your money in stocks" is not very helpful advice. Which stocks? There are big-company stocks, small-company stocks, income-oriented stocks, foreign stocks, technology stocks. These and other kinds of stocks are explored in depth in Chapter 4. A well-designed portfolio includes more than one kind.

DIVERSIFY ACCORDING TO TIME HORIZONS. In the investment markets, a month or two can be a long time. Interest rates move up and down. The stock market churns and boils, achieving new heights in July, new depths in August. National and world events can change the investment climate overnight.

You can protect your portfolio against the effects of such uncertainty by spreading your holdings across the calendar. Don't overcommit to either the long term or the short term. Mix the maturities of your bonds and certificates of deposit and continue to make regular contributions to your investment program, especially when market prices are down. They will rise again, and you will be sitting pretty when they do.

Are Your Investments in Balance?

COMPLETE THIS WORKSHEET at least once a year so you'll know how your investment mix is changing and can take action, if necessary, to bring it back into line with a mix that matches your goals and your risk tolerance.

A good year for stocks, for instance, could cause them to become a larger portion of the mix than you'd like, suggesting that you might want to sell some shares and redeploy the profits into bonds or Treasury bills.

	MARKET VALUE	% OF TOTAL
CASH		
Savings accounts	$ _____	_____
Money-market funds	_____	_____
Treasury bills	_____	_____
Total Cash	_____	_____
STOCKS		
Individual shares	_____	_____
Mutual funds	_____	_____
Total Stocks	_____	_____
BONDS		
Individual bonds	_____	_____
Mutual funds	_____	_____
Unit trusts	_____	_____
Total Bonds	_____	_____
RENTAL REAL ESTATE	_____	_____
LIMITED PARTNERSHIPS	_____	_____
PRECIOUS METALS	_____	_____
OTHER INVESTMENTS	_____	_____
COLLECTIBLES	_____	_____
Total Investments	$ _____	_____

Failing to apply the concepts described in this chapter won't necessarily deny you investment success, but the success you do manage to achieve will be due largely to pure dumb luck. If you apply these five keys to success, you'll need no more than your fair share of luck to succeed, no matter what your goals. You can be sure that every investor needs some luck. The idea is to rely on it as little as possible.

CHAPTER 3

First, Maximize Your Savings

I N CHAPTER 2, WE RECOMMENDED SETTING ASIDE THREE TO six months' living expenses in a safe place where the money earns interest and is easily accessible in case of an emergency. These are your savings, not your investments, and it's important to distinguish between the two. No one has ever explained the difference better than Will Rogers: "Forget about a return on my money," he supposedly said, "what I want is a return of my money."

The key to a successful saving strategy is finding ways to increase the return on your money without having to worry about the return of your money.

A lot of people stash this rainy-day cash in a federally insured bank, credit union or thrift account and let it go at that. They may be a little uneasy about the relatively puny amount of interest adding up, but they're willing to live with less in exchange for the peace of mind that comes with knowing their money will be there when they need it.

A safety-above-all-else approach to saving makes sense for a portion of your savings, but relying on it exclusively short-changes you and your money. You generate less money to transfer to an investment account, where you have the chance to earn a greater return. Sometimes such a practice can even cause you to lose money after inflation and taxes have taken their share of your interest payments.

The High Cost of Doing Nothing

I F YOU'VE BEEN LETTING A LOT OF YOUR MONEY LANGUISH IN A minimum-interest savings account, you're part of a very large club. As America enters the 21st century, savers have some $1.5 trillion sitting in passbook or statement savings accounts earning around 2.24%. If all the country's savers moved all that cash to certificates of deposit paying about 6%, they would earn an additional $56 billion a year. If they switched all their savings from passbook accounts to bond funds yielding around 7%, they'd grow $71 billion richer in a year.

Lucky for you, that sort of thing doesn't happen that fast. If passbook savers suddenly started moving great gobs of their money into higher-paying accounts, those accounts would begin paying less, the laws of supply and demand being what they are. Anyway, most people don't take the trouble to pay this kind of attention to their idle cash. But somewhere in the spectrum of low-risk savings vehicles, you can almost certainly find one that will pay you more than you're earning now without measurably increasing your risk.

How to Get the Most From Certificates of Deposit

C ERTIFICATES OF DEPOSIT, OR CDS, ARE A STAPLE OF MANY savers' and investors' portfolios. Available at banks, savings and loans, and credit unions, CDs are insured for up to $100,000 and they pay a higher-than-passbook rate of interest in return for your commitment to leave the money on deposit with the institution for a specified time, commonly from a minimum of a month or so to a maximum of five years. The longer you commit your money—and, in some cases, the more money you commit—the more you earn. The interest rate is usually fixed but may be variable, pegged to a market rate such as the prime rate. Minimum denominations are often $500 to $1,000, though the best rates may require higher minimums.

CDs have a lot to offer the safety- and yield-minded saver. Virtually the only catch is that if you need the money before the CD matures, you'll pay a penalty that could eliminate the advantage you thought you were getting from the higher rate.

By shutting down so many unhealthy banks and savings and loans that were paying sky-high rates to attract desperately needed depositors, federal regulators have long since taken the pressure off healthy institutions to offer similar rates. That makes the job of locating higher yields a little tougher. It can be worth the effort, though: Interest rates for CDs with similar maturities can vary by a percentage point or more. On large amounts especially, the added interest can make a big difference.

SHOPPING AROUND

You can often find a better deal simply by shopping around in your local area—either reading the ads in the paper or telephoning local institutions.

In the past, you might have thought twice about sending your money out of town in quest of a higher yield. By spending just a half-hour or so shopping for the best rates, you can probably earn an extra 1% to 2% on your next certificate of deposit (CD). With a $25,000 CD, that's an extra $250 to $500 earned in one year and from $1,275 to $2,600 over five years. Pretty good pay for a half hour's work.

Start by calling local banks and thrifts to compare rates. For each CD maturity, ask for the annual percentage rate (or APR, which reflects the compounding of interest), minimum deposit amount, the penalty for early withdrawal and how you'll be notified when the CD matures.

You should also make sure deposits are insured by the Federal Deposit Insurance Corp. FDIC insures deposits of up to $100,000 per person, per type of account (such as savings, CD and IRA) per bank. The main office and any branches count as one.

Real Protection

SOME STATES HAVE created their own deposit insurance plans for savings and loan associations and credit unions operating within their borders. But the spectacular collapse of state systems covering some s&l associations in Ohio and Maryland in the mid '80s and the sudden closing of state-insured credit unions in Rhode Island in 1991 serve as loud warnings: Do not put your money in any bank or s&l that is not insured by the Federal Deposit Insurance Corp. (FDIC; www.fdic.gov) or in any credit union that is not insured by the National Credit Union Administration (NCUA; www.ncua.gov).

Deposit Insurance for Organizations

Q: *I am on a church board, and we are "shopping" for a new bank. We're going into a building program and will have big deposits. This question came up in the process: Are we insured?*
A: Yes. Funds deposited by a corporation, partnership or unincorporated association are insured up to a maximum of $100,000. Such funds are insured separately from the personal accounts of the stockholders, partners or members.

For example, you could have a $100,000 CD in your name, keep $50,000 in a demand deposit in a joint account in your and your spouse's names and be fully insured up to $150,000. But if you had a $100,000 CD at the main bank and $50,000 CD at a branch bank, both in your own name, you'd be covered for only $100,000. (For details, call the FDIC's hotline, 800-934-3342.)

Next, broaden your search. Going national could reward you with a yield of up to 3% more. If a deposit is insured by FDIC, you're as safe with a CD offered by a bank 2,000 miles away as one around the corner.

For CD rates currently being offered by banks and thrifts around the country, check the following:

- *Kiplinger's Personal Finance Magazine* (monthly; daily updates at www.Kiplinger.com)
- the *Wall Street Journal* (daily)
- *Barron's* (weekly)
- *USA Today* (Fridays)
- the *New York Times* (Thursdays)
- Sunday editions of other major newspapers

You can find names of banks and s&l's paying the most generous yields in specialized sources. The best-known are:

100 Highest Yields (www.bankrate.com; 800-327-7717, ext. 274)

RateGram (www.bradshawbankdata.com) Formerly a newsletter and now available on the Internet.

Names of institutions you get from these publications can be checked for financial stability through Veribanc (800-442-2657), which will tell you its safety rating of financial institutions over the telephone for a charge of $10 for one rating and $5 for each additional rating. Veribanc will also send you a list of "Blue Ribbon" banks in your area for $35 or an evaluation of all the banks and s&l's in a state for $110.

BUY FROM A BROKER

A brokerage firm can generally offer you an above-average yield on a federally insured CD: about half a percentage point to a point or more higher than average, depending on the market at the time and on the maturity of the certificate. Because issuing banks pay a fee to brokers who parcel out their CDs this way, the customer usually doesn't have to pay a commission. And because brokerage firms that do this sort of packaging usually maintain an active secondary market for their CDs, you can often sell them back before maturity without paying the penalty a bank or s&l would charge for early withdrawal.

There are two possible traps here, and both are avoidable:

First, in the search for an attractive yield, the broker packaging the deal may buy up CDs from institutions you'd rather not do business with yourself. To avoid this situation, ask the broker where the CD originated and what the brokerage firm knows about the stability of the issuing institution and the status of its federal deposit insurance. Brokered CDs usually carry federal deposit insurance, but be sure to ask.

Second, the privilege of cashing in your CD early with no penalty may bear a different price. If interest rates rise between the day you purchase the CD and the day you cash it in early, you won't get back as much as you paid for it. (On the other hand, if rates have fallen, you should get more.) This is because a CD in the secondary market is in many respects a short-term bond, and the usual relationship between bond values and market rates will be at work: When interest rates rise, the value of outstanding bonds falls; when rates fall, bond values rise. For more on this relationship, see Chapter 5.

SHOULD YOU TAKE ADVANTAGE OF GIMMICKS?

Some banks and s&l's have devised yield-boosting gimmicks to attract new money.

A popular one is the "bump-up" CD. On a bump-up, banks promise to increase the rate they're paying on your CD if interest rates rise during the CD's term. Another kind of bump-up promises a yield a fraction of a percentage point higher every time you roll over the original six-month CD into a new one. In the latter deal, your initial rate is almost surely lower than the rate being offered on a CD without the bump-up feature. You'd probably be better off locking in the higher rate to begin with.

In assessing a bump-up, it's important to be aware that the deal is usually crafted to favor the bank. Whether the rate goes up, and by how much, may be entirely at the bank's discretion. A better deal is one in which you have the option to switch to the higher rate if the bank boosts the rate it's offering on a CD with the same maturity as one you're holding. In that kind of arrangement, it's up to you to keep track of the bank's current CD rates.

An even better deal on a bump-up is one in which the rate is tied to an independent index rather than one that's controlled by the bank or by you. But it's still up to you to keep track of which way rates are headed and to decide when to lock in a new, higher rate.

The latest innovation is market-indexed CDs, sold through regional brokers, requiring a minimum deposit of $5,000. They mature in 8½ years. Returns are based on the appreciation of Standard & Poor's 500-stock index during the term of the CD. But there are strings attached: You don't get credit for dividends, and because interest isn't calculated until the CD matures you don't get the benefits of compounding. If the index is lower than when you first invested, you'll get your principal back with no earnings.

Market-indexed CDs expose you to the volatility of the stock market without delivering all the potential rewards. You'd be better off putting your cash into regular CDs and your long-term savings into a stock-index fund.

PROTECT YOURSELF BY STAGGERING MATURITIES

The best way to maintain the liquidity of your savings, boost yield and protect yourself against rapid rate changes is to stagger the maturity dates of your CDs. Sometimes called "laddering," staggering maturities is really a form of diversification. You spread your money over several different maturities: say, one-fourth of your CD funds in certificates maturing in three months, one-fourth in CDs maturing in six months, one-fourth in CDs maturing in a year and one-fourth in CDs maturing in two or three years. (A profitable rule of thumb based on the history of interest-rate movements: If five-year CD rates ever reach 10% again, stock up on them.)

Normally, longer maturities pay more interest, so why not just concentrate on those? In fact, that would be a splendid strategy if you could accurately predict the direction of interest rates and your prediction was that they were going to fall. But what if they rise? By staggering your maturities, you have protected yourself in either case. If rates rise, your short-term CDs will mature in time for you to reinvest the principal at the new, higher rates. If rates fall or stay flat, you'll be sitting pretty because you've locked in the current two- or three-year rate. By the time those certificates mature, rates could well have turned in the other direction again.

Money-Market Deposit Accounts: Limited Appeal

ONE PLACE TO GET FEDERAL INSURANCE PLUS INTEREST THAT'S somewhere between a passbook account and a CD is in a money-market deposit account (MMDA). Banks and thrifts like to boast about the higher rates paid by these accounts, but in fact they rarely compete very well with certificates.

MMDAs probably compete more directly with low-rate savings accounts and interest-paying checking accounts, except for all the strings attached. You can write a limited number of checks on the account and make a limited number of withdrawals; if you exceed the limit, you pay a penalty. These limits on liquidity, coupled with the lower rates generally (but not always) paid by MMDAs compared with money-market mutual funds, add up to a high premium to pay for the federal insurance on MMDAs, considering the excellent safety record of the uninsured money-market funds.

Why You Should Use Money-Market Funds

THE REASON YOU WANT TO HAVE A PIECE OF THE MONEY MARket through a money-market fund is that it often pays more than a savings account, with no significant increase in risk. The minimum initial investment usually ranges from $1,000 to $5,000, for which you get a slice of a portfolio containing a number of investments you could never afford on your own.

Money-market mutual funds take your cash and invest it in the money market, which is a collective name that describes all the different ways in which governments, banks, corporations and securities dealers borrow and lend money for short periods. Money-market loans may be due in a few days, a few weeks or a few months, but never more than a year. Thus, short-term certificates of deposit are considered to be in the money market. Treasury bills, which mature in three, six, nine or 12 months, are money-market instruments; Treasury bonds, which mature in ten or more years, are not.

A typical money-market portfolio contains a variety of short-term investments:

Certificates of deposit and commercial paper (short-term corporate IOUs), which are among the favorites;

Treasury bills and notes (government IOUs) within a few months of maturity;

Other federal government securities (short-term securities issued by individual government agencies or government-sponsored organizations such as Fannie Mae);

Banker's acceptances (a somewhat esoteric instrument used to finance international commercial transactions);

Repurchase agreements, or "repos" (also somewhat esoteric ways of selling financial holdings for a day or two with a pledge to buy them back at a higher price);

Eurodollar CDs (issued by the foreign branches of U.S. banks); and

Yankee CDs (issued by U.S. branches of foreign banks).

Some money-market funds pay tax-free earnings because they invest exclusively in short-term municipal bonds issued by state and local governments.

One of the most attractive features of money-market funds is that you can sell your shares anytime by writing a check drawn on your account. You pay no sales fees either buying or selling. The funds' managers, who decide which money-market instruments to buy, charge a modest management fee, on the order of 1% or so. All that makes the funds liquid, convenient and relatively economical to own. But money-market funds often engage in transactions that individual savers and investors comprehend only dimly, if at all. Thus, it is important to know what could go wrong with them, how likely that is to happen and how you might be hurt if something does go wrong.

ASSESS THEIR SAFETY

Actually, money-market funds have a reputation for being about the safest uninsured, non-Treasury investment around, and it's a well-earned reputation. Since they were created in 1972, no individual investor has lost a cent of principal in any of the hundreds of funds you now have to choose from. So safe are they thought to be that savers and investors have stashed hundreds of billions of dollars into them.

This safety record was built partly on restrictions that govern the funds and partly on the fund sponsors' determination to keep the public's faith in funds strong.

Securities laws dictate that the average maturity of a money fund's holdings may not exceed 90 days, and any individual debt instrument owned by a fund must mature within 13 months. Short maturities help insulate the value of money funds from movements in interest rates. (Prices of interest-paying investments, such as bonds, fall when rates rise, and vice versa; the shorter the maturity, the smaller the move.)

This relative stability allows money funds to keep the value of a share constant from day to day, even though, in fact, net-asset values do fluctuate a little. (The net asset value, or NAV, is the value of one share in a fund; see page 139.) Under a widely accepted accounting procedure known as "penny rounding," a fund may report a value of $1 a share as long as its actual value does not drop below $0.995 per share or rise above $1.005.

The short maturities also make it unlikely that a fund will be caught holding the debt of an issuer that gets into financial trouble. If a fund buys 30-day commercial paper issued by an apparently healthy company, chances are slim that the firm's financial condition will deteriorate so quickly that it defaults before the debt matures.

DEFAULT RISKS. But a slim chance doesn't mean no chance. In January 1997, Strong Heritage Money Fund, the nation's top-yielding retail money-market mutual fund, and two other Strong funds found themselves holding large amounts of suddenly worthless commercial paper issued by Mercury Finance Corp., which defaulted on a $17 million payment.

The fund's sponsor bought back the failed debt at face value and swallowed the losses so that shareholders wouldn't be hurt, keeping the money-market fund industry's safety record intact.

In the unlikely event that a money-market fund holds securities that go into default, it helps to have your money invested with a well-capitalized company, such as Dreyfus, Fidelity, T. Rowe Price, Strong, or others that we recommend.

INTEREST-RATE RISKS. There is another way funds can get clobbered. The chief worry is a sudden spike in interest rates. When rates soar, even the relatively short-term holdings of money-market funds can suffer a decline in value so severe that the fund has difficulty maintaining its net asset value. The longer the average maturity of the fund at the time of the spike, the greater the danger. If investors flee from the fund in search of higher yield elsewhere, forcing a sale of holdings at distress prices, the problem is compounded.

THE IMPACT OF AN INTEREST-RATE SPIKE. What would happen if a fund got caught in a rate bind these days? What would it take to do real damage? A fund with an average maturity of 60 days could suffer a half-cent loss of net asset value if short-term rates were to quickly ratchet up three percentage points, according to Standard & Poor's. In fact, says S&P, short-term rates in the U.S. have surged as much as four percentage points in as few as five days. The share value of a fund with an average maturity of 90 days, now the maximum allowed, would drop less than a half cent if rates jumped two points within a few days.

For all this, the odds of losing principal in a money-market fund remain very slight. A fund would have to suffer several defaults among its holdings or own a portfolio with an extremely long average maturity at a time when rates suddenly skyrocketed. Furthermore, the fund's sponsor would have to abandon the industry's unwritten policy of bailing out money-market funds in the event of a loss. Even in such circumstances, losses to investors would be modest, probably on the order of 1% or 2%. That's a small enough chance to take compared with the dead certainty of losing out on one, two or more percentage points of yield by keeping all your money in a savings account or a bank money-market deposit account.

Play It Super-Safe

To diminish the risks even further, follow these routes to the safest money-market funds. As you do, remember that each restriction you place on a fund can, under certain market conditions, hold down the yield. Government-only funds, for instance, pay slightly less than others because their portfolios are safer. For a list of money-market funds that fit the descriptions below, see pages 42-43.

To limit the risk of default, check the prospectus carefully to see what kinds of debt the fund will buy. If the fund invests in commercial paper, make sure it's limited to issues receiving the highest ratings (they will be labeled A-1 and P-1) from the major rating services, such as Standard & Poor's or Moody's Investors Service. Call the fund and ask about its current policy, which may be more or less conservative than is permitted by the prospectus.

Standard & Poor's follows several dozen money-market funds and ranks them for safety. For a list of the S&P ratings, write to Standard & Poor's, Managed Funds Ratings, 13th Floor, 25 Broadway, New York, NY 10004.

Online, check out:
www.bankrate.com
the Money Fund Selector™ (www.ibcdata.com)

Money-Market Funds: A Starter Kit

HERE IS A SAMPLING of the hundreds of money-market funds available to investors today. The funds on this list are among the largest in each category, and most have well-established track records for safety and performance. We have chosen funds that accept a minimum initial investment of $2,500 or less. The best way to choose a fund you'll like is to identify several that fit your objectives, telephone for prospectuses and make your choice based on investor services that fit your needs.

GENERAL TAXABLE FUNDS	MINIMUM INITIAL DEPOSIT	MINIMUM CHECK AMOUNT
Cash Equivalent (Kemper) 800-621-1048; www.kemper.com	$ 1,000	$ 250
Centennial Money Market Trust (Oppenheimer) 800-525-7048; www.oppenheimerfunds.com	1,000	250
Dreyfus Liquid Assets 800-645-6561; www.dreyfus.com	2,500	500
Dreyfus Worldwide Dollar Money Market 800-645-6561; www.dreyfus.com	2,500	500
Fidelity Cash Reserves 800-544-8888; www.fidelity.com	2,500	500
IDS Cash Management (American Express) 800-225-5437; www6.americanexpress.com/advisors/	2,000	100
Kemper Money Market 800-621-1048; www.kemper.com	1,000	500
Oppenheimer Money Market 800-525-7048; www.oppenheimerfunds.com	1,000	100
Prudential Money Market Assets 800-225-1852; www.prudential.com	1,000	500

To eliminate default risk entirely, look for funds that invest only in federal government securities. Some of these invest in a variety of government-issued securities, such as Treasury bills, and government-sponsored debts of agencies such as the Federal Farm Credit Bank, and repurchase agreements backed by Treasury issues. Another type of government-only fund buys just Treasury bills—the ultimate in credit safety.

GENERAL TAXABLE FUNDS	MINIMUM INITIAL DEPOSIT	MINIMUM CHECK AMOUNT
Reserve Fund 800-223-5547; www.reservefunds.com	**$ 1,000**	**no minimum**
Schwab Money Market 800-435-4000; www.schwab.com	1,000	no checks
Scudder Cash Investment Trust 800-225-2470; http://investments.scudder.com	2,500	$ 100
T. Rowe Price Prime Reserve 800-638-5660; www.troweprice.com	2,500	500

GOVERNMENT-ONLY FUNDS	MINIMUM INITIAL DEPOSIT	MINIMUM CHECK AMOUNT
Capital Preservation (American Century) 800-472-3389; www.americancentury.com	**$ 2,500**	**$ 100**
Cash Equivalent/Government (Kemper) 800-621-1048; www.kemper.com	1,000	250
Dreyfus 100% U.S. Treasury 800-645-6561; www.dreyfus.com	2,500	500
Fidelity U.S. Government Reserves 800-544-8888; www.fidelity.com	2,500	500

TAX-FREE FUNDS	MINIMUM INITIAL DEPOSIT	MINIMUM CHECK AMOUNT
Calvert Tax-Free Reserves 800-368-2748; www.calvertgroup.com	**$ 2,000**	**$ 250**
Dreyfus Municipal Money Market 800-645-6561; www.dreyfus.com	2,500	500

To control interest-rate risk, look into the fund's policy on the average maturity of its portfolio. Most prospectuses allow money funds to extend maturities to the maximum 90 days. As a matter of policy, however, many funds keep average maturities at 40 to 60 days. You can also find current average maturities in tables of money-market fund yields, which are published weekly in many newspapers.

The difference between well-paying funds and bad-paying funds is often a good guess at the direction of interest rates and absorption of fees by the management company. Bottom line: Some money-market funds are better managed and make more money, and some pay out more to attract investors.

Shift Some Cash Into Short-Term Treasuries

I F YOU HAVE ACCUMULATED MORE THAN $1,000 IN SAVINGS, YOU should consider eliminating the management fees charged by money-market funds by owning Treasury bills yourself. T-bills and other securities issued by the U.S. Treasury are even safer than CDs because they're backed by the full faith and credit of the federal government. For that reason, they generally yield a little less than CDs, but they still have a couple of advantages.

For one thing, rates are determined by the market rather than by a rate-setting committee at a bank. For another, earnings from Treasuries, although subject to federal tax, are exempt from state and local income taxes—a definite benefit in high-tax states such as California, Massachusetts and New York.

WAYS TO BUY THEM

You can buy T-bills from a bank or a broker for a modest fee, and there is one good reason to consider doing so. Banks and brokers are selling bills from their own inventory, which is likely to contain a variety of maturities. New bills mature in three, six, nine or 12 months. That's a nice variety, but the timing may not be to your liking. Suppose you know you're going to need the money in three weeks? Or five months? Theoretically, a bank or a broker should be able to find you a bill that matures within a few days of when you want your money back.

If timing isn't that important, you can save the $50 or so a broker would charge by buying directly from the Treasury. To purchase T-bills, which come in maturities of one year or less, you can buy them by telephone or online. Or you may fill out a simple form and send a certified check or cashier's check for $1,000 (the minimum investment) to the government. For information on how to do this and on how to purchase other securities directly from the government, see page 103 of Chapter 5.

A NOTE OF CAUTION

Although the interest from Treasury securities that you buy your-self is not subject to state and local taxes, you can't assume the same is true for dividends earned through a U.S. government securities mutual fund. Most states exempt the earnings, but a number of them don't. In states that do, only funds that limit their investments to securities issued directly by the Treasury and certain government agencies qualify for exemption.

Saving With Savings Bonds

U.S. SAVINGS BONDS ARE ALSO EXCELLENT SAVING VEHICLES. EE bonds pay a market-based rate of interest. Interest is free of state and local taxes, and federal taxes can be deferred until you cash in the bonds. What's more, interest earned on bonds purchased in your name may escape income taxes entirely if you meet certain income tests and use the pro-ceeds to pay college tuition and fees for your children. This tax break is diminished if you plan to use the education tax credits, an Education IRA or a state college savings plan. The income tests and a way to avoid paying more taxes than required are described in Chapter 13.

PART TWO

Build a Successful Portfolio

CHAPTER 4

Stocks: The Main Ingredient

UY STOCKS. NO OTHER INVESTMENT AVAILABLE TO intelligent amateurs with average resources, average willingness to take risks and limited time to spend on active management holds as much promise as stocks over the long run. Not real estate. Not gold. Not bonds. Not savings accounts. Stocks aren't the only things that belong in your investment portfolio, but they are the most important.

Ibbotson Associates has delved into investment records going back to 1926, calculating the compound annual returns (including reinvested dividends and interest) of large- and small-company stocks, corporate and government bonds, and Treasury bills. Ibbotson then matched all the returns against each other and, for good measure, against the inflation rate.

The graphs on page 50 show the results through 1998, a period that includes the two biggest stock-market crashes in history, plus the Great Depression. Stocks win by a large margin, with small-company stocks edging out those of big companies by less than a couple of percentage points. Even that small difference looms large when it is compounded over the years: $1,000 growing at 11.2% a year for 20 years becomes about $8,300. At 12.4%, it becomes $10,300. During the 72-year period covered by the bottom graph, $1,000 invested in a representative sampling of big stocks would have grown to an eye-catching $2.1 million. The same $1,000 riding along with small stocks would have become more than $4.5 million.

All that's pretty impressive, but unless your main concern is

Stocks Are the Long-Term Winners

WHETHER YOU TAKE the long-term view represented by the graph on the top or the extra-long-term view, shown in the graph on the bottom, it's clear that stocks beat other financial assets, and that the stocks of small companies tend to outperform the stocks of large compa- nies. Since 1966, small-company stocks returned 13.8%, on average, while large-company stocks topped 12.2%. The figures reflect total return, which means that any dividends or interest paid by the investment being measured were plowed back into the same investment.

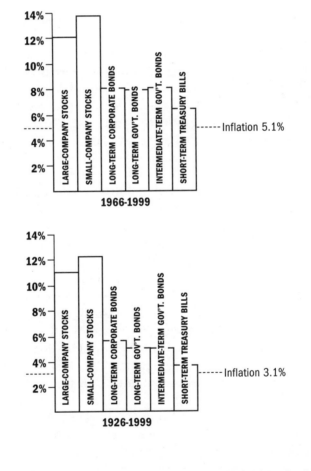

1966-1999

1926-1999

Source: Ibbotson Associates

the financial welfare of your great-grandchildren, you'd probably prefer a faster pace than 72 years. If you can pick better-
than-average stocks, you will beat the average return.

In fact, the payoff from even mediocre stocks often beats the
long-term averages (which, remember, cover bad times as well as
good). From 1994 through 1998, the return on the 30 big-
company stocks that make up the Dow Jones industrial average
topped 22% per year with dividends reinvested, and the 500
stocks in the S&P 500 topped 24%. For the '90s as a whole, both
indexes returned about 19% per year.

This chapter will show you how to pick good stocks that can
reasonably be expected to beat the averages during a decade in
which it is reasonable to expect the stock market to generate
decent returns. You don't have to beat the market by much to
prosper over time. An ambitious but achievable goal is to do two
to five percentage points better than the market. By that measure, your goal over the long range should be to earn an average
return of 12% to 15%—not every single year, but on average.
There is risk involved, as there is in all investments, but the
important thing is to accept the risks as the path to the higher
returns you seek. And if you stick to the techniques described in
this book, you can reduce those risks.

Different Kinds of Stocks

FIRST IT'S IMPORTANT TO UNDERSTAND WHAT A STOCK IS.
When investors talk about stocks, they usually mean "common" stocks. A share of common stock represents a share
of ownership in the company that issues it and ties the investor's
fortunes to those of the company. The price of the stock goes up
and down, depending on how the company performs and how
investors think the company will perform in the future. The
stock may or may not pay dividends, which usually come from
profits. If profits fall, dividend payments may be cut or elimi-
nated.

Many companies also issue "preferred" stock. Like common
stock, it is a share of ownership. The difference is that preferred
stockholders get first dibs on company dividends in good times
and on assets in bad times, if the company goes broke and has to
liquidate. Theoretically, the price of preferred stock can rise or

fall along with the common. In reality it doesn't move nearly as much because preferred investors are interested mainly in the dividends, which are fixed when the stock is issued. For this reason, preferred stock is really more comparable to a bond than to a share of common stock.

It's hard to think of a reason to buy preferred stocks. They generally pay a slightly lower yield than the same company's bonds and are no safer. Their potential equity kicker (the chance that the preferred will rise in price along with the common stock) has been largely illusory. Preferred stock is really better suited for corporate portfolios because a corporation doesn't have to pay federal income tax on most of the dividends it receives from another corporation. For these reasons, this chapter will concentrate on common stocks.

Stocks are bought and sold on one or more of several "stock markets," the best known of which are the New York Stock Exchange (NYSE), the American Stock Exchange (AMEX), and the widely dispersed telecommunications system known as Nasdaq. There are also several regional exchanges, ranging from Boston to Honolulu. Stocks sold on an exchange are said to be "listed" there; stocks sold through Nasdaq are often called "over-the-counter" (OTC) stocks.

There are lots of reasons to own stocks and several different categories of stocks to fit investors' goals. Sometimes the reasons for buying a particular kind of stock are obvious from the definition of the category.

Growth stocks have good prospects for growing faster than the economy or the stock market in general. Investors buy them because of their good record of earnings growth and the expectation that they will continue generating capital gains over the long haul. More stocks seem to fit this definition than you can shake a stick at, ranging from the very well known and much commented upon, such as Procter & Gamble and Wal-Mart Stores, to the comparatively obscure.

Blue-chip stocks are a more loosely defined universe, including solid performers that could also be classified as growth stocks, such as Merck and Coca-Cola. Investors with an eye on the long term and little tolerance for risk buy these stocks for their undeniable high quality. They tend to generate decent dividend income, some growth and, above all, safety and reliability.

Income stocks worthy of the name pay relatively high dividends and raise them regularly. Electric utilities, automobile manufacturers and banks often fall into this category, which is favored by retirees and others in need of relatively high income from their stocks.

Cyclical stocks are called that because their fortunes tend to rise and fall with those of the economy at large, prospering when the business cycle is on the upswing, suffering in recessions. Automobile manufacturers are a prime example, which illustrates the important fact that these categories aren't mutually exclusive. Other industries whose profits are sensitive to the business cycle include airlines, steel, chemicals and any business dependent on home building.

Defensive stocks are theoretically insulated from the business cycle because people go right on buying their products and services in bad times as well as good. Utility companies fit here (another overlap), as do companies that sell food, beverages and drugs. The major problem with this category is that to maximize profits, you need to buy them on the verge of an economic downturn, which requires an ability to predict that is rare even among experts.

Value stocks earn the name when they are considered underpriced according to several measures of value described later in this chapter. For instance, a stock with an unusually low price in relation to the company's earnings may be dubbed a "value stock" if it exhibits other signs of good health.

Speculative stocks may be unproven young companies in a fast-growing area, such as the Internet or telecommunications. They may be erratic or down-at-the-heels old companies exhibiting some sort of spark, such as the promise of an imminent technological breakthrough or a brilliant new chief executive. Buyers of speculative stocks have hopes of making a killing. In recent years investors have driven up the prices of several high-tech stocks even though profits for the companies were acknowledged to be years away. Most speculative stocks don't do well in the long run, so it takes big gains in a few to offset your losses in the many.

A Smart Way to Buy Stocks

T
HE SECRET TO CHOOSING GOOD COMMON STOCKS IS THAT there really is no secret to it. The winning techniques are tried and true, but it's how you assemble and apply them that makes the difference. The techniques don't work all the time, but they work often enough so that the methods employed by successful stock investors tend to be more alike than different.

Information is the key. Having the right information about a company and knowing how to interpret it are more important than any of the other factors you might hear credited for the success of the latest market genius. Information is even more important than timing. When you find a company that looks promising, you don't have to buy the stock today or even this week. Good stocks tend to stay good, so you can take the time to investigate before you invest.

You get the information you need to size up a company's prospects in many places, and a lot of it is free. The listing on the following pages offers a guide to the most readily available sources of the data described below.

WHAT YOU NEED TO KNOW

The Kiplinger way to succeed in the stock market is to invest for both growth and value. That means concentrating the bulk of your portfolio in stocks that pass the tests described below and holding them for the long term—three, five, even ten years. For those in search of income, not growth, it means applying the same tests so that you don't make any false and risky assumptions about the stocks you buy. This method is not based on buying a stock one day and selling it the next. It does not depend on your ability to predict the direction of the economy or even the direction of the stock market. It does depend on your willingness to apply the following measures before you place your order. If you do that, you'll find most of your choices falling into the growth, income and blue-chip categories described earlier. The aim: an average 12% to 15%

annual total return (price increases plus dividends) on your investments when the market is performing in its historical range, plus the opportunity for much bigger gains when the economic forces described in Chapter 1 push it to much greater heights.

You'll have no trouble finding candidates for your investment dollars. In fact, you can't escape the daily barrage of recommendations from newspapers, television and radio, not to mention a growing pack of financial magazines. Most of the information you need to check out these possibilities is readily available from the sources listed on pages 56 and 57 or can be calculated from the data you find there.

You'll quickly discover that the number of stocks that meet all these tests at any given time will be low. So what you're really looking for are stocks that exhibit most of the following signs of value and come close on the others. These should form the core of your portfolio. Many investors have profited mightily in the past few years by ignoring signs of value and buying the stock of companies that are too new to have a track record but are engaged in an exciting new business such as e-commerce—stocks that would qualify as "speculative" according to the definitions presented earlier. The rules go out the window in sizing up issues like this, as the clues to success lie more in your faith in a concept or your gut instincts than on the company's balance sheets. Be on the watch for such stocks; they make investing fun. But remember the pyramid of risk described earlier, and don't let them grow to be a significant part of your portfolio.

EARNINGS PER SHARE. This is the company's bottom line—the profits earned after taxes and payment of dividends to holders of preferred stock. Earnings are also the company's chief resource for paying dividends to shareholders and for reinvesting in business growth. Check to be sure that earnings come from routine operations—say, widget sales—and not from one-time occurrences—such as the sale of a subsidiary or a big award from a patent-infringement suit. The exhaustive stock listings in *Barron's* give the latest quarterly earnings per share for each stock, plus the date when the next earnings will be declared. Historical earnings figures are available in annual reports, Standard & Poor's and Mergent FIS (formerly Moody's Investors Service) publications, and *Value Line Investment Survey*,

Where to Get the Facts You Need

THIS CHAPTER RECOMMENDS using certain key facts about a company to size up prospects for its stock. Here's where to find those facts. In most cases you won't need more than one or two of the sources listed.

SOURCE	WHAT'S IN IT AND WHERE TO GET IT
Company's annual report	Basic information about the company, including audited financial data for the most recent year and summaries of prior years. Available from brokers and the investor relations office of the company.
Form 10-K	Extensive financial data, required to be filed annually with the Securities and Exchange Commission. Includes two years' worth of detailed, audited financial balance sheets, plus a five-year history of the stock price, earnings, dividends and other data. To order copies, contact Disclosure Information Services (800-638-8241; www.sec.gov).
Analysts' reports	Commentaries by brokerage firms' research departments, containing varying amounts of hard data to accompany the analysts' recommendations to buy, sell or hold stocks followed by the firm. Available from brokers.
Value Line Investment Survey	A vast collection of data, including prices, earnings and dividends, stretching back nearly 70 years, along with analysis and several unique features, such as a "timeliness" rating for each stock. Follows 1,700 stocks. Available from libraries, or from *Value Line* ($570 a year, ten-week trial subscriptions are $55; P.O. Box 3988, Church St. Station, New York, NY 10008-3988; 800-535-8760; www.valueline.com).
Standard & Poor's	*S&P Stock Reports* offer a wealth of current and historical data covering the three major exchanges (NYSE, AMEX and OTC) in three volumes that are updated every six weeks. The monthly *S&P Stock*

plus the databases offered by many Internet services.

Value Sign #1: Look for companies with a pattern of earnings growth and a habit of reinvesting a chunk of earnings in the growth of the business. Compare earnings per share with the dividend payout. The portion that isn't paid out to shareholders gets reinvested in the business.

SOURCE	WHAT'S IN IT AND WHERE TO GET IT
	Guide is a compendium of similar data on more than 5,000 stocks, but with no analysts' commentary. The guide provides most of the hard data you need to check out a company. Available from libraries, brokers or by subscription from S&P (25 Broadway, New York, NY 10004; 800-221-5277; www.standardpoor.com).
Mergent FIS publications (formerly Moody's Investors Service)	Mergent FIS publishes eight *Moody's Manuals* containing current and historical data on thousands of companies. *The Handbook of Common Stocks* covers nearly 1,000 stocks, and the *Dividend Record* keeps track of current dividend payments of most publicly traded companies. *The Handbook of Dividend Achievers* is widely used by individual investors. Available from brokers, libraries or from Mergent FIS (60 Madison Ave., Sixth Floor, New York, NY 10010; 800-342-5647, Ext. 7601; www.fisonline).
Financial newspapers	The stock listings of the *Wall Street Journal, Barron's* and *Investor's Business Daily* contain current information on prices, dividends, yields and price-earnings ratios, as do the stock listings of most daily newspapers. What sets these three apart is the accompanying depth of coverage of the investment markets. Available from newsstands or libraries, or by subscription.
Computer online data bases	There are many, the largest of which is probably Thompson Financial Securities Data, which provides historical and current data, information on file at the SEC, market news, analysts' reports and other features. Available from Dow Jones News/Retrieval (800-522-3567) and CompuServe (800-848-8990) or directly by subscription (800-662-7878). Prodigy (800-776-3449) charges a flat fee for its Strategic Investor service. America Online (800-827-6364) and the other commercial services also offer stock and investment information, as do countless Internet sites.

PRICE-EARNINGS RATIO. Many investment pros consider the price-earnings ratio to be the single most important thing you can know about a stock. It is the price of a share divided by the company's earnings per share. If a stock sells for $40 a share and the company earned $4 a share in the previous 12 months, the stock has a P/E ratio of 10. Simply put, the P/E ratio tells you how much money investors are willing to pay for each dollar of a

How to Read the Stock Listings

A A small "s" next to the listing means the stock was split or the company issued a stock dividend within the past year. This is your signal that the year's high and low prices have been adjusted to reflect the effect of the split.

B An "x" indicates that the stock has gone "ex-dividend." Investors who buy the stock now won't get the next dividend payment, which has been declared but not paid. Most listings stick the "x" next to the figure in the volume column.

C Sometimes a stock has been issued so recently that it doesn't have a full year's history on which to base its pricing. In such a case the 52-week high and low prices date from the beginning of trading and the stock gets a little "n" to the left of the listing.

D The dividend listed is the latest annual dividend paid by the stock.

E The yield is the stock's latest annual dividend expressed as a percentage of that day's price.

F The price/earnings ratio is the price of the stock divided by the earnings per share reported by the company for the latest four quarters.

G Most prices—and price changes—are reported in increments of one-eighth of a point. One-eighth of a dollar is 12.5 cents.

	52 Weeks Hi	52 Weeks Lo	Stock	Sym	Div (D)	Yld % (E)	PE (F)	Vol 100s	Hi (G)	Lo (G)	Close (G)	Net Chg (G)
	28 3/8	12 1/8	ChileTel ADR	CTC	.39e	1.7	...	3019	22 15/16	22 1/2	22 15/16	+ 7/16
	14 15/16	4	ChinaEstrnAir	CEA		...	...	117	12 1/4	12 1/8	12 1/4	+ 1/4
	12 1/2	4 15/16	ChinaFund	CHN	.08e	.7	...	150	10 15/16	10 7/8	10 15/16	...
	13 15/16	3 1/16	ChinSAir ADS	ZNH		...	...	147	10 1/8	10 1/16	10 1/8	+ 1/8
	66 1/2	23	ChinaTelecm	CHL		...	...	256	61 3/4	61 1/4	61 3/4	– 13/16
	9 1/8	3 9/16	ChinaTire	TIR	.08	1.2	...	74	6 3/4	6 3/8	6 11/16	+ 1/4
	2 13/16	3/8	ChinaYuchai	CYD		...	...	153	1 5/8	1 1/2	1 5/8	...
	12 13/16	6 15/16	ChiquitaBrd	CQB	.20	2.8	dd	692	7 1/8	7	7 1/8	+ 1/8
▼	42 3/8	29 11/16	ChiquitaBrd pfA		2.88	9.9	...	16	29 1/4	29	29	– 11/16
	50 1/8	37	ChiquitaBrd pfB		3.75	9.6	...	9	39 7/16	39 1/4	39 1/4	– 3/16
	33 5/8	25 7/16	Chittnden	CHZ	.88	3.1	cc	213	29 1/4	28 5/8	28 11/16	– 9/16
	10 7/8	4 3/4	ChockFull	CHF		...	cc	53	10 3/8	10 3/8	10 3/8	...
	19 3/4	9 5/8	ChoiceHtl	CHH		...	19	321	17	16 3/4	17	...
	69	37 3/8 ♣	ChoicePoint	CPS		...	25	474	64 1/4	62 7/8	63 11/16	+ 1 1/2
	53 1/2	38 5/8	ChrisCrft	CCN	stk	...	93	1012	50 3/8	48 15/16	50	– 3/8
	18 1/2	11 7/8	Chromcrft	CRC		...	9	9	12 11/16	12 11/16	12 11/16	– 1/16
	76 3/8	54	Chubb	CB	1.28	2.2	14	8773	59	57 5/8	58 1/4	– 13/16
	50 9/16	27 1/16	Church&Dwt	CHD	.56f	1.2	24	2731	47 7/16	46 1/2	46 1/2	– 1/4
	3 1/8	1 1/8	Chyron	CHY		...	dd	128	1 3/8	1 1/4	1 1/4	– 1/16
	33 5/16	13 5/16	CIBER	CBR		...	29	1628	19 15/16	19 1/4	19 7/16	– 7/16
B — (x)	65	48 3/8	Cilcorp Inc	CER	2.46	3.8	39	1904	64 11/16	64 1/2	64 5/8	+ 7/16
A — (s)	26 1/2	8 67/128	CincBell	CSN	.40	2.2	19	14449	19	18	18 1/2	– 1/2
	26 1/2	24 9/16	CincGE deb	JRL	2.07	8.3	...	13	24 15/16	24 11/16	24 13/16	+ 1/8
	78	68	CinnGE pfA		4.00	5.5	...	z50	72 5/8	71 3/4	72 5/8	– 3/8
	39 7/8	27 5/16	CINergyCp	CIN	1.80	5.8	14	9474	31 7/16	30 5/16	31 3/16	+ 13/16
	8	**3 1/2**	**CirctCityCrmx**	**KMX**		**...**	**dd**	**3234**	**3 11/16**	**3 1/2**	**3 1/2**	**– 3/16**
s	52 31/32	14 13/32	CircuitCity	CC	.07	.1	cc	17372	47	44 5/8	46 3/4	+ 7/8
	26 13/16	22 5/8	CiticpCap pfA		1.78	7.4	...	180	24 1/16	23 7/8	23 241/256	– 5/128
C — (n)	24 7/8	21 3/8	CitigpCap pfX		.68e	3.0	...	425	23	22 13/16	22 7/8	+ 1/16
s	51 3/4	19	Citigroup	C	.56	1.1	27	[illegible]	[illegible]			
	25 11/16	21	CitignCap [illegible]									

Reprinted with permission of the Wall Street Journal
©1999 Dow Jones & Company, Inc.

company's earnings. It is such a significant key to value that it's listed every day in the newspapers along with the stock's price.

Any company's P/E needs to be compared with P/Es of similar companies, and with broader measures as well. Market indexes, such as the Dow Jones industrials and the S&P 500, have P/Es, as do different industry sectors, such as chemicals or autos. Some online brokers, including Charles Schwab & Co., post P/E ratios for some industries on their Web sites; see page 326). Knowing what these are can help you decide on the relative merits of a stock you're considering.

It's hard to say what the "right" level is for a company's P/E ratio, or for the market as a whole. You should expect to pay more to own shares of a company you think will increase profits faster than the average company of its type. But high-P/E stocks carry the risk that if the earnings of a company disappoint investors, its share price could plunge quickly. Just one poor quarter—or a rumor of one—can mean a vicious pounding for a stock with a sky-high "multiple." By contrast, investors don't expect a low-P/E company to grow so rapidly and are less likely to desert the company on mildly unfavorable news. If profits rise faster than expected, investors may bid up that low P/E. The combination of higher earnings and a growing P/E can push a stock's price up fast.

Other things being equal, analysts often recommend the stock with the lowest P/E in its industry, if they like the business and if several companies look good. For example, the auto and truck industry normally trades at a P/E of around 12 or 13, while the food-processing industry usually has a multiple of about 20. Therefore, if General Motors has a P/E of 10, it is actually selling at a slight discount to its industry and thus is relatively cheap. If General Mills has a P/E of 20, it is right in line with its industry, neither expensive nor especially cheap at that time. (Caution: A low P/E is not by itself a sign of value. A stock's price may be low relative to its earnings because investors have little faith in the reliability of those earnings, and investors could be right.)

You don't make any money from the stellar performance of a company before you buy its stock. You want it to do well after you buy it. So look not only at the "trailing" P/E, which is based on the previous 12 months' earnings, but also at P/Es based on analysts' future-earnings estimates. Those could be wrong, of course, but they are another piece of information on which to base your decision to buy or not to buy. Brokers will happily provide the forecasts of their firms' analysts, and you can find other forecasts in many of the sources listed on pages 56 and 57.

There are other factors to weigh before deciding which stocks to buy. But P/E ratios are the natural starting point because they provide a quick way to separate stocks that seem overpriced from those that don't.

Value Sign #2: For "keeper" stocks, look for companies with P/E ratios lower than other companies in the same industry.

DIVIDEND YIELD. This is the company's dividend expressed as a percentage of the share price. If a share of stock is selling for $50 and the company pays $2 a year in dividends, its yield is 4%. In addition to generating income for shareholders, dividends are a good indicator of the strength of a company compared with its competitors. A long history of rising dividends is evidence of a strong company that manages to maintain payouts in good times and bad. Even better is a company with a history of rising dividends and rising earnings per share to match. A stock's current dividend payout and yield are included in the daily stock listings in the newspaper. For historical information, the *S&P Stock Guide* and *Value Line* are excellent sources, as are the stock data bases of the online services.

Analysts' dividend forecasts play an important role in creating expectations for a stock's future performance. If analysts expected the $50 stock mentioned earlier to raise its quarterly dividend to 55 cents, its price might creep upward in anticipation of the increase. Then, if the company's profits rose only enough to permit it to pay 52 cents per share, disappointed investors might sell, thus causing the stock's price to fall, even though profits and dividends rose!

Sometimes the opposite can happen. Shortly after the death of its 92-year-old founder, Armand Hammer, Occidental Petroleum slashed its dividend almost in half and its price quickly rose. Investors apparently felt that Hammer had kept dividends artificially high and deemed the move (which was part of a larger plan to close down some unprofitable operations and write off debts) a smart step toward a stronger company in the future. Thus, a cut in dividends isn't always a sign of weakness in a company. It's important to know what's behind it.

Although dividends occasionally are paid in the form of additional shares of stock, they are usually paid in cash; you get the checks in the mail and spend the money as you please. Many companies encourage you to reinvest your dividends automatically in additional shares of the company's stock, and have set up programs that make it easy to do so. Such arrangements, called dividend reinvestment plans, or DRIPs, are described later in this chapter.

Value Sign #3: For long-term investments, look for a dividend to generate income to reinvest in the company. The target: a pattern of rising dividends supported by rising earnings.

BOOK VALUE. Also called shareholders' equity, book value is nothing more than the difference between the company's assets and its liabilities (which includes the value of any preferred stock the company has issued). Book value per share is the number most investors are interested in.

Normally, the price of a company's stock is higher than its book value, and stocks may be recommended as cheap because they are selling below book value. Such stocks often attract takeover bids from big investors and corporate raiders, which in turn attract other investors who bid up the price of the shares. But the hope of a profitable takeover is not by itself a good reason to buy such a stock. A company's stock may be selling below book value because the company shows little promise, and you could wait a long time for your profits to materialize. You need to look for other signs of value to confirm that you've found a bargain-priced stock.

The idea of buying shares in a company for less than what they're really worth has a certain appeal. At any given time, there will be stocks selling below book value for one reason or another, and they aren't all dogs. Some may be good small companies that have gone unnoticed or good big companies in an unloved industry. How can you tell? If the company has a low P/E ratio, a healthy dividend with plenty of earnings left to reinvest in the business and no heavy debts, it may be a bargain whose down-and-out status is a temporary condition that time and patience will correct.

On the other end of the scale, you want to stay away from companies whose price is too far above book value per share. It's difficult to say what's too high because the standards vary so much with the industry, and in some industries—insurance and finance, for instance—book value per share isn't considered particularly significant. Nor does it count for much in software companies, such as Microsoft, whose greatest assets reside in the brains of their employees and not in buildings or machinery. In start-up companies, book value is utterly meaningless. Not only do they have few or no assets, they may have very high liabilities as a result of borrowing to get started. Still, in general, when the figure is available, you want it to be on the low side.

Value Sign #4: For stocks with good long-term potential, look for book value per share that is not out of line with that for similar companies in the same business.

RETURN ON EQUITY. This number is the company's net profit after taxes, divided by its book value, and it can usually be found in the annual report. It shows how much the company is earning on the stockholders' stake in the enterprise. If return on equity is growing year after year, the stock's price will tend to show long-term strength. If the number is erratic or declining even though profits are steady, you may have uncovered problems with debt or profit margins and you should stay away from the stock.

Value Sign #5: Look for a return on equity that is consistently high, compared with the return for other companies in the same industry, or that shows a strong pattern of growth. A steady return on equity of more than 15% is a sign of a company that knows how to manage itself well.

DEBT-EQUITY RATIO. The debt-equity ratio shows how much leverage, or debt, a company is carrying, compared with shareholders' equity. For instance, if a company has $1 billion in shareholders' equity and $100 million in debt, its debt-equity ratio is 0.10, or 10%, which is quite low. In general, the lower this figure the better, although the definition of an acceptable debt load varies from industry to industry. You'll find data on debt in company annual reports, *Value Line, Moody's* and S&P publications, and in stock reports provided by the on-line services.

Value Sign #6: Look for companies that have debts amounting to no more than about 35% of shareholders' equity.

PRICE VOLATILITY. Probably the most widely used measure of price volatility is called the beta. It is calculated from past price patterns and tells you how much a stock can be expected to move in relation to a change in the market as a whole (usually represented by the S&P 500, which is assigned a beta of 1.00). A stock with a beta of 1.50 historically rises or falls half again as much as the index. A stock with a beta of 0.50 is half as volatile as the index; it would be expected to go up only 5% if the index rose 10% or down 5% if the index fell 10%. A few stocks have negative betas, meaning they tend to move in the direction opposite to that of the market.

Betas are published by several stock-tracking services such as those mentioned on pages 56 and 57 and are usually available from a broker. The key thing to remember about betas is that the higher the beta, the bigger the risk.

Value Sign #7: Whenever you assume the risk that goes with an oversized beta, it should be in expectation of receiving an oversize reward. For the most part, stick with stocks that have betas of around 1.00.

More Clues to Value in a Stock

THERE YOU HAVE THE NUMBERS-CRUNCHING, BALANCE-SHEET approach to finding value in the stock market. Those numbers are extremely important, but they aren't the only facts you need. If the stock meets most of the above tests, look for these additional signs of value.

The company's industry is on the rise. Even though you can make lots of money in a declining industry (as cigarette sales dropped, Philip Morris managed to maintain profitability, in part by taking market share away from other companies), you're more likely to succeed in big and growing markets than in small or shrinking ones. Exciting young industries such as Internet-based commerce, biotechnology and telecommunications may still offer exciting profit potential, but the staying power of any particular company is hard to predict.

The company is a leader in its industry. Being number one or two in its primary industry gives a company several advantages. As an industry leader it can influence pricing, rather than merely react to what others do. It has a bigger presence in the market: When the company introduces new products, those products stand a better chance of being accepted. Also, the company can afford the research necessary to create those new products.

The company invests in research and development. Any company worthy of your investment dollars should be concerned about product development and future competitiveness. Compare the company's spending on research and development—both in actual dollars and as a percentage of earnings and sales—with that of other firms in its industry. If expenditures seem quite low, think twice about buying the stock.

Low-Risk Strategy #1: Dollar-Cost Average

NOW THAT YOU KNOW THE SIGNS OF A GOOD STOCK, YOU HAVE to address the question of how to go about buying them. One of the biggest worries is timing. Suppose you're unlucky enough to buy at the very top of the market? Or suppose something unexpected happens to dash the price of your shares overnight? How can you protect yourself against bad things happening to good stocks while you're holding a basketful of them?

Dollar-cost averaging is a time-tested method of smoothing out the roller-coaster ride that awaits those who try to time the market. You don't have to be brilliant to make it work, and you don't even have to pay especially close attention to what's happening in the market or in the economy. With dollar-cost averaging, you simply invest a fixed amount regularly, depending on your saving schedule. The trick is to keep to your schedule, regardless of whether stock prices go up or down.

Because you're investing a fixed amount at fixed intervals,

your dollars buy more shares when prices are low than they do when prices are high. As a result, the average purchase price of your stock will be lower than the average of the market prices over the same time.

For example, say you invest $300 a month over a six-month period in SureThing Enterprises, a stock that ranges in price from a low of $20 to a high of $30. Here's a look at what dollar-cost averaging would do. (This example ignores brokerage commissions, which can be distressingly high on small trades like these. See Chapter 16 for help in reducing brokerage fees.)

First month: The stock is trading at $30 a share. Your $300 investment buys ten shares of SureThing.

Second month: The market has taken a tumble and the price of your stock has fallen to $25. You buy 12 shares.

Third month: Things have stabilized. The price of your stocks is still $25, and you buy another 12 shares.

Fourth month: On news of a takeover bid by another company, the price soars to $33. Your $300 buys you only nine shares, with a little change left over.

Fifth month: The takeover bid falls through and the price dips back down to $25. You pick up another 12 shares.

Sixth month: Uh-oh. An earnings report that falls short of analysts' expectations causes a couple of mutual funds to bail out of your stock, pushing the price down to $20 a share. You acquire 15 shares.

Let's add it up: So far you've spent, in round numbers, $1,800 (not counting commissions) and you own 70 shares of SureThing, which means you paid an average of $25.71 a share. Compare that with other ways you could have acquired the stock: If you had bought ten shares during each of those six months, you'd own 60 shares at an average price per share of $26.33. If you had invested the entire $1,800 at the start of the period, you'd own 60 shares at $30 per share. You can begin to see the advantages of dollar-cost averaging. The only reliable way to beat it over the long haul is to buy consistently at the bottom and sell at the top—not a very realistic expectation.

Now, you might have noticed that at the end of the sixth month you were holding stock for which you had paid an average price of nearly $26 in a market that was willing to pay you only $20 a share. What now? Should you sell and cut your losses? Not necessarily. Now is a good time to reassess your faith in SureThing; carefully reexamine the fundamentals described earlier in this chapter. If the fundamentals still justify your faith, this dip in the price represents a good opportunity to buy more shares.

Dollar-cost averaging won't automatically improve the performance of your portfolio. But don't underestimate the value of the added discipline, organization and peace of mind it gives you. It's natural to be frightened away from owning stocks when prices head down, even though experience has shown that such times can be the best time to buy.

Stock Splits

Q: *A friend recommended that I buy some stock in a company because he thinks it's going to split 3 or 4 to 1. Should I buy it now? Is the price of a stock likely to rise after a split?*
A: A company will split its stock if it thinks a lower price will attract more investors, but a split by itself doesn't really affect the value of the stock. If you own 100 shares of a $40 stock, it's worth $4,000. If the stock splits 4 for 1, you have 400 shares of a $10 stock— still worth $4,000. Stocks sometimes experience short-term jumps when a split is announced, especially when it's in combination with a hike in the dividend. Over the longer term, though, the company's fundamentals—profits, growth, business prospects—will determine the share price.

Because they charge no sales commissions, no-load mutual funds (see Chapter 6) are actually better suited for dollar-cost averaging than stocks. You'd incur relatively large commissions to buy a small number of shares of stock, and your fixed monthly investment might not buy whole shares. You can buy fractional shares in a mutual fund. Many funds will let you arrange to have money transferred regularly from a bank account, and some can arrange payroll deductions.

Although dollar-cost averaging lets you put your investments on autopilot, you shouldn't leave them there indefinitely. Inflation and increases in your salary make your fixed-dollar contribution less meaningful over time, and you shouldn't continue to buy any stock merely out of habit. Reexamine the company's investment prospects on a regular schedule—at least once a year—and adjust your investment accordingly.

If you have a lump sum to invest, such as a pension payout or an inheritance, you can take advantage of dollar-cost averaging by parking the sum in a money-market fund and taking some of it out in regular installments to buy stocks.

Low-Risk Strategy #2: Reinvest Your Dividends

A NOTHER INVESTMENT STRATEGY THAT, LIKE DOLLAR-COST averaging, pays little attention to the direction of prices uses corporate dividends to boost profits over the long haul. It's called the dividend reinvestment plan, or DRIP. More than 1,000 companies offer these special programs. Instead of sending you a check for the dividends your initial shares earn, the company automatically reinvests your money in additional shares. Because most companies pay dividends quarterly, your portfolio grows every 90 days without your having to lift a finger.

In a DRIP, shares are held in a common account. You receive regular statements but no stock certificates unless you request them. Companies seldom promote their DRIPs, so unless you ask about them you may not know that they exist. But most big-name firms, from AT&T to Xerox, have them.

DRIPs have other advantages:

Small dividends buy fractional shares, a boon to small investors.

Many DRIPs let you make additional investments on your own. A handful of companies further sweeten the pot by offering DRIP shares at discounts of 3% to 5% from the market price, although few permit the discounts on additional purchases.

You reduce risk by investing via a DRIP because it's a form of dollar-cost averaging.

Some plans charge small fees, such as a maximum $2.50 administrative fee per transaction, or $1 to $15 if you want possession of stock certificates. Brokers who hold stocks that are in a DRIP charge little or nothing to add these shares to your account each dividend period.

DIRECT-PURCHASE PLANS

While hundreds of no-fee DRIPs are still available, the trend recently has been away from them. The new plans that are displacing many DRIPs offer some of the features that have made mutual funds so popular. Most retain the dividend-reinvestment option but allow investors to avoid brokerage fees entirely by purchasing even the first share of stock directly from the company. They are called direct-purchase plans (DPPs), or no-load stocks. Most of the new plans allow investors to make additional cash purchases on a weekly or monthly schedule via electronic debiting of their bank account. Some even allow you to set up an IRA or sell shares over the telephone. A few offer discounts on the price of the stock and allow participants to borrow against the value of their shares, as they would with a margin account at a brokerage.

HOW YOU JOIN. Joining a DRIP is easy. Check the company's Web site or call its shareholder relations department for a prospectus and application, and send back the completed form. You must already own some stock before you can sign up.

You'll probably have to buy your first shares through a broker, register the stock in your own name (not in the broker's "street" name), and then transfer it to the DRIP. A small but growing number of companies will handle an initial purchase directly. They include, for instance, Ameritech, Exxon, Fannie Mae and Procter & Gamble.

HOW YOU GET OUT. DRIPs can be a drag when it's time to sell. Since most DRIP investors are long-termers, companies are not geared toward sales. It can take weeks to get your money. In some cases you need only write a letter stating the number of shares you wish to sell, and the company will send you the proceeds. But other firms merely mail you a stock certificate, which you must then sell through a broker. A few also limit selling to specified amounts, such as 100-share lots. But selling needn't be troublesome if you think ahead.

If you don't plan to hold the stock for at least five years, a DRIP may not be for you. Remembering the rules of each plan can be confusing if you belong to several, and there's no guarantee those rules won't change. You may be limited to buying additional shares only at monthly or quarterly intervals that coincide

with dividend payment dates. Money for voluntary cash purchases is often held by the company—at no interest—until the
plan's purchase dates.

All reinvested dividends are taxable for the year they're paid,
even though you don't see the money. And if the shares were
bought at a discount from the market, the amount of the discount is included in your taxable income in the year of purchase.

HOW TO PICK A DRIP. Don't buy a stock just because it offers a dividend reinvestment plan. Evaluate the company's fundamentals,
and consider the following points:

The best choices. Look for stocks with good track records of steadily rising dividends. Companies offering DRIPs that also have
outstanding dividend-raising records include H&R Block,
Emerson Electric, Minnesota Mining & Manufacturing, Mobil
Corp. and Merck. These companies may or may not be good
buys right now based on fundamentals.

Check the limits if you plan to invest additional cash through a
DRIP. Some companies will let you kick in as little as $10 per
month. Others have higher minimums. Nearly all have maxi-
mums, ranging from $1,000 to more than $5,000 per month.
AT&T, for example, permits optional cash purchases of up to
$250,000 a year. Plans with the lowest minimums will be more
attractive to small investors. Ask for the company's dividend
record dates—when dividends are recorded on the books. By
sending voluntary payments just before the record date you can
cut down on waiting time for reinvestment. The same applies
when you first sign up.

DRIPs change. Some companies that once offered a discount no
longer do. Overall, the number of firms offering shares at a discount has diminished in recent years. If you're shopping for a
discount, check to see whether it is still being offered.

Check the prospectus. A few plans let you receive part of your dividends in cash and have part reinvested.

WHERE TO GET MORE INFORMATION. Several sources can provide a list of companies offering dividend reinvestment plans, plus details of those plans. Consult the most recent edition of:

The Directory of Companies Offering Dividend Reinvestment Plans, by Sumie Kinoshita ($32.95, plus $2 shipping; Evergreen Enterprises, P.O. Box 763, Laurel, MD 20725; 301-549-3939; no Web site)

The Moneypaper Guide to Dividend Reinvestment Plans ($27; Vita Nelson's *The Moneypaper,* 1010 Mamaroneck Ave., Mamaroneck, NY 10543; www.drp.com; 800-388-9993 or 914-381-5400)

Charles Carlson's *DRIP Investor Newsletter* ($79 for a one-year subscription, $135 for two years; 7412 Calumet Ave., Hammond, IN 46321; www.dripinvestor.com; 800-233-5922 or 219-852-3200)

Web sites. You can find a list of the companies that offer DRIPs online at www.dripcentral.com and www.netstockdirect.com. You can find a list of companies that charge no fees to DRIP investors at www.moneypaper.com.

When to Sell a Stock

DECIDING WHEN TO SELL IS JUST AS IMPORTANT AS DECIDING which stocks to buy in the first place. The refusal to sell, whether it's due to unrealistic expectations, stubbornness, lack of interest or mere inattention, is the undoing of many an investor.

As a long-term investor, you don't want to cash in every time your stock moves up a few dollars. Commissions and taxes would cut into your gain and, besides, you'd have to decide where to put the proceeds. By the same token, you don't want to bail out in a panic in the aftermath of a market plunge.

Brokerage houses' research departments are slow to issue sell signals unless a company faces serious problems. When analysts get uneasy about a stock, they often equivocate with phrases like "weak hold." You should take that to mean, "Don't buy any more shares and if you've got a profit, seriously considering selling this stock."

How You Can Judge When to Sell

Here are some clues that it is time to consider selling a profitable stock no matter what the analyst's report says.

THE FUNDAMENTALS CHANGE. Whether you own America Online or Coca-Cola or a company most people have never heard of, you need to follow the corporation's prospects, its earnings progression and its business success as reflected in market share, unit sales growth and profit margin. Annual reports, news stories, research updates from brokerage houses, and investment newsletters are fertile sources of such information, along with the references listed on pages 56 and 57.

If the company's fundamentals start to weaken, it's time to reconsider your investment. An example might be a fast-expanding retail chain whose sales per store, after rising for years, suddenly decline. Maybe the profit margin has slacked off after a series of consistent increases. These problems could signal that the business has peaked.

THE DIVIDEND IS CUT. The progression and security of its dividend are important to any stock's prospects. A dividend cut or signs that the dividend is "in trouble"—meaning that analysts or creditors are quoted as saying they don't think the company can maintain its payout to shareholders—can undermine the stock price (but see the example of Occidental Petroleum on page 60).

YOU REACH YOUR TARGET PRICE. Many investors set specific price targets, both up and down, when they buy a stock; when the stock reaches the target, they sell. A good target is to double or triple your money, or to limit your patience with a stock to a loss of 20%. Such guidelines can prompt you to take your gains in a timely fashion and to dump losers before the damage gets too painful.

You can take the simple step of setting a "mental protective stop." Watch the stock listings and sell any stock that hits your mental stop point. You can set your sell level anywhere, perhaps arbitrarily choosing a price level that will double your money, for example. Once you've reached your objective, take the money. If the goals you set are ultraconservative, you might miss some gains from time to time, but that's better than holding on too long and falling victim to the Wall Street maxim that says: "Bulls make money, bears make money, pigs get slaughtered."

HOW THE PROS DECIDE TO SELL

Over the years we have asked successful investment professionals how they decide that it's time to sell a stock. Here are some highlights of what they've said:

SELL IN STAGES AS THE PRICE GOES UP. The chairman of a family of mutual funds: "Almost all stocks move in two-steps—two years of appreciation, two years of digestion, two more years of growth. So after a run-up in price, we sell 50% of our position, even though we may be investing for a longer term, and let the other half run."

SELL WHEN EVERYONE ELSE IS BUYING. The executive director of investments for a large pension fund: "Heavily promoted investments give me a warning signal. By the time they gain notoriety, the smart money has gotten out. You wind up holding something at the top of the market that you don't want."

SELL WHEN MOMENTUM SLOWS. The stock portfolio manager of a mutual fund company: "When growth slows, we sell." As an example, he cited a major shortage of liability insurance that once sent premiums soaring: "In this litigious age, people don't go without insurance. So the sales and earnings of major casualty insurance companies swelled—and continued for about a year and half. Then growth in revenues and premiums slowed and we sold them all."

SELL WHEN THE GRASS IS GREENER ELSEWHERE. The chairman of an international group of mutual funds: "Sell when you've found something better. We sell a stock to buy one that shows better potential for appreciation. We used to sell a stock to buy another that we thought had 30% more potential. We did not reach our goal of being right two-thirds of the time, so we changed our criterion to 50%. Let's say you own a $10 stock that has an appraised value of $20. Then you find another $10 stock with a $30 value—50% better than the first one. That's when we sell the first stock."

A note of caution: Fund managers and other professional investors are by the nature of their work more active traders than individual investors should be. We present their comments because we think they can provide some insight into the professional's mind and methods, not because we think you should always emulate their behavior.

How Much Money Did You Make?
Keep your eye on the total return.

SOME INVESTORS MAKE THE MISTAKE OF THINKING THAT THE change in price between the time they buy and the time they sell represents the sum total of how well or poorly their stocks perform. If a stock goes from $20 to $30, you've made $10 a share; if it goes to $15, you've lost $5 per share. That way of looking at investment results doesn't go far enough.

The quickest way to recognize the shortcomings of looking only at price changes is to imagine buying a utility stock that pays a dividend of 6%. You buy it at $20 and hold it for a year, then sell it for $22. Was your gain limited to $2 a share? Clearly not, because you collected that 6% dividend, which amounted to $1.20 per share. Assuming you owned 100 shares for a year, you pocketed $120 in dividends, plus the $200 profit from the price increase. Thus your *total return* was $320. Expressed as a percentage of your purchase price, you made 10% on the price of the shares, but your total return was 16%.

Counting dividends (whether you receive them as cash or reinvest them in additional shares) and interest as part of your investment return is really the only accurate way to figure it, whether you're dealing with stocks, bonds or mutual funds. Most compilations of investment results, including those you'll find in this book, are compilations of total returns, and assume that earnings are reinvested in additional shares of the same investment and compound at the same rate.

On the other side of the equation, forgetting to take commissions and taxes into account is a common way to *overstate* your profits. Commissions are discussed in Chapter 16. How taxes affect your investments is the subject of Chapter 12.

Advanced Investing I:
Timing the Market—Sort of

P ROFESSIONAL PORTFOLIO MANAGERS HAVE SO MUCH DIFFI-
culty deciding whether the stock market is poised to go up
or poised to go down that at first glance it seems prepos-
terous for individual investors to even try to guess. But the temp-
tation is often irresistible because the payoff looks so lucrative.

In his book, *Stock Market Logic* (Dearborn), Norman G. Fosback
calculated that if you had bought a portfolio representative of the
average stock on the New York Stock Exchange in 1964 and held
it for 20 years, you would have earned an average of 11% per year.
That means $10,000 would have grown to $87,500.

If you had anticipated the three bear markets that occurred during
that period, sold all stocks and held cash, then bought stocks
when the next bull market started, you would have achieved a
21% average annual return and your $10,000 would have grown
to nearly $490,000.

If you had "sold short" (a technique by which you make money
when stock prices fall) during those three bear markets, that
$10,000 would have multiplied to nearly $1,400,000.

If you had correctly anticipated every 5% swing in the market up or
down, buying stocks on the upswings and selling them short on
the downswings, you would have reaped a profit of more than
$5 billion in 20 years!

Such perfect timing is impossible, of course, and that was
Fosback's point. But the promise that good timing can spark up
returns has spawned numerous investment newsletters and fills
the sleep of small investors with dreams of riches. In fact, there
is an entire industry devoted to the idea of perfect timing.

MEET THE TECHNICIANS

Examining the financial balance sheets of individual companies
to determine their strengths and weaknesses is the hallmark of
"fundamental" stock analysis because it looks at financial funda-

mentals for clues to a company's prospects for growth. Another school of thought, called "technical" analysis, looks at patterns created by the movements of the market for indications of what's going to happen next.

Technicians study past trading patterns in hopes of spotting relationships that appear ready to repeat themselves, thus creating money-making opportunities for those who know what's going to happen next. For example, many technicians believe that if the number of stock issues rising in price exceeds the number of decliners by a certain amount for a certain length of time, the market is probably headed up for a while. This advance-decline theory is also said to work on the downside.

The Dow Theory, named after one of the founders of Dow Jones, is one of the most widely followed methods of technical analysis. It holds that a significant market move up or down (a bull or bear market) is under way when a change in the primary direction of the Dow Jones industrial average (which reflects price changes of 30 large-company stocks) is "confirmed" by the Dow Jones transportation index (which is composed of 20 transportation-industry stocks) moving in the same direction at the same time. Disciples of the Dow Theory don't claim that it will predict a change in market direction, just that it will confirm it in time for attentive investors to take advantage of the primary trend.

Large brokerage houses have technicians on their staffs of analysts, and their reports are available on request. Technical analysts usually try to make money on short-term moves in the stock market rather than on the long-term potential of a particular stock.

LOOK FOR MAJOR MARKET SHIFTS

Although it is unrealistic to think that you—or anyone, for that matter—can consistently spot minor ups and downs in the market before they occur, it is often possible to anticipate the major moves. You won't be able to do it every time and you won't be able to predict the timing of the change with great precision. But the early signs of major market changes have enough characteristics in common that paying close attention to what's going on can often give you a jump on the crowd and a higher-than-usual investment return.

In the early stages of a bull market, you can increase your profit opportunities by stepping up the pace of your dollar-cost averaging plan or shifting more cash into stocks. In the early stages of a bear market, you'll want to be careful about committing new cash to stocks, and you might even consider selling parts of your most profitable holdings and moving the proceeds into the kinds of cash vehicles described in Chapter 3.

HOW TO SPOT A RISING MARKET IN ADVANCE. Here are four signs that, when they occur together, suggest that the market has been down far enough and long enough that the next major move should be up:

1. Stocks are cheap. "Cheap" means that price-earnings ratios are low and dividends are high, compared with the market's averages over the past several months.

2. Interest rates are low. This makes stocks more attractive than bonds, especially when coupled with high dividend yields. In addition, low interest rates tend to encourage borrowing, which creates economic activity, and that's good for the stock market. A sustained drop in both short- and long-term rates can usually be counted on to give the market a boost.

3. Pessimism is rampant. Talk of a new Great Depression and widespread abandonment of the stock market are often signs that things are about to bottom out. Cash levels of mutual funds and other institutional investors are high and the opinions of market newsletter writers are low.

4. The market seems to be falling apart. This is called the selling climax: In a final burst of gloom, the market experiences breathtaking drops on huge volumes of selling. On one or more days, the Dow Jones industrial average may plunge 300, 400 or 500 points or more on New York Stock Exchange volume of a billion shares. This is usually a good time to buy.

HOW TO PROTECT YOURSELF IN A FALLING MARKET. The uncertainty of the stock market and the difficulty of predicting the direction of its next move are good arguments for taking the long-term view, but some kinds of markets call for especially cautious tactics.

On average, bear markets since 1950 have led to a 27% decline in the Standard & Poor's 500-stock index. You don't want to get caught in a crunch like that.

The onset of most of those bear markets was followed by a recession within seven to 12 months. Stock prices bottomed out and began rising before the end of each of those six recessions, usually three to eight months in advance of an economic upturn. Wouldn't it be nice to be able to protect yourself while the market is down, and be in a position to ride it back up when it changes direction? There are some things you can do:

Steer clear of stocks with high price-earnings ratios. The market will clobber them if they report disappointing earnings the next time around.

Beware, too, of stocks with relatively few shareholders. Their prices could be devastated by a few big sell orders. Annual reports and stock prospectuses available from brokers should tell you how many shares of the company are in the hands of the public.

Ask these questions about the stocks you own in a bear market: Would the company's sales be hurt by higher unemployment? By higher energy prices? By less spending on the part of businesses? Some common sense applied to the information you can get from the sources on pages 56 and 57 will help you rank your stocks by degree of risk in a bear-market recession. (See the definition of defensive stocks on page 53.)

WHY NOT SELL YOUR STOCKS AND SIT OUT THE STORM? Whether you should do that depends on how much risk you're willing to take. Getting out of stocks altogether carries risk, too—of lost opportunity for profits if all your investments are sitting in a money-market fund when stock prices head up again. When down markets do end, the bull reemerges with a bang. Yale Hirsch noted in *Don't Sell Stocks on Monday* that in the bull markets that began between 1949 and 1982, the Dow Jones industrial average rose 38% on average in the first 12 months and that those gains constituted two-thirds of the entire upward move before the next bear market started. Ironically, panicky selling of stocks when the urge to throw in the towel is almost too great to resist usually occurs at the very end of bear markets—precisely the wrong moment.

WHAT ABOUT MONEY YOU WANT TO LEAVE IN STOCKS? Look into these investment possibilities:

Recession-resistant companies. Their profits can grow in just about any economic environment because they provide basic goods or services people need or want no matter what: drug makers, food processors, grocery chains, beverage companies and hospital-management firms.

Utility stocks and electric companies do well in down markets, thanks partly to their high yields, but thanks also to the fact that demand for electricity remains fairly steady because people continue to wash clothes, watch TV and turn on the lights.

Dividend raisers. Using the signs of value described in earlier sections of this chapter, look for companies that regularly raise their dividends through fat times and lean times, .

Value stocks. As described earlier, these are stocks with low P/E or low price-to-book-value ratios but good prospects. Their earnings could fall in a recession but can usually be counted on to recover.

Advanced Investing II:
Companies That Own Their Markets

W E'D ALL LIKE TO HAVE A PIECE OF THE PROFITS OF BUSI-nesses that are near-monopolies. In fact, you can. The companies won't be giants like General Motors or General Electric but more likely unglamorous companies that churn out such products as recycled plastic bottles, round cartons for premium ice cream, stamp pads, football uniforms, free-laying carpet tiles, binders used in desktop publishing, and even tennis-ball fuzz.

What sets such companies apart from the crowd is simply this: They have a lock on their lines of business. Because they make things nobody else does or make them so much better or cheaper, their positions are almost unassailable. Operating outside Wall Street's limelight, they often trade at modest price-earnings ratios. Debt is minimal or nonexistent. And because of their dominance, profits tend to rise steadily.

There's a term for such companies: "niche" stocks. True niche companies are resistant to competition—they got there first. They have the technological and marketing edge, plus a proven ability to parlay those advantages into fat profit margins. Many combine the ability to make lots of money in good times with the strength to muddle through in hard times.

Don't make the mistake of confusing a niche with a fad. Remember video-game parlors? Gasohol refiners? Condominium converters? Fads attract "me-too" competitors. So the trick is to separate the enduring from the transitory and not pay too much when you buy the stock.

> ## Triple Witching Hour
>
> **Q:** *I am new to investing and was puzzled to see a recent market swoon attributed to a "triple witching hour." Are these regular happenings or are they sporadic events? How can I anticipate them?*
>
> **A:** "Triple witching hours" occur four times a year on a Friday afternoon with the simultaneous expiration of options, index options and index futures (see Chapter 11). They often add volatility to the market, but knowing that they're coming won't help you much because the volatility moves prices both ways and it's virtually impossible to know which way the market is going in the last hour of any particular day. The best strategy is to hang on and remember that whatever happens on a given day, the fundamental strengths (or weaknesses) of the market will eventually prevail.

How Companies Own Their Markets

There's no textbook technique, but look for these qualities:

It sticks to the business it knows best. A firm that tries to make something for everyone or spread into too many unrelated fields becomes too tied to the business cycle to be a niche stock. Beware of companies that, having conquered one business, take on entrenched opponents in others. McDonald's doesn't deliver packages and Federal Express doesn't sell hamburgers.

It has the dominant market share. The company should be the biggest seller in its market niche. This isn't always easy to determine: Check annual reports of the company and any competitors you can think of, and compare sales figures.

It's tough to break into the business. If a business is lucrative, other companies will want to jump in, so look for markets in which the financial or technical obstacles to competitors are formidable. For instance, Calgon Carbon is the leading producer of activated carbon for water purification systems. It's a lucrative business, but one that analysts estimate would take tens of millions of dollars to break into. That's some barrier. For computer software companies, by contrast, the costs of starting up are relatively low.

It is financially strong. A company that takes full advantage of a secure market should show a long record of rising earnings. Also critical is a balance sheet earmarked by low debt as a percentage of total capital—or no debt at all. In short, it should meet the tests of value described earlier in this chapter.

It shows a high profit margin. A corporation that does its thing better, cheaper or faster than everyone else should get a premium price and control its costs. Compare the company's profit margins, which you can find in the annual report or get from a stockbroker, with the industry averages listed in *Value Line Investment Survey*.

It has a record of stability. A decade or so of product leadership would be ideal. That's too much to expect from a health-related or high-technology company, where business conditions change rapidly. But it's possible in such prosaic industries as packaging or chemicals.

How to Find Niche Companies

Your own knowledge about a product line or an industry can lead you to a niche company. So can annual reports and 10-K forms, research departments of regional brokers, investment newsletters or reference sources like *Value Line*. Mutual fund reports to shareholders can also give you some leads, especially reports from funds that specialize in finding such companies themselves.

Advanced Investing III:
When Bad Things Happen to Good Stocks

T HIS VARIATION ON VALUE INVESTING ENTAILS LOOKING FOR good companies whose prices have been beaten down by nonrecurring events that don't necessarily reflect on the long-term quality of the management. Sometimes a company's underlying strengths are enough to pull it through unexpected catastrophes that would sink a weaker one. And sometimes these setbacks can create once-in-a-lifetime buying opportunities.

The theory behind this approach is that the stock market is not always efficient (contrary to what a technician would say) because investors often shun otherwise solid companies plagued with temporary setbacks, such as mothballed nuclear power plants or flawed birth-control devices, that drive their stocks' prices down to bargain-basement levels.

CONSIDERING THREE CASE STUDIES

Prominent examples from the past decade or so include Union Carbide, Gerber and General Public Utilities. Each came roaring back from the brink of disaster.

UNION CARBIDE. In 1984, a leak of toxic gas at a pesticide plant in Bhopal, India, killed more than 2,000 people and injured tens of thousands more. The tragedy was a shocking blow to Connecticut-based Union Carbide, which owned 51% of the Indian plant. Within days, billions of dollars' worth of lawsuits were filed against Union Carbide on behalf of Bhopal victims.

Union Carbide's stock price quickly fell 21%, including a drop of nearly $6 per share in a day. In Bethesda, Md., analysts at the Robert E. Torray & Co. investment firm, one of few that specializes in buying stocks hit by bad news, did their analysis, then started writing checks. Over a couple of weeks, Torray bought more than a million shares of Union Carbide at a price in the low teens—and doubled its money in less than five years. In 1992, the stock traded as high as $29 and as low as $10. Within two years, it had topped its previous high once more and reached almost $36. In August 1999 the stock was selling above $60 a share when Union Carbide and The Dow Chemical

Company announced a merger that would create the world's second largest chemical company, to be known as The Dow Chemical Company.

GERBER. After a New York City woman charged that she found glass slivers in Gerber baby food in October 1984, Gerber Products' stock price dived 15% in two days to $22. Five years later, the price had risen better than threefold. In 1994, Sandoz, the giant Swiss drug company, purchased Gerber for ten times its share price in 1984 (adjusted for splits).

GENERAL PUBLIC UTILITIES. Limping along after a disaster at its Three Mile Island nuclear-power-generating plant the previous year, GPU shocked investors in 1980 by suspending dividends. The news, more ominous to investors than the Three Mile Island disaster itself, drove GPU's stock price down 36% to a modern low of $3.38 per share. In early 1991, the company, now known simply as GPU, sold for $27 per share after splitting two shares for 1. By mid 1999, it was trading above $40 and paying a dividend yield around 5%. (In 1999, GPU sold the last of its troubled stake in Three Mile Island for $121 million.)

BUYING ON BAD NEWS

Buying good stocks on bad news can pay off big, but it's not for the fainthearted, and it's something to try with only a small portion of your portfolio. A few years ago, Kiplinger looked to see what had happened to stocks on the New York Stock Exchange that fell 25% or more in price during any one-week period three years earlier, figuring that was long enough for a beaten-down stock to demonstrate its ability to climb back. Some companies had made fabulous comebacks, often because they had become takeover targets of other companies: A. H. Robins, for instance, which was bought by American Home Products, and Essex Chemical, which was bought by Dow Chemical. But half the casualties either barely survived or had fallen even further three years later. As a group, this portfolio of snakebit companies grew 21% during the period, while the Dow Jones industrials grew 40%.

Clearly, careful selection is the key. Finding a solid investment prospect among a list of torpedoed stocks isn't all that different

Lost Stock Records

Q: *My daughter has lost her AT&T stock purchase records and several stock certificates. She also lost records of an assortment of the Baby Bell stocks and some AT&T stock she received after the AT&T breakup. She sold most of the Baby Bell stocks for which she had certificates, but she has no records of purchase for reporting capital gains to the IRS. Can she get this information?*

A: Ordinarily when stock certificates are lost, the company that issued them can send replacements. Your daughter should write to Boston EquiServe, transfer agent for AT&T, at: Shareowner Records, Boston EquiServe, L.P., P.O.Box 8032, Boston, MA 02266-8032. Your daughter should include her social security number and, if available, the account number, issue date and number of shares she owned.

Or she may call AT&T Shareholder Services (800-348-8288) for the information she needs and arrange for replacements for the lost stock certificates. The company can also provide her with a booklet that will inform her of any stock splits that affected her and help her estimate her costs for tax purposes. The booklet as well as other information can be downloaded from AT&T's Web site at www.att.com.

If she has lost certificates for the other Baby Bells she may obtain information by calling their individual shareholders-service numbers.

from ordinary investing homework. You need to look at the underlying values of the company.

LOW DEBT LOAD. Using the sources listed on pages 56 and 57, look for cash flow three to four times larger than interest payments on debts. Avoid highly leveraged companies and high-flying stocks with big price-earnings ratios. Debts and high P/Es just make things worse.

SUBSTANTIAL ASSETS. Look to see if the company has substantial assets that could be sold to raise cash if necessary. Saleable assets include interests in other companies, subsidiaries with well-defined markets, or even plants and equipment that can be sold and leased back to the company from their new owner.

FEW COMPETITORS. Don't buy down-on-their-luck companies that are highly vulnerable to foreign competition. The tougher the marketplace, the tougher it is to come back. On the domestic front, public utilities are often good bets because they have few competitors in their markets and can be expected to be around for years to come.

Mistakes Even Smart Investors Make

I T'S A SAD FACT THAT MANY PEOPLE FAIL TO LIVE UP TO THEIR investing potential because of common mistakes even smart people make. Here's our list of the six transgressions we see most often:

ACTING ON TIPS. Investors get compelling, authoritative tips from friends. You get "cold calls" from aspiring young brokers pushing companies you've never heard of. You get friendly calls from your own broker about stocks you know nothing about. You get urgent messages or "extra-hot" advice from an online newsgroup discussion. If you act on those suggestions without first investigating, you're begging for trouble. If your friend or broker knows this hot tip, so do a lot of other people. Assume that this information is already fully reflected in the stock's price. And if that's the case, is the stock still worth buying?

GETTING SENTIMENTAL. Falling in love with a stock is a common transgression of retired employees who have accumulated lots of stock in the company they worked for all those years. Children who later inherit those shares have the same strong, sentimental attachment to the firm and tend to hang on. Don't do it. Weed out the poor performers in your portfolio, wherever they came from originally.

FORGETTING TAXES AND COMMISSIONS. Say your 100 shares of a $20 stock go up to $22, so you claim bragging rights to a 10% profit. However, when you figure in commission, your shares really cost more like $2,050. If you sold for a $50 commission, you'd get $2,100—a 5% gain, pretax, that makes the simplicity and safety of bank CDs look good.

Fooling yourself this way is expensive and makes it difficult for you to choose well among competing investments. Get an accurate idea of the tax and administrative costs of your investment when figuring your gains and losses.

FAILING TO DIVERSIFY. All your life, people have warned you against putting all your eggs in one basket. You no doubt understand the concept, believe in it and are thoroughly sick of such simplistic preachments. But note this amazing fact: Many investors still put all their eggs in one basket. They tend to invest in clumps of things, thinking in terms of individual investments rather than in terms of industries. A carefully researched portfolio of auto-industry and airline stocks could all get beaten up at the same time by some common transportation plague such as increased fuel costs. A diverse list of stocks could all be clobbered if they aren't balanced by certificates of deposit or other investments that will protect you if stock prices fall through the floor.

LOSING PATIENCE. It's normal to feel let down when nothing much happens to your stocks right away. Don't lose heart, though. Make an investment not on the basis of a stock's performance over a few months or even a year. If you selected it carefully and the fundamentals are still sound, hang in there. With a long-term outlook, you can ride out the interim slides.

TAKING A FLIER ON A PENNY OR MICROCAP STOCK. These are low-priced, not widely owned and not traded on any stock exchange. True, a $3,000 investment in a $3 stock gets you 1,000 shares. If the stock goes up a dollar, you've got a 33% profit. A little bit of this kind of speculation is fine. But the fact is, a dirt-cheap stock price is more likely a tip-off to a troubled company than to an undiscovered Microsoft. These are discussed in more detail in Chapter 11. Go for it if you must, but don't bet the kids' college tuition fund on it.

CHAPTER 5

Bonds: For Balance

ONDS BELONG IN YOUR INVESTMENT PLAN FOR GOOD reasons, but maybe not for the reasons you think.

Bonds are a natural choice to diversify and hedge your stock holdings. The kinds of economic forces that depress stock prices—the early stages of a recession, for instance—tend to boost bond prices.

Bonds can generate impressive profits from capital gains. As we will point out, sometimes you can even calculate those gains years in advance, on the day you buy the bonds.

Bonds can provide a predictable stream of relatively high income you can use for living expenses or for funding other parts of your investment plan.

Some kinds of bonds offer valuable tax advantages and unparalleled opportunities to take advantage of the time value of money, that is, to invest a modest amount with a reasonable prospect of collecting a large amount a few years later (see Chapter 2).

Note that the word "safety" doesn't appear on the list. A lot of people think bonds are about the safest investment around, but such a notion can be costly. Bonds entail several kinds of risks, each of which will be dealt with in this chapter. First, though, you have to master the lingo, and the vocabulary of bonds is different from the vocabulary of stocks.

What You Need to Know About Bonds

ONDS ARE IOUs ISSUED BY CORPORATIONS, STATE AND CITY governments and their agencies, and the federal government and its agencies. When you buy a bond, you become a creditor of the corporation or government agency; it owes you the amount shown on the face of the bond, plus interest. You get a fixed amount of interest on a regular schedule—every six months, in most cases—until the bond matures after a specified number of years, at which time you are paid the bond's face value. If the issuer goes broke, bondholders have first claim on the issuer's assets, ahead of stockholders.

Bonds typically have a face value of $1,000 or $5,000, although some are larger. Investors may actually receive a bond certificate or they may not. Usually, bond ownership is in the form of a "book entry," meaning the issuer keeps a record of buyers' names but sends out no certificates. Treasury bonds, for instance, are issued in book entry form.

A long-term bond typically matures in 20 to 40 years, although some are issued for shorter periods. A bond due to mature in three to ten years is called an intermediate-term bond. After bonds are issued, they can be freely bought and sold by individuals and institutions in what's called the secondary market, which works something like a stock exchange.

DIFFERENT KINDS OF BONDS

Bonds share those basics, but they come in a variety of forms:

Secured bonds are backed by a lien on part of a corporation's plant, equipment or other assets. If the corporation defaults, those assets can be sold to pay off the bondholders.

Debentures are unsecured bonds, backed only by the general ability of the corporation to pay its bills. If the company goes broke, debentures can't be paid off until secured bondholders are paid. Subordinated debentures are another step down the totem pole. Investors in these don't get paid until after holders of so-called senior debentures get their money.

Zero-coupon bonds may be secured or unsecured. They are issued at a big discount from face value because they pay all the interest at maturity, with no payments along the way. (Although buying such a bond may sound a little nutty, in fact zero-coupon bonds offer a number of potential advantages to investors, as we will see later on in this chapter.)

Municipal bonds are issued by state or city governments or their agencies and come in two principal varieties:

- **General obligation bonds** are backed by the full taxing authority of the government.
- **Revenue bonds** are backed only by the receipts from a specific source of revenue, such as a bridge or highway toll, and thus are not considered as secure as general obligation bonds.

The interest paid to holders of both revenue and general obligation municipal bonds is exempt from federal income taxes and, usually, income taxes of the issuing state.

U.S. Treasury bonds, which in maturities of a year or less are called Treasury bills and in maturities of under ten years may be called notes, are backed by the full faith and credit—and the printing presses—of the federal government.

Agency securities are issues of various U.S. government–sponsored organizations, such as Fannie Mae (formerly the Federal National Mortgage Association) and the Tennessee Valley Authority. Although they are not technically backed by the full faith and credit of the U.S. Treasury, they are widely considered to be moral obligations of the federal government, which presumably wouldn't let an agency issue fail.

Short-Term vs. Long-Term Bonds

Q: *What are the advantages of short- and intermediate-term bonds over longer-term issues?*

A: In general, the shorter the maturity, the less the bonds are subject to price fluctuations due to interest-rate changes and inflation. Bonds with maturities of 20 to 30 years usually offer the highest yields, but sometimes they pay only slightly more than you can earn on intermediate-term bonds (those with maturities of three to ten years). And sometimes those higher rates can disappear. Most long-term bonds can be redeemed early, or "called," on specified dates. If interest rates fall, you can expect the issuer to refinance its debt at lower rates. In that case, bondholders would be paid off, but they'd lose the high rates they had counted on.

Convertible bonds are corporate bonds that can be swapped for the same company's common stock at a fixed ratio—a specified amount of bonds for a specified number of shares of stock. Convertible features make some companies' bonds more attractive by offering the possibility of an equity kicker: If the price of the stock rises considerably after you buy the convertible bonds, you can profit by swapping your bonds for stock.

For example, suppose you buy five convertible bonds issued by AT&T at $1,000 each. The bonds pay 7% and each is convertible into 20 shares of AT&T stock. When you buy the bonds, AT&T is selling at $45 a share. Because break-even conversion price is $50, you've paid $5 a share for the conversion privilege. If AT&T stock climbs above $50, you can make a profit by converting your bonds to stock. If the price were to go to, say, $60, you could quickly turn your $5,000 bond investment into $6,000 worth of stock.

Because their fate is so closely tied to that of the stock price of the issuing firm, convertible bonds tend to be more closely in sync with the stock market than the bond market. There's more about convertibles later on.

Callable bonds. Bonds can often be "called," meaning they can be redeemed by the issuer before they mature. A company might decide to call its bonds if, for instance, interest rates fell so far that it could issue new bonds at a lower rate and thus save money. This is obviously to the corporation's advantage, not yours. Not only would you lose your comparatively high yield, but you'd also have to figure out where to invest the unexpected payout in a climate of falling interest rates. And if the bond is called for more than you paid for it, you'd also owe tax on the difference.

Unlocking the Potential of Bonds

WHEN A NEW BOND IS ISSUED, THE INTEREST RATE IT PAYS is called the coupon rate, which is the fixed annual payment expressed as a percentage of the face value. A 5% coupon bond pays $50 a year interest on each $1,000 of face value, a 6% coupon bond pays $60 and so forth. That's what the issuer will pay—no more, no less—for the life of the bond. But it may or may not be the yield you can earn from that issue, and understanding why is the key to unlocking the real potential of bonds.

Take a new bond with a coupon interest rate of 6%, meaning it pays $60 a year for every $1,000 of face value. What happens if interest rates rise to 7% after the bond is issued? New bonds will have to pay a 7% coupon rate or no one will buy them. By the same token, you could sell your 6% bond only if you offered it at a price that produced a 7% yield for the buyer. So the price at which you could sell would be whatever $60 represents 7% of, which is $857.14. Thus, you'd lose $142.86 if you sell. Even if you don't sell, you suffer a paper loss because your bond is now worth $142.86 less than you paid for it. It is selling at a "discount."

But what if interest rates were to decline? Say rates drop to 5% while you're holding your 6% bond. New bonds would be paying only 5% and you could sell your old bond for whatever $60 represents 5% of. Because $60 is 5% of $1,200, selling your 6% bond when interest rates are at 5% would produce a $200 capital gain. That $200 is called a premium.

Actual prices are also affected by the length of time left before the bond matures and by the likelihood that the issue will be called. But the underlying principle is the same, and it is the single most important thing to remember about the relationship between the market value of the bonds you hold and changes in current interest rates:

As interest rates rise, bond prices fall; as interest rates fall, bond prices rise. The further away the bond's maturity or call date, the more volatile its price tends to be.

VARIETIES OF YIELD

Because of this relationship, the actual yield to an investor depends in large part on where interest rates stand the day the bond is purchased, so the vocabulary of the bond market needs more than one definition for yield.

Coupon yield (the annual payment expressed as a percentage of the bond's face value) is only one way to look at a bond's payout. These are the others:

Current yield is the annual interest payment calculated as a percentage of the bond's current market price. A 5% coupon bond selling for $900 has a current yield of 5.6%, which is figured by taking the $50 in annual interest, dividing it by the $900 market price and multiplying the result by 100.

Yield to maturity includes the current yield and the capital gain or loss you can expect if you hold the bond to maturity. If you pay $900 for a 5% coupon bond with a face value of $1,000 maturing five years from the date of purchase, you will earn not only $50 a year in interest but also another $100 when the bond's issuer pays off the principal. By the same token, if you buy that bond for $1,100, representing a $100 premium, you will lose $100 at maturity.

The yield to maturity can dramatically affect investment results. You can figure it out with a financial calculator, or your broker will gladly do it for you. To get a close approximation of yield to maturity, divide the discount by the number of years the bond has left to maturity. Call that result the "annually accumulated discount" and then apply the following formula:

$$\text{Yield to maturity} = \frac{\text{annually accumulated discount} + \text{annual interest payment}}{\text{average of face value} + \text{current price}} \times 100$$

In the case of the bond selling for $900 with a coupon yield of 5% and five years to go to maturity, the yield to maturity would be 7.4%:

$$\frac{(20 + 50)}{\frac{(1,000+900)}{(2)}} \times 100 = 7.4\%$$

If you bought the premium bond for $1,100, your current yield would be 4.6%, but the yield to maturity would be only 2.86%. (To apply the formula to a premium bond, you subtract the annually accumulated premium from the annual interest payment.)

Why would you ever want to buy a premium bond? For one thing, it's possible that the low yield to maturity could be counterbalanced by the extra interest you collect prior to maturity. That assumes the current yield on the issue exceeds yields available elsewhere. Also, tax considerations could make the capital loss valuable to you a few years down the road, when it could be used to offset income from other sources.

Yield to call is the same as yield to maturity, except it is calculated on the assumption that the bond will be redeemed by the issuer on the first possible call date.

GLEANINGS FROM THE BOND LISTINGS

The daily bond listings in most newspapers show the maturity date for each issue, the coupon rate, the current yield and the current price. You have to figure out yield to maturity yourself, get it from a broker or look it up in a standard investor's reference, such as Standard & Poor's monthly *Bond Guide,* which is available at libraries. This is what the listings might look like for a couple of bonds issued by American Telephone & Telegraph:

BOND	CURRENT YIELD	VOL	CLOSE	NET CHANGE
ATT 55/804	5.7	20	99¼	¼
ATT 7s05	6.7	25	104⅛	⅛

The first bond, listed as "ATT55/804" was issued to pay 5.625% on its face value (also called par value and shown as 5⅝ in the listing) and will mature in the year 2004 (the "04" in the listing).

The next column reveals that it is paying a current yield of 5.7%, which means that investors are buying it at a discount. And, sure enough, skip to

The "Close" column, which shows the price of the bond at the time the market closed that day, shows that it was selling for 99¼%, or 99.25% of $1,000, which is $992.50 for each $1,000 bond.

The yield to maturity on this issue, taking into account the fact that you will collect $1,000 per bond in the year 2004, isn't shown. (It would be 5.8%.)

The listing also doesn't show whether the bond is callable, but that is probably a moot point in this case. A company is unlikely to call in a bond on which it is paying only 5.625% interest.

A Key to the Bond Listings

A Current yield is the annual yield you'd get if you bought the bond at that day's price. If the bond is selling at a discount from the issue price, the price shown in the column labeled "Close" will be less than 100. If the bond is selling at a premium, the price will be more than 100.

B Each number in the "Vol" (volume) column stands for $1,000 worth of bonds traded that day. Bonds are usually priced at $1,000 each.

C The first number after the name of the issuer shows the interest rate at which the bond was issued, known as the coupon rate. The letter "s" following the rate is used as a spacer to avoid confusion between the rate and the next set of numbers if there is no fraction there to serve the same purpose.

D This is the year in which the bond matures.

E The notation "cv" indicates that the issue is a convertible bond, meaning it can be exchanged for a fixed number of shares of common stock of the issuer.

F A "zr" listed before the maturity date indicates a zero-coupon bond.

A B C D E F

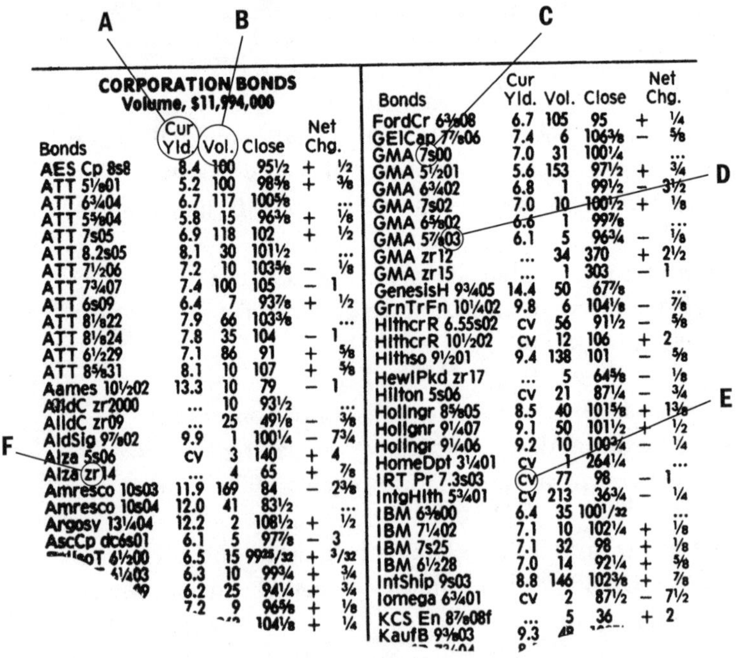

CORPORATION BONDS
Volume, $11,994,000

Bonds	Cur Yld.	Vol.	Close	Net Chg.
AES Cp 8s8	8.4	100	95½	+ ½
ATT 5⅛01	5.2	100	98⅝	+ ⅜
ATT 6¾04	6.7	117	100⅝	...
ATT 5⅝04	5.8	15	96⅜	+ ⅛
ATT 7s05	6.9	118	102	+ ½
ATT 8.2s05	8.1	30	101½	...
ATT 7½06	7.2	10	103⅝	− ⅛
ATT 7¾07	7.4	100	105	− 1
ATT 6s09	6.4	7	93⅞	+ ½
ATT 8⅛22	7.9	66	103⅜	...
ATT 8⅛24	7.8	35	104	− 1
ATT 6½29	7.1	86	91	+ ⅝
ATT 8⅝31	8.1	10	107	+ ⅝
Aames 10½02	13.3	10	79	− 1
AlldC zr2000	...	10	93½	...
AlldC zr09	...	25	49⅛	− ⅜
AldSig 9⅞02	9.9	1	100¼	− 7¾
Alza 5s06	cv	3	140	+ 4
Alza zr14	...	4	65	+ ⅞
Amresco 10s03	11.9	169	84	− 2⅜
Amresco 10s04	12.0	41	83½	...
Argosy 13¼04	12.2	2	108½	+ ½
AscCp dc6s01	6.1	5	97⅞	− 3
...lsoT 6½00	6.5	15	99²⁵/₃₂	+ ³/₃₂
... 4¼03	6.3	10	99¾	+ ¾
...49	6.2	25	94¼	+ ¾
	7.2	9	96⅝	+ ⅛
		[illegible]	104⅛	+ ¼

Bonds	Cur Yld.	Vol.	Close	Net Chg.
FordCr 6⅜08	6.7	105	95	+ ¼
GEICap 7⅞06	7.4	6	106⅜	− ⅝
GMA 7s00	7.0	31	100¼	...
GMA 5½01	5.6	153	97½	+ ¾
GMA 6¾02	6.8	1	99½	− 3½
GMA 7s02	7.0	10	100½	+ ⅛
GMA 6⅝02	6.6	1	99⅞	...
GMA 5⅞03	6.1	5	96¾	− ⅛
GMA zr12	...	34	370	+ 2½
GMA zr15	...	1	303	− 1
GenesisH 9¾05	14.4	50	67⅞	...
GrnTrFn 10¼02	9.8	6	104⅛	− ⅞
HlthcrR 6.55s02	cv	56	91½	− ⅝
HlthcrR 10½02	cv	12	106	+ 2
Hlthso 9½01	9.4	138	101	− ⅝
HewlPkd zr17	...	5	64⅝	− ⅛
Hilton 5s06	cv	21	87¼	− ¾
Hollngr 8⅝05	8.5	40	101⅝	+ 1⅜
Hollgnr 9¼07	9.1	50	101½	+ ½
Hollngr 9¼06	9.2	10	100¾	− ¼
HomeDpt 3¼01	cv	1	264¼	...
IRT Pr 7.3s03	cv	77	98	− 1
IntgHlth 5¾01	cv	213	36¾	− ¼
IBM 6⅜00	6.4	35	100¹/₃₂	...
IBM 7¼02	7.1	10	102¼	+ ⅛
IBM 7s25	7.1	32	98	+ ⅛
IBM 6½28	7.0	14	92¼	+ ⅝
IntShip 9s03	8.8	146	102⅜	+ ⅞
Iomega 6¾01	cv	2	87½	− 7½
KCS En 8⅞08f	...	5	36	+ 2
KaufB 9⅜03	9.3	[illegible]	[illegible]	

The "Vol" column shows the number of bonds that changed hands that day (20 for the first issue listed and 25 for the second).

The "Net Chge." (meaning net change) shows that the price went down 25 cents.

The second listing can be interpreted the same way. These are bonds issued to pay 7% of face value ($70 per bond) each year until they mature in 2005. Twenty-five bonds sold that day. The last price paid was $104.125, producing a current yield of 6.7%. (The yield to maturity would be 6.2%.)

How to Reduce the Risks in Bonds

INTEREST-RATE CHANGES CREATE ONE OF THE CHIEF RISKS YOU face as an investor in bonds: The market value of the bonds you own will decline if interest rates rise. This unalterable relationship suggests the first of several risk-reducing steps you can take as a bond investor:

DON'T BUY BONDS WHEN INTEREST RATES ARE LOW OR RISING. Put your cash in a money-market fund or in certificates of deposit maturing in three to nine months. The ideal time to buy bonds is when interest rates have stabilized at a relatively high level or when they seem about to head down.

STICK TO SHORT- AND INTERMEDIATE-TERM ISSUES. Maturities of three to five years will reduce the potential volatility of your bond holdings. They fluctuate less in price than longer-term issues, and they don't require you to tie up your money for ten or more years in exchange for a relatively small additional yield.

ACQUIRE BONDS WITH DIFFERENT MATURITY DATES TO DIVERSIFY YOUR BOND HOLDINGS. A mix of issues maturing in one, three and five years will protect you from getting hurt by interest rate movements you can't control. Mutual funds, which are discussed in the next chapter, are an excellent way to achieve diversity in your bond investments.

BUY HIGH-RATED BONDS TO REDUCE THE RISK OF DEFAULT. Interest-rate

What the Ratings Mean

S&P	MOODY'S	WHAT IT MEANS
AAA	Aaa	The highest possible rating, indicating the agencies' highest degree of confidence in the issuer's ability to pay interest and repay the principal.
AA	Aa	A very high rating, only marginally weaker than the highest.
A	A	High capacity to repay debt but slightly more vulnerability to adverse economic developments.
BBB	Baa	The lowest investment-grade rating, indicating "adequate" capacity to pay principal and interest but more vulnerability to adverse economic developments.

rises aren't the only potential enemy of bond investors. Another risk to consider is the chance that the organization that issued the bonds won't be able to pay them off. It's not realistic to expect that you could do the kind of balance-sheet analysis it takes to size up a company's ability to pay off its bonds in ten, 20 or even 30 years. Assessing the creditworthiness of companies and government agencies issuing bonds is a job for the pros, the best known of which are Standard & Poor's and Moody's. Fitch Investors Service Inc. also rates bond issues for default risk. If the issuer earns one of the top four "investment grades" assigned by the companies—AAA, AA, A or BBB from Standard & Poor's and Fitch, and Aaa, Aa, A or Baa from Moody's—the risk of default is considered slight.

The box above gives a detailed breakdown of the companies' rating systems for issues considered to be worthy of the investment-grade designation. (Sometimes the ratings will be supplemented by a "+" or a "–" sign.)

Ratings below investment grade indicate that the bonds are considered either "speculative" (BB, Ba or B) or in real danger of default (various levels of C and, in the S&P ratings, a D, indicating that the issue is actually in default). You can consider any issue rated speculative or lower to be a "junk" bond, although brokers and mutual funds usually call them "high-yield" issues.

Sometimes the term "junk" is more suitable. In May 1999,

during a booming economy with the Dow hitting 11,000, there came some surprising and disturbing news. Companies were defaulting on their bond payments at a rate that had not been seen since the early 1990s. Until then the market for junk or high-yield bonds had been strong.

One high-yield issue, Vencor, Inc., a huge nursing home chain, defaulted on its payments and Vencor's bonds fell to 15 cents on the dollar.

Moody's Investor Services reported that nearly 4% of companies that had junk bonds outstanding defaulted on their payments between April 1998 and April 1999. Moody's predicted that defaults for 1999 would top 4.5%, the highest level since 1992.

Analysts said the problem was caused by a combination of a search by investors for higher, riskier returns and an effort by more small, unstable companies to finance themselves through the bond market. The junk had become junkier.

Junk bonds are very risky and it's best to avoid them unless you're willing to study the company's prospects very closely. Even then, junk bonds should never occupy more than a sliver of your portfolio.

Bond safety ratings aren't guarantees; they are based on the informed opinions of the rating companies' analysts. At Standard & Poor's, for example, about 1,100 analysts globally are involved in rating and continuously monitoring bonds. They spend days or even months examining the debt structure and earning power of a corporation or municipality before assigning a rating.

Check the rating of any bond you're considering purchasing. A broker can give you the rating, or you can look it up in the Moody's or S&P bond guides found in many libraries. Online sources for ratings include S&P's at www.personalwealth.com and www.bondsonline.com. Moody's has a Web site, too, at ww.moodys.com, although you may find it difficult to search for ratings of individual companies. For a mutual fund, the prospectus (see Chapter 6) will describe the lowest rating acceptable to the fund's managers, and the annual reports should list the bonds in the fund's portfolio, along with their ratings.

In general, the lower the rating, the higher the yield a bond must offer to attract investors. For example, in the same week in 1999 that a long-term U.S. Treasury bond sold at a price that

How to Ride the Yield Curve

WHETHER YOU'RE BUYING corporate bonds or Treasuries, knowing a little bit of economic esoterica can help with your decisions about when to buy and which maturities to choose. The yield curve is a simple device used by economists to keep track of what's happening to interest rates. You can use it, too. The yield curve is nothing more than a line graph formed by plotting bond interest rates on the vertical axis against maturities on the horizontal.

Normally, the longer the maturity the higher the rate, so the line on the graph slopes upward to the right. But from time to time the line will flatten or even slope the other way, creating what's called an inverted yield curve.

Yield curves generally become flat or inverted when a nervous Federal Reserve Board pushes up short-term rates to slow down a hot economy and to cool inflationary pressures, as happened in 1997-98. Meanwhile, long-term rates don't change much because investors don't expect the current inflation to persist for 20 or 30 years. An inverted yield curve (short-term rates are higher than long-term rates) creates opportunities for money-market

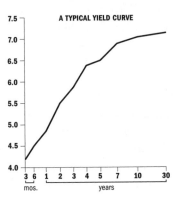

A TYPICAL YIELD CURVE

investors to earn high interest, but it also creates some danger to the economy. If the Fed overreacts and raises short-term rates too high, it risks pushing the economy into a recession. The yield curve has been inverted five times since 1953, and four times a recession followed within 12 to 28 months.

This sort of situation has practical implications for investors. An obvious strategy when the yield curve is inverted is to stick with short maturities, putting your cash into money-market funds, CDs or Treasury bills, where it will earn high interest.

But don't concentrate on short-term bonds exclusively. When a recession is in the offing, long-term rates are likely to decline. The appearance of an inverted yield curve may represent a good opportunity to lock in current rates by using new money to "go long"—say, to maturities of ten years or so. A middle course would be to dollar-cost-average out of a money-market fund into a long- or intermediate-bond fund, which would permit you to earn high short-term rates on your money without committing yourself too far down the road while you wait for the situation to clarify.

paid a current yield of 5.8%, an AAA corporate bond of the same maturity yielded 6%, a BBB-rated corporate yielded 7.4% and a B-rated corporate was priced to yield 8.5%.

DIVERSIFY BY BUYING BONDS FROM SEVERAL ISSUERS. The fact that a municipal or corporate bond has a high rating is no guarantee that it is completely safe. For example, the municipal bonds of Orange County, Cal., were rated Aa by Moody's. Orange is one of the world's richest counties and investors felt safe buying its municipal bonds. But in 1995, Orange County was forced to delay payment on several of its obligations and even filed for bankruptcy. The county's voters balked at approving tax increases to pay the debt, temporarily leaving security holders in the lurch. But they were eventually paid with new issues of debt. Orange County had one of the best bond ratings but still ran into financial difficulty. This is an example of why diversification by issuer is important (unless the issuer is the U.S. government).

Highly rated corporate bonds also can provide unpleasant surprises for investors. Lightning struck holders of RJR Nabisco bonds in 1988 when that company became the object of the largest leveraged buyout ever. (In a leveraged buyout, the buyers typically take on huge debts in the company's name to pay off the sellers. A bid to take over a company may be good for stockholders, who can sell their stock at the high takeover price. But a takeover paid for with additional debt can be disastrous for bondholders.) This LBO sparked lawsuits for restitution by investors who got burned when some RJR bonds fell below 36 cents on the dollar.

(One way to diversify your bond investments is to buy shares in bond mutual funds. A discussion of bond funds is included in Chapter 6.)

PAY ATTENTION TO THE NEWS. The rating agencies keep track of the issues they've rated, raising or lowering ratings when they think a change is justified. Hundreds of "fallen angels" get downgraded each year, and hundreds get upgraded. The last thing you want is to have the rating of a bond issue lowered while you're holding it in your portfolio. Even a slight downgrade can affect a bond's value. For example, Aeroquip-Vickers, a global manufacturer of engineered components and systems for industrial aerospace and automotive markets, was acquired by Eaton Corp. in early April 1999. The bonds of Aeroquip-Vickers were downgraded from A to BBB+, which sent bonds with a maturity of 2012 from 107⅞ to 103. To guard against downgrading, you have to pay attention to the company's prospects after you buy the bond.

CONSIDER OTHER FACTORS. Ratings aren't the final word on good bond buys. In fact, the market often recognizes problems with bond issues before the rating services can react. In 1989, Integrated Resources Inc., a huge financial services firm that has since declared bankruptcy and disappeared, defaulted on nearly $1 billion dollars' worth of debt. The default wasn't entirely without warning, but the firm's CCC rating at the time gave little notice that a complete collapse was imminent.

Such a possibility underscores the importance of considering a bond's rating in the context of other information about bond issues you might buy:

Compare the bond's price and yield with those of bonds with identical ratings to see which is the better buy. If the issuing company seems a likely target for a takeover—it's undervalued, has well-known brand names in its stable of products or has divisions that could be sold separately—look for what's called poison put provisions in the bond. Essentially, poison puts guarantee that anyone holding bonds in a company that is taken over can redeem those bonds at par (face value). Such a provision protects investors and discourages takeovers at the same time.

Make sure you're looking at the bonds' current credit rating. Buying on the basis of an outdated rating can be an expensive mistake.

Make sure there's a market for the bond. This advice sounds obvious, but one thing that can cause junk bonds to lose so much of their value so fast is a situation in which there are suddenly many, many sellers and very few buyers, as when bad news hits.

Should You Buy Convertible Bonds?

CONVERTIBLE BONDS COMBINE THE FEATURES OF STOCKS AND bonds in one investment. They are redeemable for a set number of shares of stock of the same company, or at a specified ratio—25 shares of stock for each $1,000 in bonds, for example. If the price of the company's stock rises, so will the price of its convertible bond, although not dollar for dollar. If the stock falls, the convertible will fall, too; but because it is a bond, its movement will also be affected by interest rates. Thus, fundamental or economic factors that are bad for stocks (recession, for instance) may be balanced by factors that are good for bonds (falling interest rates). If the stock rises high enough, you can exchange your bonds for stock and, if you wish, sell the stock and pocket the profits.

It sounds like the best of both worlds, but before you rush out to buy, consider a few more facts about convertibles:

They are usually debentures, meaning they are not backed by the assets of the company.

They are usually subordinated debentures, meaning other, unsubordinated debts will be paid off ahead of them in case of bankruptcy.

Default risks aside, most convertibles are callable on short notice. The issuer is unlikely to allow its stock price to climb very high above the conversion price; as a result, your profit potential is limited.

You pay a price for these hybrid securities: They pay less interest than you could get from the same company's bonds, and you can expect to pay a higher price to buy the convertible than its value as either a stock or a bond. That higher price is called the conversion premium or, in the parlance of Wall Street, "water." It represents the distance the stock price has to climb to reach the break-even point for converting the bond.

This doesn't mean that convertible bonds aren't worth considering. It does mean that the investment decision is more complicated than the decision to buy stock or bonds issued by the same company. As a cross between the two, convertibles demand that you be concerned not only with the ability of the company to pay its debts but also with the anticipated direction of interest rates and the price appreciation potential of the company's stock. In a climate in which interest rates are declining and prospects look good for stock prices, as happens near the end of a recession, for example, carefully selected convertibles offer price potential and relatively small downside risk. But the interplay of interest rates, call provisions, conversion premiums and stock prices is so complex that it's safe to assume that individual investors get talked into buying convertibles by their brokers more often than they think of doing it themselves. In short, convertibles require more time and attention than most investors are willing to give them.

Treasuries: The Safest Bonds of All

O NE WAY TO ELIMINATE THE DEFAULT RISK ENTIRELY IS TO stick with IOUs from the U.S. Treasury. Because they are backed by the federal government, there is virtually no chance that you'll miss a payment of interest or principal or that Uncle Sam's credit rating will be lowered, no matter how many billions of dollars he is in the red. (Remember, he owns the presses that print the money.)

Buying Treasuries doesn't eliminate market risk, however; once issued, their value fluctuates with interest rates, just as is true of corporate bonds. But the risk of default is nil.

Treasuries have other attractive features as well. Interest (but not capital gains) is exempt from state and local income taxes. Because the market for them is so vast, they are easy to buy and easy to sell. Commissions tend to be modest. In fact, you can buy Treasuries direct at regularly scheduled auctions (you don't have to attend) and eliminate commission charges entirely.

All these advantages do come at a price: Treasuries tend to yield a little less than corporate bonds with comparable maturities, even AAA-rated corporates. But for the peace of mind they provide, that's a small price millions of investors are happy to pay.

YOUR CHOICES

Here's an overview of the choices in Treasury IOUs, followed by advice on the best ways to buy and sell them.

TREASURY BILLS. These mature within a year—three- and six-month T-bills are the most common. Minimum purchase is $1,000. A key feature of T-bills that sets them apart from most other issues is that they pay the interest up front. You pay the face value of the bill minus the interest; when the bill matures, you collect the face value.

Here's how the system works: The Treasury holds regularly scheduled auctions at which investors bid for the bills. If the bids determine that the interest on that week's bills is 5%, you pay $9,500 for a $10,000 bill (assuming the maturity is a year; for shorter maturities, the payment would be adjusted accordingly). Then, when the bill matures, the Treasury sends you a check for $10,000.

The 5% interest you earn is called the "auction," or "discount," rate, and it actually understates your yield. Because you're earning 5% on $10,000 but had to lay out only $9,500 to get it, you're a little ahead of the corporate-bond buyer, who would have had to ante up the entire $10,000. You can calculate the bond-equivalent yield for a T-bill by figuring the interest earned on the actual cash investment. In this case, you're putting up $9,500 in exchange for $500 in interest. Thus your bond-equivalent yield is about 5.3%.

TREASURY NOTES. Treasury notes, like corporate bonds, pay interest semiannually. Notes are issued in medium-term maturities of two to ten years and are sold about once a month in minimum denominations of $1,000 for maturities of four years or more, $5,000 for shorter maturities. They can't be called.

TREASURY BONDS. These have maturities of more than ten years, although some can be called in early by the Treasury. The minimum purchase is $1,000.

How to Buy Treasuries

The easiest way to buy a newly issued Treasury bill, note or bond is by phone or over the Internet. If you have a touch-tone phone, you can call 800-943-6864 and make the purchase by debiting your bank account. If you have access to the Internet, you can go to www.publicdebt.treas.gov and buy online. You can also pay a broker or bank to buy them for you. You'll probably be charged about $50 per transaction, which lowers your yield a bit. Some institutions also levy fees for collecting interest payments on your behalf. If you want to sell the Treasury before it matures, you simply notify the bank or broker and it will be done for you.

How to Sell T-Notes and T-Bonds

Q: *I have been purchasing Treasury bills and two-year Treasury notes under an account with the Federal Reserve Board Treasury Direct Bookkeeping Securities System. I hesitate to purchase intermediate- or long-term notes or bonds because I have been unable to determine how I can sell them prior to maturity. Is there a simple procedure for selling notes or bonds?*
A: In order to sell Treasury securities before they mature you can use the Treasury Direct "Sell Direct" service or you can transfer the securities out and have your bank or brokerage sell them.

To use Sell Direct, fill out and mail to the Federal Reserve Bank of Chicago a properly certified security transfer request form (PDF 5179-1). For each security that FRB Chicago sells in the secondary market, it will charge you $34.

If you prefer to use a bank or brokerage to sell the securities, you must set up an account there, then transfer your notes and bonds out of the Treasury Direct bookkeeping system. Your bank or brokerage can then sell the security for you for a fee, which which usually runs around $50.

To transfer your notes or bonds, fill out Form PDF 5179, "Security Transfer Request," available from the Federal Reserve Branch where you purchased your note or bond. Include your financial institution's routing number and handling instructions.

It's not terribly complicated to buy Treasuries by phone or mail from any of the country's 12 Federal Reserve banks, at their 36 branches or at the Treasury Department in Washington. You can get details by contacting the Capital Area Servicing Center, Bureau of the Public Debt, Department N, Washington, DC 20239-1500, or by calling 202-874-4000 for recorded information. Check your phone book's blue pages for the closest Federal Reserve bank or branch.

Whether you deal by mail or in person, you'll be required to fill out a tender, or bid, for the bill, note or bond you're buying. Most individuals submit what are known as noncompetitive bids, which means you'll get the average interest rate produced by the auction. The auction announcement states the date and time you must deliver in-person tenders. If you buy by mail, your envelope must be postmarked no later than the day before the auction and received by the date the security is issued. You can pay by check (for T-bills it must be a certified check) or with cash if you're buying in person. You can get a pretty good idea of the yield you're likely to get on newly issued Treasuries by checking newspaper tables of Treasury prices for comparable maturities in the secondary market.

How Do You Collect Your Interest?

Under the Treasury Direct system, you supply on your tender form the number of your bank or money-market account, along with the name and nine-digit identification number of the financial institution you want to receive the funds (the number is on the institution's checks). The Treasury then deposits interest and principal payments directly to your account. Treasury Direct also lets you sign up for automatic reinvestment of proceeds in new Treasury bills without filling out new forms.

U.S. Agency Securities

Federal agency securities offer a way to step up the yield a bit over Treasuries without really increasing the risk. Agency debt isn't backed by the full faith and credit of the government, but no one believes that the government could ever let one of its agencies default. Still, because agency securities are not quite so risk-free as Treasuries, they generally must pay a little more interest to attract investors.

The chief issuers of agency securities are the Federal Farm Credit System and the major mortgage-related agencies, which include Fannie Mae (formerly known as the Federal National Mortgage Association), the Government National Mortgage Association (Ginnie Mae) and Freddie Mac (the Federal Home Loan Mortgage Corp.). Maturities range from one to 40 years; minimum purchase requirements range from $1,000 to $25,000. The interest from issues of some agencies, such as the Student Loan Holding Corp. and the Tennessee Valley Authority, is exempt from state and local income taxes. You purchase agency securities through brokers, and they are issued in book-entry form, like Treasuries, meaning that a record is made of your ownership but you don't actually receive the securities.

Pass-Through and Participation Certificates

Technically, the mortgage-related agencies just named don't deal in bonds as such. They package mortgage loans they've purchased in the secondary market and sell "pass-through" or "participation" certificates to investors interested in receiving

See Chapter 6.

Alternative to Savings Bonds

Q: *I am 25 years old, single, and have just started investing. I am buying U.S. savings bonds each month through payroll deductions. Would I be better off putting my money elsewhere?*

A: Savings bonds are one of the safest, most convenient ways to invest, but someone your age, who can afford to take some risk, should consider a stock mutual fund for long-term investing with higher rewards. Many funds rival the convenience of savings-bond payroll deduction by allowing you to invest a regular amount each month via automatic bank drafts. See Chapter 6.

income from mortgage-backed securities. Ginnie Mae, for instance, insures pools of FHA and VA mortgages. If a borrower in the pool misses a payment, Ginnie Mae will make good if necessary, which isn't likely because the FHA and VA mortgages in the pool are backed by the government to begin with.

Pass-through and participation certificates start at $25,000, so that for many people a Ginnie Mae mutual fund or unit trust is a more practical way to invest in mortgage-backed securities. The minimum for funds is usually $1,000.

Once bought, mortgage-backed securities behave a lot like bonds: Their market value declines as interest rates rise, and vice versa. But they carry their own unique risk as well: As mortgage rates decline, many homeowners take advantage of the situation by refinancing. They pay off their old, high-rate mortgages, which then drop out of the pool. Investors get their principal back, but their interest payments may decline. As a result, the price of mortgage-backed securities can drop at the same time that the price of other bonds is rising.

When homeowners pay off mortgages in a pool, the effect is the same as when a corporation calls its bonds: Investors get part of their principal back before they want it. In addition, cash flow is hard to predict. Because of this intrinsic unpredictability, Ginnie Maes and other mortgage pools generally pay a higher yield than Treasury bonds of comparable maturity. Over the years, this extra interest has attracted a lot of investors who didn't understand the risks involved. In turn, those risks have led to the creation of an instrument designed to make mortgage-backed income more predictable, the collateralized mortgage obligation (CMO).

CMOs are Ginnie Maes that are split into several different classes, or tranches. Investors choose a tranche according to whether they want a short-, intermediate- or long-term investment. All investors get interest income, but prepayments of principal go first to the short-term investors until they are paid off, then to the intermediate-term investors, and so on. The real estate mortgage investment conduit, or REMIC, is a variation on the CMO idea that may not limit itself to Ginnie Mae mortgages. The minimum investment in CMO-type instruments is usually $1,000.

For a more on mortgage-backed securities, see Chapter 9.

Savings Bonds: New Spark for an Old Idea

ONCE THOUGHT OF CHIEFLY AS A HAVEN FOR SCAREDY-CATS and an obvious gift for kids' birthdays and bar mitzvahs, savings bonds have been finding their way into serious investors' portfolios since the government floated interest rates in the early 1980s. Today, series EE bonds offer a competitive yield, unquestioned safety and a couple of unique tax features that make them especially suited for savers with an eye on college costs or retirement some years away.

COMPETITIVE INTEREST RATES. EEs earn interest for 30 years at a floating rate. In the first five years, EEs issued after May 1995 through April 1997 earn 85% of the average of six-month Treasury security yields. Interest is added every six months. After five years, the bonds earn 85% of the average five-year Treasury rate. The savings-bond rate is adjusted twice a year, in May and November, to reflect current market rates.

Series EE savings bonds bought on or after May 1, 1997, will earn interest based on five-year Treasury security yields right from the start. The new rate for EE bonds will be 90% of the average yields on five-year Treasury securities for the preceding six months. EE bonds will increase in value every month instead of every six months. Interest is compounded semiannually. If you cash a bond before it's five years old, you'll pay a penalty equal to three months' interest.

Current rate information is available by phone at 800-487-2663 or online at www.publicdebt.treas.gov. For interest rates on EE bonds issued before May 1, 1997, contact your local bank or write to Savings Bonds, Parkersburg, WV 26106-1328. This

Maximizing Interest When Selling Bonds

Q: *I've been purchasing U.S. savings bonds through payroll deduction. When is the best time to redeem the bonds to get the most interest?*

A: You'll receive the maximum interest if you redeem your bonds on the exact date that you are credited with interest or as soon as possible after that. Series EE bonds accrue interest twice a year, starting six months after purchase. A bank can tell you your bonds' redemption dates as well as their guaranteed minimum interest rates, if any.

You can order the tables of redemption values for series EE bonds for $2.75 from the Superintendent of Documents, P.O. Box 371954, Pittsburgh, PA 15250. You can also get a free copy of *The Best Times to Redeem or Exchange Savings Bonds,* which explains how to maximize the interest, by writing to the Savings Bond Marketing Office, Bureau of Public Debt, 999 E Street, N.W., Room 354, Washington, DC 20239. This information is also available online at www.publicdebt.treas.gov.

information also is found on the Comprehensive Savings Bond Value Tables that can be downloaded, using Adobe Acrobat, from the Treasury Direct Web site (www.publicdebt.treas.gov).

Bonds bought before November 1982 and held for five years after that date also qualify for the variable rates. The exceptions are bonds issued more than 40 years ago, which are no longer earning interest and should be redeemed right away.

CONVENIENT TO PURCHASE. Many people buy EE bonds via automatic payroll deduction, a virtually painless way to accumulate bonds little by little as the years go by. For others, buying a bond is as easy as making a trip to the bank. EEs come in denominations as small as $50 and as large as $10,000. You pay half the face amount and collect the accumulated interest when you redeem the bond, which you can do at any bank, with no commission charges on either side of the transaction.

SAFETY. Savings bonds are protected against default by the full faith and credit of the U.S. government. The only way you can lose the principal is to lose the bond, and if you do lose the bond (or if it is stolen or destroyed), you can get it replaced by completing form PDF 1048 and mailing it to the Bureau of the Public Debt, Savings Bond Operations Office, Parkersburg, WV 26106-1328. You can download this form from the Web at www.publicdebt.treas.gov or you may request that it be mailed to you.

CONVERTIBILITY INTO AN INCOME STREAM. Series EE bonds pay no current income—that is, you have to cash them in to get your interest. But $500 or more worth of EE bonds can be converted directly into series HH bonds, which pay 4% interest in semiannual installments. (Bonds issued before March 1, 1993, pay 6% or 7%.)

SPECIAL TAX FEATURES. This is where savings bonds really earn their spurs. Interest is exempt from all state and local income taxes, and your options for paying federal income taxes are unique to savings bonds. You can either pay the tax each year as the interest accrues, or postpone paying the tax until you cash in the bond or give it to someone else, or until it matures. Or you could exchange your EE bonds for HH bonds and continue putting off the tax until you cash in the HHs (although the semiannual interest payments are taxable) or until they reach maturity after 20 years. This is a possibility for retirees to consider, but tax savings shouldn't blind you to the fact that you may be able to earn more than 4%, after taxes, elsewhere.

SPECIAL DEAL FOR COLLEGE SAVINGS. The practice of buying savings bonds to finance the kids' college education is an American insti-

Swap EE Bonds for HH Bonds?

Q: *For more than 15 years my husband and I purchased U.S. savings bonds with plans to cash them in after retirement. We're retired now, and our oldest bonds won't mature for a few more years. Should we exchange the bonds for HH bonds so that we can put off paying federal tax on the accumulated interest and receive the semiannual interest payments? Or should we cash in all the bonds now, pay the tax and put the proceeds in a tax-free mutual fund?*

A: We wouldn't recommend either option. If you exchange your E and EE bonds for HH bonds, you put off federal taxes on the amount you roll over. But you earn only 4% interest on HHs, which is paid semiannually and taxable in the year you receive it. If you cash in the bonds and put the money in a tax-exempt fund, paying taxes would leave you with less to invest (in the 28% bracket, you'd have only $720 to invest for every $1,000 of accumulated savings-bond interest). And tax-exempt interest, unlike savings bonds' tax-deferred interest, is counted as income in the formula that determines how much of your social security benefits is taxed. Instead, consider redeeming your EEs periodically over the years as you need the money. Your tax liability would be spread out more evenly than if you cashed them in all at once, and you could redeem the bonds with the lowest guaranteed interest rate first.

tution. Parents and grandparents buy bonds in the name of the child, who can often count the interest as tax-free because the child doesn't have enough income to incur any tax. As an alternative, the child's tax bill can be deferred until he or she reaches age 14, when the so-called kiddie tax disappears (see Chapter 13). The child may pay tax then, but probably in the lowest bracket.

If you buy series EE bonds in your own name (not the child's), all income from them will be tax-free if the bonds are redeemed to pay college tuition or fees, as long as your income is under certain levels. See Chapters 12 and 13 for a more complete explanation.

Making Money With Municipals

MUNICIPAL BONDS ARE ISSUED BY STATES, COUNTIES, CITIES and other political jurisdictions, and their agencies, which may include school districts, airport authorities, bridge and highway departments, and sewer districts.

The main attraction of municipal bonds is well known: The interest earned from them is exempt from federal income tax and, in most cases, from income taxes of the issuing state as well. (The only exceptions are Illinois, Iowa, Oklahoma and Wisconsin, which grant limited exemptions.) One way to look at the federal tax exemption is this: The states and cities don't tax the interest from Treasury issues, so the federal government returns the favor by not taxing the interest from municipal bonds. (In fact, the exemption is based on the U.S. Constitution, which bars the feds from interfering with state revenues, and vice versa.)

Because tax-exempt interest is worth having only if it exceeds the after-tax yield of taxable interest, figuring the taxable-equivalent yield of a municipal bond is the first step in deciding whether to buy it. If it doesn't pass this test, there's no need to evaluate it further. Thus, it is crucial to know how to perform the following calculation, although a broker will gladly do it for you:

$$\text{Taxable-equivalent yield} = \frac{\text{yield from municipal bond}}{1-\text{your federal tax bracket}}$$

Example: A municipal bond is offered at a yield of 6%. Let's say your taxable income is $50,000 on a joint return, which puts you in the 28% bracket. To work the equation, you convert your bracket to a decimal, or .28. So the taxable equivalent yield is 6 divided by (1 − .28) = 6 ÷ .72 = 8.33. To match the 6% tax-free yield, you'd need a taxable bond paying at least 8.33%.

The calculation actually understates your taxable equivalent if your state doesn't tax municipal-bond interest. In high-tax states such as Massachusetts, New York, Ohio, Oregon, Pennsylvania and Rhode Island, the double-tax-free status of municipal bonds issued within the state can add to the allure considerably. If you live in a city or county that also levies an income tax, the triple-tax-free status of bonds issued by your own state or local jurisdiction raises the taxable-equivalent yield even higher.

HOW TO PICK A MUNI BOND

Municipals, like corporate bonds, vary in quality according to the economic and financial soundness of the project or the creditworthiness of the issuing jurisdiction. Also, like corporate issues, they are rated for default risk by Standard & Poor's and Moody's, on the same scale as corporates: Bonds considered least risky get rated AAA or Aaa, and so forth, as described earlier in the chapter. The higher the bond's rating, the less interest it needs to pay to attract investors, and vice versa.

In addition to its ratings by the credit agencies, a major point to check about a tax-free bond is whether it is a general obligation issue or a revenue bond. As explained earlier, a general obligation bond gets the full backing of the jurisdiction's ability to tax, but a revenue bond has the backing only of the revenues generated by the project it supports—a bridge, an airport or a sewage treatment plant, for instance. Every revenue bond project is different and needs to be analyzed on its economic merits.

Ask your broker for any reports that his or her firm has generated on the project. The official statement from the issuer describes the bond, the project and the municipality in detail. If the bond is a new issue, your broker is required to give you a copy of the statement, just as he or she is required to give you a copy of the prospectus for a new corporate stock or bond issue. But this document, unlike a corporate prospectus, has no standardized format. And municipal bond issuers are not required to provide the kind of detailed financial information corporations must report to bondholders. Disclosure rules have been toughened in the past couple of years, but the onus is still on you to stay current on the financial condition of the issuer of any bonds you may hold.

If you have only a few thousand dollars to commit to municipals, their $5,000 minimum face value suggests that buying into pooled arrangements such as mutual funds and unit trusts makes more sense than chasing after individual bonds. Funds and trusts offer diversified portfolios while providing liquidity and controlling commission costs. They are described in the next chapter.

INSURED MUNICIPAL BONDS

Defaults are rare with municipal bonds, but they happen. Calamities such as the bankruptcy of Orange County, Cal., in 1994 helped to create an active demand for municipal bond insurance. At this writing, state and local economies are doing well, but things could change if the economy takes a downturn. The American Municipal Bond Assurance Corp. (AMBAC) was the first to insure municipal bonds, starting in 1971. The Municipal Bond Insurance Association (MBIA), another major insurer of municipals, appeared three years later.

To insure its bonds, an issuer or underwriter pays a premium based on the type of issue, rating of the issuer, and market conditions—generally 0.1% to 2% of total principal and interest. In return, the insurance company agrees to pay principal and interest to bondholders if the issuer defaults. Policies remain in effect for the life of the bond. Insured bonds get the top (AAA) rating from S&P, even if the bond has a lower rating based on its own creditworthiness. The insurance that makes a bond less risky also makes the bond more attractive to investors. As a result, its yield will be a little lower than a comparably rated uninsured issue.

Municipal bond insurance guarantees that your principal and interest will be paid. It doesn't protect the market value of your bond. (The week Orange County collapsed, mutual funds holding tax-free bonds—especially California bonds—got clobbered.) Interest-rate changes or a downgrading of the issuer's credit rating will still affect the market value of insured bonds, although if you hold the issue until maturity you won't lose a cent.

TAXABLE MUNICIPAL BONDS

Until a few years ago, all municipals were tax-free, but these days it's necessary to differentiate. The interest earned from municipal bonds issued to finance private business activities, such as shopping malls, is generally taxable on the federal level, though it may still be exempt from state and local taxes. The income from certain kinds of private activity bonds, such as those issued to finance the building of a hospital or to back certain kinds of mortgages, is still exempt. For investors in high brackets who have a lot of tax-sheltered income, however, the interest from such bonds issued after August 7, 1986, may be subject to taxation through the alternative minimum tax (AMT). The AMT taxes so-called preference income above a certain level at 26% or 28%, depending on income. Most taxpayers are not subject to the AMT, but make sure you find out the purpose for which your bonds were issued.

How to Use Zero-Coupon Bonds

BONDS NORMALLY PAY INTEREST EVERY SIX MONTHS. ZERO-coupon bonds, known as zeros, don't pay any interest at all until they mature, at which time they pay all accumulated interest at once. Zeros come in denominations as low as $1,000 and are sold at discounts from face value of 50% to 75%, depending on how long you have to wait for maturity. A $1,000 zero yielding 6.15% and maturing in 20 years, for example, costs just $294.10.

Their huge discounts from face value make zeros an excellent long-term investment when you know that you'll need the money at a particular date in the future. The catch is, the IRS taxes the interest year by year as it accrues, just as if you had received it. Because it makes little sense to pay tax on income you haven't yet received, investors buy zeros mainly to keep in their individual retirement accounts, which allow tax-free buildup of earnings within the account (see Chapter 14).

Outside of IRAs, zero-coupon municipal bonds can be a good way to take advantage of the time value of money by paying 50 cents or so today to collect a dollar of face value some years down the road. Tax-free zeros are relatively rare, however, so you may have trouble finding ones that mature when you'll need the money. They usually can be called early, too, making their maturity dates even less reliable.

Zeros as a College Financing Tool

The tax consequences of zero-coupon bonds needn't be so onerous as they first appear if the bonds are used as a part of a college financing plan for young children. Buy the bonds in the child's name so that the income will be taxable to the child. Your broker can set up a free or low-cost custodial account. The first $700 of investment income a child reports each year is tax-free. For a child under age 14, the next $700 is taxed at his or her own rate, probably 15%, and investment income in excess of $1,400 is taxed at the parent's rate—probably 28% or 31%.

The way the IRS requires zero-coupon bond interest to be reported works to your advantage. Consider a 6% zero that grows over 20 years from $312 to $1,000. You don't report one-twentieth of the $688 difference ($34) each year. Instead you report interest as it actually accrues. The first year, a $312 investment earning 6% compounded semiannually earns about $19. The second year, your investment would be $331 ($312 + $19), and $20 of interest would accrue. (You'll get a notice each year from the issuer or your broker showing how much interest to report to the IRS.) It would take quite a few years for the income to trigger much tax, even if you buy, say, ten bonds with a total face value of $10,000. (Chapter 13 provides more details about using zeros as a college savings plan.)

Choosing a Zero

The most popular zeros are those issued directly by the U.S. Treasury and their close cousins created by brokerage firms, who strip the income from regular Treasuries and sell the bare bonds. The direct Treasury issues are called STRIPS. The brokers' versions go by names like TIGRS and CATS. Beyond the security of having the federal government behind them, STRIPS are noncallable; they can't be paid off early if interest rates decline.

Zeros issued by corporations offer slightly higher yields than government zeros of similar maturities. Pay special attention to the ratings of corporate zeros; if the company goes broke, you may never get your money, or you may get only pennies on the dollar. Check for call features, too. If you consider any callable bond, be certain you understand when and at what price it can be called.

You can also buy zeros through a mutual fund. For example, the American Century Target Maturities Trust (800-472-3389; www.americancentury.com), formerly known as the Benham Target Maturity Trust, offers zero funds with several different maturity years. With such funds, you buy shares at a price that is expected to grow to $100 at the end of the target year. Although share prices can fluctuate day to day, if you hold on to your shares until the fund matures, you should earn the yield promised when you bought them. (Benham Target Maturity's minimum initial investment for regular accounts is $2,500; for custodial accounts and IRAs it is $1,000.)

Unless you buy shares in a fund, you'll need to use a broker to buy zeros. You may need more than one, in fact, to compare the availability and yields of bonds that fit your plans. Don't assume all STRIPS or broker-made Treasury zeros yield the same amount. Yields can vary with the commissions built into the price.

The search for tax-free zeros will be tougher. The supply isn't abundant and the call features can be troubling. You must find a broker willing to do the spadework to find appropriate bonds.

As an alternative, you could do your own spadework to find a mutual fund that finds the kinds of bonds you're looking for. The next chapter will show you how.

CHAPTER 6

Mutual Funds: For Many, All You'll Need

UTUAL FUNDS ARE THE HIRED GUNS OF THE INVEST-
ment business: They do the dirty work for
you. A lot of people with neither the time nor
the inclination to slog through reports on
thousands of stocks and bonds in search of a handful of good
ones turn the job over to one or more mutual funds. The funds'
professional portfolio managers pool your money with that of
other investors and assemble portfolios designed to achieve specific investment objectives, which are spelled out in each fund's
prospectus. Thus, instead of digesting thousands of reports, you
need digest only a few.

Funds can make investing easier, but it's a mistake to think
they make it easy. In their quest to attract investors of every conceivable stripe, mutual funds have multiplied so rapidly that
they now outnumber the 3,000-plus stocks listed on the New
York Stock Exchange. The Investment Company Institute
(ICI), the national association to which most funds belong, lists
more than 7,300 of them as members. The ICI sorts funds into
a couple of dozen categories according to investment objectives,
ranging from aggressive stock funds that buy the shares of
promising but unproven new companies to conservative bond
funds that restrict their investments to the municipal bonds of
a single state.

Why Mutual Funds?

BECAUSE THEY PROVIDE expert portfolio management, mutual funds are a better choice than individual stocks or bonds for beginning investors who are still unsure of their own stock- and bond-picking prowess.

Because they provide instant diversification, well-selected mutual funds are a better choice than individual stocks or bonds for investors with modest amounts of money to place at risk.

Convenience, shareholder services and a wide choice of portfolios tailored to different investment goals make mutual funds a suitable substitute for individually selected stocks and bonds, even for experienced investors. Your own investment style should determine whether you should use funds for part or all of your portfolio.

What Funds Have to Offer

IN ADDITION TO THIS AMAZING RANGE OF INVESTMENT PORTFOLIOS, funds offer a combination of shareholder services that is impossible to find anywhere else.

EXPERT PORTFOLIO MANAGEMENT. Mutual funds are sponsored by management companies that hire the experts who make the investment decisions. Sometimes a manager will guide the fund to such sterling performance for so long that the manager's name becomes practically synonymous with the fund's: Peter Lynch, who retired from Fidelity Magellan fund in 1990 after 13 years at the helm, and John Neff, who ran Vanguard Windsor fund for 30 years, are examples. Other funds bear the names of founders who established their credentials as stock market gurus before setting up publicly available mutual funds. John Templeton, Mario Gabelli and Martin Zweig fit that description. The vast majority of mutual fund portfolio managers don't share this celebrity status. They labor in relative obscurity, which is probably just fine with them.

AUTOMATIC DIVERSIFICATION. Owning shares of a mutual fund gives you a small ownership interest in all the stocks, bonds and other investments in the fund's portfolio. Whether your aim is to own a cross section of growth stocks or utility stocks, corporate bonds or gold-mining shares, you can find a fund or funds to suit you.

EASE OF PURCHASE AND SALE. You can buy funds through a broker, a bank or the mail. You can sell them the same way, or with a phone call. By law, a fund must buy back its shares when you want to sell them. The price at which fund shares are bought and sold is based on the fund's net asset value, or NAV, which is the market value of the fund's holdings, minus management expenses, divided by the number of fund shares outstanding. A few specialized funds calculate their NAV hourly, but for the most part the price you pay or receive will be based on the net asset value calculated at the close of trading on the day you place your order. (A major difference between "load" and "no-load" funds, which are discussed in detail later in this chapter, is that you buy and sell no-load funds at their net asset value; you buy load funds at net asset value plus a commission, but sell them back to the fund at net asset value.)

OPEN-END VS. CLOSED-END FUNDS. Because most mutual funds are regularly issuing new shares and buying back old ones, the number of shares is constantly changing. Thus, they are "open-end" funds. This distinguishes them from "closed-end" funds, which issue a fixed number of shares and don't promise to buy them back. Once issued, closed-end shares are bought and sold on a stock exchange or over the counter. The distinction between open-end and closed-end funds sometimes gets muddled by the fact that some open-end funds reach a point at which they don't want any additional cash to invest and declare themselves "closed" to new investors. In recent years, the Fidelity Contrafund and Magellan funds decided to close in that way (although Fidelity has created a Contrafund II that is open to new investors). They did not become closed-end funds, however, because they stand ready to redeem or issue shares for their current shareholders. There's more on closed-end funds later in this chapter.

SMALL MINIMUM PURCHASES. Some funds will accept a minimum initial investment of as little as $250 or $500. A typical minimum to open an account is $1,000, with minimum additional investments of $50 or $100. Minimums are often less for IRA accounts. Thus, mutual funds are ideal vehicles for long-term accumulation programs through dollar-cost averaging (see Chapter 4). And because funds will issue fractional shares, you can invest a flat amount regularly without worrying about whether you're buying whole shares. For instance, $250 will buy 15.63 shares when a fund is selling for $16 a share. If it's selling for $15.50 the next time you buy, your $250 gets you 16.13 shares.

AUTOMATIC REINVESTMENT OF EARNINGS. Dividends paid by stocks in the fund's portfolio, interest from bonds, and capital gains earned from selling securities can be automatically reinvested for you in more shares. Reinvesting earnings is a critical element in any long-term investment plan. Reinvesting is discussed in more detail later in this chapter.

AUTOMATIC PAYMENT PLANS. If you'd like to receive regular income from your shares, funds will set up automatic payment plans for you. If dividends and interest earned aren't enough to cover your payments, the fund will sell shares to cover them.

SHAREHOLDER SERVICES. Most funds are happy to hear from their shareholders and have set up well-staffed telephone systems to handle inquiries about everything from current account balances to requests for descriptive brochures and order forms. Funds love individual retirement accounts or Keogh accounts (because they know such accounts are likely to stay there for some years) and have simplified the custodial paperwork to the point that it is virtually painless. Companies that manage a group of funds, often called a family of funds, make it easy for you to switch your money from one member of the family to another—say, from a stock fund to a money-market fund—usually with a phone call.

EASY ACCESS TO INFORMATION. Fund prices are published in the newspaper every day, just like the prices of the stocks and bonds that funds buy and sell for their portfolios. (See the sample listing on page 128.) Most funds maintain toll-free numbers to facilitate requests for information about the fund; in fact funds are supposed to provide you with a prospectus before selling you any shares (see pages 126 and 127 for an explanation of what to look for in a prospectus).

Several tracking services follow funds and report their results over periods ranging from a month to ten years. The list of newspapers and magazines that publish comparative fund performance information in every single issue is long and diverse, ranging from broad-based personal finance publications such as *Kiplinger's Personal Finance Magazine,* which publishes a monthly list of top performers in various categories and an annual compilation of results for all funds, to business and investment publications such as *Forbes, Barron's, Business Week,* the *Wall Street Journal* and *Investor's Business Daily.* The box on page 130 describes a number of publications that contain comprehensive listings of funds, including, in some cases, performance results.

The Cost of Mutual Fund Investing

IN RETURN FOR ALL THIS EXPERTISE AND CONVENIENCE, MUTUAL funds charge a variety of fees. Like cars, hotels and stockbrokers, some funds give you more for your money than others.

SALES CHARGES. It's tempting to divide funds neatly into two camps: load funds, which are sold mostly through brokers and charge you a commission when you buy shares, and no-load funds, which are sold directly to the public via advertising and don't charge a sales commission. Unfortunately, making the distinction is not that simple anymore. The marketing of funds has become so sophisticated that before you can know what you're paying, you need to check the prospectus for front-end loads, back-end loads and other kinds of fees that can sneak up on you if you don't watch out.

FRONT-END LOADS. Of the more than 3,000 funds ranked by Kiplinger in 1998, more than half charged a front-end load. A typical load is about 3.00% to 5.75%, often charged on a sliding scale that decreases with the size of the investment. For instance, one fund charges 5.75% on purchases of less than $50,000, 4.5% for a $50,000 to $100,000 investment, and so on until the load disappears for investors with $1 million or more. It's important to be aware that the load is calculated on the gross amount of your investment. If you invest $1,000 in a fund with a load of 5.75%, then $57.50 will be deducted as a sales charge and $942.50 will be invested in the fund's shares. Calculated as a percentage of your investment, that $57.50 actually represents a commission of 6.1% paid to the fund.

Choose Your Load

IF YOU ARE INVESTING for capital gains, a fund that charges a front-end load costs you less than a fund that charges a redemption fee because the front-end load will be based on a smaller amount.

If you are investing for income, a back-end load may be preferable to a front-end load because more of your initial investment goes to work earning interest.

Other things being equal, a no-load fund is preferable to either a front- or back-end load. Because the sales load reduces the size of your initial investment, you earn less in a load fund over time than you would by placing the same amount of money in a no-load fund that produced the identical performance record.

BACK-END LOADS. Funds prefer to call these redemption fees. They are levied against the net asset value when you sell, thereby reducing your profit or adding to your loss. Several funds give investors a choice: paying a load to get in, or paying a load to get out.

DEFERRED LOADS. Sometimes called contingent deferred sales fees, these are deducted from the amount of your original investment if you redeem shares within a specified time after you buy them. The amount of the charge and the conditions under which you'll have to pay it are described in the prospectus. The purpose, clearly, is to discourage you from jumping into and out of the fund.

MANAGEMENT FEES. Most of the fees just described go to the broker who sells you the fund, although some funds that sell directly to the public also charge commissions. All funds, both load and no-load, must charge a management fee to compensate the managers for their services, pay the rent, pay brokerage commissions on portfolio transactions, and so forth.

A typical management fee is 0.5% to 1.0% of the fund's assets. It may be either a flat rate or a sliding scale that shrinks as the size of the fund's portfolio grows. Most American Century equity funds, which are no-load, charge about 1% for instance. Investment Company of America, which carries a 5.75% load, charges 0.39% for management. Scudder Large Company Value Fund, a no-load, charges about 1%. Fidelity Investment Grade Bond Fund, a no-load fund, charges 0.44%. Clearly, a fund's policy on management fees has nothing to do with its policy on sales fees. Careful inspection of the prospectus is the best way to ferret out these fees.

MARKETING FEES. Some funds deduct the costs of advertising and marketing the fund directly from the fund's assets rather than absorbing them in the management costs. These charges, called 12b-1 fees, are typically around 0.25% to 0.30% but range as high as 1.25%. Sometimes a portion of the fee is paid to the broker who sold you the fund.

EXPENSE RATIO. The expense ratio is the cost of running the fund expressed as a percentage of the fund's assets. It's the best tool you have for comparing the management costs you'll incur by investing in different funds. The ratio includes management and 12b-1 fees, but not sales loads. The expenses are deducted from net assets and reflected in the percentage returns reported by the funds. Expense ratios can range up to 2.5% or more; the higher the ratio, the less the fund has left to pay its shareholders out of earnings.

How to Find the Right Funds for You

IN A WAY, WORRYING ABOUT MANAGEMENT FEES AND EXPENSE ratios is putting the cart before the horse. The first task in choosing a mutual fund that's right for you is to narrow the field of thousands to a few appropriate candidates. You do that by concentrating on the funds whose investment objectives and willingness to take risks match your own. After you've done

---

12b-1 Fees

Q: *My friend says I should never invest in funds that have 12b-1 fees because they'll eat my profits. Is he right?*
A: Not necessarily. Some funds have relatively small 12b-1 fees, and the performance results reported by funds must take them into account. In choosing a fund, look at its overall expense ratio and performance record. You'll occasionally find funds that, despite the 12b-1 fees, have expense ratios far below those of the average fund and thus are less costly than other funds without 12b-1 fees.

How Loads Affect Performance

Q: *Why is a fund's load fee not counted in most performance calculations? Doesn't that omission distort the actual results?*
A: It's important to take fees into account when calculating your own gain, but in comparing the performance of funds, keep in mind that a fund's total return is a fund's total return, period.

A sales fee doesn't mean that the percentage return on your investment will be lower; it means that less of your money is invested initially. Example: You invest $10,000 in a fund with a 6% sales fee, and the fund has a 10% total return the first year you own it. The broker kept $600, so only $9,400 of your money got into the fund. You still earned 10% on the amount invested. Suppose someone else did the same thing, but a year earlier than you. He earned 10% on his entire investment in the second year because he didn't pay another sales fee.

The point is not that fund loads should be ignored but that they affect different investors in the same fund in different ways, depending on when they put their money in. It is very difficult to account for such differences in a ranking system based on portfolio performance.

that, you should compare performance records, expense ratios and shareholder services before deciding where to put your money. The resources listed on page 130 will help you get that information.

WHAT IS THE FUND'S INVESTMENT OBJECTIVE?

Most of the categories used by the Investment Company Institute to describe funds give a pretty good clue to the kinds of investments they make: growth, aggressive growth, corporate bond and long-term municipal bond, for example. The investment objective is a crucial piece of information, and all the sources listed on page 130 include it. A fund's goals should match yours. Later in this chapter, we suggest some funds with good long-term records to consider for various investment objectives.

WHAT IS THE FUND'S PERFORMANCE RECORD?

You want two pieces of information here: the fund's performance in relation to the market as a whole, and the fund's performance in relation to other funds of its type. The industry-sponsored guides, such as the ICI's *Mutual Fund Directory*, don't include this sort of information; the independently published guides, such as the *Individual Investor's Guide to Low-Load Mutual Funds*, do include it, either as part of a ranking system or in a form you can use to discern relative performance.

Compare the total return (price changes plus reinvested earnings) over several years, not just for a year or two, and consider what was going on in the market during the periods being measured. A fund that maintains a good total return in good markets and bad has earned further consideration. Look for stock funds that consistently do well when compared with their peers (funds of the same type).

How Risky Is the Fund?

Again, you won't find comparative information on the risk-reward relationship in the industry-sponsored guides. You'll have to look to the magazines and newsletters listed and to the data collection services. Like stocks, mutual funds have betas, which measure volatility relative to the market as a whole (see Chapter 4). But fund trackers go much further than that, producing risk ratings for bull and bear markets, and volatility groupings ranging from low to high, on the basis of standard deviations from expected results. These risk measurements are useful indicators of how much volatility to expect from a fund, but a low risk ranking is not a guarantee of safety. If the market plunges, you can be virtually certain that it will take low-risk stocks—and the funds that own them—down with it.

Of all the measures of relative risk in mutual funds, *volatility rankings* are probably the most common. Standard & Poor's Micropal, which tracks fund performance for Kiplinger and other clients, measures variations in each fund's total return relative to other funds over the most recent five-year period. (If a fund is less than five years old, its return is measured for as many years as it is available.) The wider a fund's up-and-down swings over the period, the more volatile, or risky, it is considered to be. Micropal assigns each fund a ranking from 1 (least volatile) to 10 (most volatile).

Bond funds typically earn a 1 because their prices tend to

What to Look for in a Mutual Fund Prospectus

A MUTUAL FUND PROSPECTUS is an awkward cross between a sales pitch and a legal treatise. It is the basic information document that all fund sellers must provide to prospective investors. In it you'll find a summary of fees and expenses, instructions for buying and redeeming shares, plus descriptions of fund objectives, management and shareholder services. These once were impenetrable documents written by lawyers, but the Securities and Exchange Commission has ordered them to be written in "plain English."

The prospectus shouldn't be the only thing you read from or about the fund, but it is among the most important. Here's what you can get out of it:

How do the fund's objectives match your own?

Every prospectus has a discussion of the fund's objectives. It may appear in a section labeled "objectives," "highlights" or "summary." Read this section very carefully, because it reveals how the fund intends to make money and what kinds of risks it will take. Will the fund invest in high-dividend stocks? Will it look for fast profits or long-term growth? Will it take chances you'd rather not take? Pay especially close attention to the fund's guidelines concerning the quality of its investments.

How risky is the fund's strategy?

Many prospectuses include a general discussion of risks. Pay attention to it. In other prospectuses, you may have to ferret out this information. What could go wrong with the fund's plans? Studying the fund's performance can give you a sense of how well it has handled risks in the past.

How much will it cost you to invest?

Tables in every prospectus will tell you whether the fund imposes a load, or charge, when you buy, reinvest or redeem shares; they'll also spell out annual operating costs. As a rule, a company that keeps its expenses at 1% or less of its assets is considered a low-cost fund; the average stock fund charges 1.56%.

change little. A volatility ranking of 10 is relatively rare but is awarded from time to time to very aggressive stock funds that take big risks in search of big payoffs. A ranking of 5 indicates that the fund carries an average risk.

One measure of volatility in a bond fund that isn't often included in the fund's literature is a number called *duration*. Call the fund and ask for it. Used by all professional bond managers, duration is an indication of how sensitive the fund's portfolio would be to a one-percentage-point change in interest rates—the bigger the number, the greater the sensitivity. A duration of six years, for example, means the fund can be expected to gain 6%

How has the fund done in the past?

A performance table shows how you would have fared had you owned shares of the fund over the past decade, assuming it has been around that long. Dividends, capital-gains distributions and the share price at the beginning and end of each year are included. Also listed is the fund's portfolio turnover rate, which is a measure of how often it buys and sells securities. Generally, the higher the rate, the greater the fund's expenses. A rate exceeding 100%—meaning the fund replaced the equivalent of its entire portfolio in the period measured—is a sign of an aggressively managed fund or a fund operating in perilous markets. For instance, a bond fund would tend to log a low turnover rate in a period of steady or declining interest rates but a high turnover when rates head up.

The performance section lists yield and total-return figures. Total return includes income and changes in share price during the period being measured and assumes that such payouts are reinvested in additional shares.

How do you buy and redeem shares?

The key information here is the minimum purchase accepted and minimum subsequent purchases. In the case of a money-market fund, also check the minimum redemption amount. If you plan to use the fund as an interest-earning checking account, for example, you probably won't want one that imposes a $1,000 minimum on redemptions by check.

What securities does the fund own?

One thing you won't find in the prospectus is a listing of what securities the fund actually owns. You can get that information, though, in the fund's Statement of Additional Information and its latest quarterly or annual reports. Ask for copies when you request the prospectus, but keep in mind that portfolio holdings change often and your report is bound to be at least a little out of date. Information regarding a fund's top ten holdings is often available free online at the fund's Web site or on AOL's Morningstar Mutual Funds feature, a scaled-down version of Morningstar's by-subscription service (see page 130).

in market value if rates on comparable bonds fall by one percentage point, or lose 6% if rates fall by a point. Duration is far more accurate than a portfolio's weighted average maturity in determining how its value will change when rates rise or fall. But because the duration is not commonly distributed to individual investors and because it's harder to understand, most investors stick to average maturity.

Make sure you compare apples with apples: Compare long-term funds with other long-term funds and short-term funds with other short-term funds. The most useful number to know is a fund's *weighted average maturity,* which essentially tells you how

How to Read the Mutual Fund Listings

MOST DAILY NEWSPAPERS publish mutual fund tables in the business pages. Some have devised their own presentations. Here's a guide to the rest:

NAV is net asset value per share, that is, what a share of the fund is worth.

The **offering price** is what you pay per share.

NL in the pricing column means there is no up-front sales load.

NAV Chg., daily chg or net chg is the change in the fund's NAV from the previous day.

YTD%ret is the year-to-date return.

p next to the fund's name means that it charges a yearly 12b-1 fee. Funds may be listed as NL even if they charge this fee

so long as it isn't more than 0.25% of assets.

r stands for redemption charge, which may be permanent or temporary. It may start as high as 6% and decline gradually. A fund can have a redemption fee but still be called no-load.

p and **r** mean that the fund levies both 12b-1 and redemption fees. In most cases, p and r listed together refer to a fund with a contingent deferred sales charge. Such a fund may not be listed as no-load.

Some newspapers substitute **t** for funds with both p and r charges.

x stands for "ex-dividend," meaning only current shareholders get the fund's next dividend payout, which is imminent. New buyers won't get it.

NAV	Net Chg	YTD%ret

Name	NAV	Net Chg	YTD %ret	Name	NAV	Net Chg	YTD %ret	Name	NAV	Net Chg	YTD %ret
SmCap	11.30	+0.03	+17.3	**Conseco Fund Group:**				EmgMkt	14.14	+0.10	+48.4
USA Gbl	19.93	+0.22	+22.2	20A	p	16.24	+0.10	+26.9	FL Int r	13.06	+0.03	— 1.1
BldProLoan	14.48	+0.09	— 0.9	AstAlcA	p 12.69	+0.07	+ 9.6	GlbGrth	p 36.51	+0.41	+ 5.0
Burnhm	p 36.94	+0.46	+13.8	ConvSecA	p 13.13	+0.22	+21.3	GnCa r	12.69	+0.06	— 3.4
CCB Funds:				EquityA	p 14.29	+0.03	+14.3	GMBd t	13.55	+0.05	— 3.4
Equity	23.07	+0.12	+ 8.6	EquityY	14.48	+0.03	+14.8	GNY t	19.17	+0.06	— 3.0
CDC MPT + Fds:				FixIncA	p 9.86	+0.05	— 0.3	GNM	p 14.22	+0.05	+ 1.3
AggEql r	10.16	+0.14	NS	FixIncY	9.90	+0.05	+ 0.1	GrInc	20.38	+0.21	+10.5
CoreEql r	10.14	+0.14	NS	HiYldA	p 9.95	+0.01	+ 4.7	GthOp	10.69	+0.14	+10.7
GlobIndl r	10.08	...	NS	HiYldB	p 9.92	+0.01	+ 4.5	HiYld	11.78	+0.03	+16.6
CG Cap Mkt Fnds:				Copley	37.68	+0.55	+ 1.7	InShTV A	1.97	...	+ 1.9
BalInv	11.72	+0.07	+ 5.2	**Cornerstone Funds:**				InsMu t	17.29	+0.07	— 3.0
EmgMkt	6.85	+0.12	+36.5	NYMun	p 0.71	...	—10.9	InterGr	t 13.41	+0.11	+ 6.9
HighYld	7.34x	—0.07	+ 0.6	**Countrywide Funds:**				InflIndex r	14.45	+0.01	+ 8.7
IntrFx	7.89x	—0.01	— 0.5	EqfyA	23.49	+0.38	+11.4	IntlVal	17.45	...	+15.3
IntlEq	12.50	+0.07	+ 9.1	GroVal	p 19.27	+0.16	+14.6	IT Inc	12.41	+0.06	+ 2.9
IntlFx	8.06x	—0.07	— 7.6	IntBd	p 9.53	+0.06	— 2.6	DBaGn	14.66	+0.05	+ 1.8
LgGrw	25.38	+0.48	+12.4	IntGvtA	p 10.38	+0.05	— 1.9	LTGrR	19.19	+0.14	+ 8.6
LgVal	14.19	+0.05	+ 8.8	Oh TF A	11.57	+0.04	— 2.1	LTIncR	13.75	+0.06	+ 2.4
LTBnd	7.89x	+0.05	— 6.2	TF IntA	p 10.79	+0.02	— 1.0	LTGrInR	18.07	+0.10	+ 4.0
MtgBkd	7.84x	+0.01	+ 0.7	Utility A	17.81	+0.36	+ 1.8	LrgCoVl	24.53	+0.08	+ 6.6
MunI	8.22x	+0.01	— 3.8	CuFdAdl	9.93	+0.01	+ 2.9	MA Int r	13.25	+0.01	— 1.4
SmGrw	18.41	+0.08	+ 9.3	CuFdST	9.84	+0.01	+ 2.8	MldcpVl r	22.36	—0.11	+25.6
SmVal	10.78	—0.02	+ 1.2	CutlerEl	15.54	+0.18	+ 5.1	Mas Tx r	16.02	+0.06	— 3.0
CGM Funds:				CutlerValue	18.63	—0.02	+11.3	MunBd r	11.71	+0.05	— 3.7
AmerTF	9.08	+0.04	— 4.0	**DLB Fund Group:**				NJ Int r	13.51	+0.03	— 0.8
CapDv	23.58	+0.03	— 5.5	Disc Gr	17.79	+0.19	+12.0	NJ Mun r	12.59	+0.05	— 2.6
	9.44	+0.09	— 7.8	FixInc	10.27	+0.05	— 1.1	NwLd r	47.78	+0.02	+16.0
		+0.7	+4.0	Growth	13.20	+0.21	+ 3.0	NYInt t	10.68	+0.05	— 3.0
				MicroCap	9.34	+0.02	+ 8.5	NY Tax r	14.69	+0.05	— 2.0
					1.94	—0.04	+ 0.4				
					3.03	+0.03	+10.7				

Reprinted with permission of the Wall Street Journal©1999 Dow Jones & Company, Inc.

long the average bond holding in the fund has until its maturity date. A bond's maturity date is the date on which the issuing company or government is due to pay off all it owes on a bond. This date is set before bonds are sold—although often issuers are allowed to redeem bonds early. (A fund's maturity is "weighted," meaning bonds that make up a larger portion of the portfolio count for more than bonds that are a smaller part of the fund.) The higher a fund's weighted average maturity, the longer-term the fund is, and the more it will fluctuate in value as interest rates change. Other things being equal, long-term bond funds—those with high weighted average maturities—tend to be riskier than short-term bond funds.

DOES THE FUND CHARGE A FRONT- OR BACK-END LOAD?

Sales loads do make a difference. Consider two stock funds with similar records for the five years ended in the spring of 1999. Enterprise Growth Fund had a five-year annual average return of 28.36%, while for the same time period, Janus Growth & Income had a return of 28.02%. Enterprise Growth seems to be the winner by a whisker, but it charges a 4.75% front-end load, while Janus has no sales fee. Say you put $1,000 into each fund at the beginning of the period. Enterprise immediately deducts $47.50 for the commission, leaving you with $952.50 working in the fund. Five years later, that amount has grown to $3,319. Not bad. But because Janus has no sales fee, your entire $1,000 goes to work there, and in five years you'll have $3,439. That's $120 more despite the fractionally inferior return.

Of course, the hope is that paying a load will help you find a superior fund you might otherwise overlook. But loads don't pay for more research or more-talented fund managers; they pay for the advice of the broker or financial planner who sells you the fund. In the case of low-load funds, the money goes directly to the sponsor.

It would be difficult to make a case that loads get you better management. In a study of five-year results done for *Kiplinger's Personal Finance Magazine* a few years ago, 14 of the 25 top equity funds—picked on the basis of their percentage returns—were load funds. But after factoring the effect of front- and back-end loads into those five-year returns, only 11 funds with sales charges

Keep Up With Mutual Funds

INFORMATION ABOUT MUTUAL FUNDS abounds in the popular press, online and in reference sources.

Magazines and Web sites

Several personal finance and investment magazines rank the top-performing mutual funds monthly and rank most funds annually. Several commercial online services also provide fund-ranking and search capabilities.

Among the popular periodicals covering funds on regularly are *Business Week, Forbes, Kiplinger's Personal Finance Magazine* and *Money. Barron's* publishes fund rankings quarterly. All of them have Web sites:

barrons.com offers financial information and portfolio tracking for a fee.

Businessweek.com offers a mutual fund interactive scoreboard and selected fund stories free; you must subscribe to get access to the rest of the site.

kiplinger.com, forbes.com and money.com offer free financial information, portfolio tracking, and financial calculators.

Directories

The following publications and services provide comprehensive directories to funds. They are available in libraries, directly from the publisher, and, in some cases, on the Internet or in bookstores.

Directory of Mutual Funds ($10; 1401 H St., N.W., Suite 1200, Washington, DC 20005; www.ici.org). A comprehensive guide to 7,225 funds, including money-market funds, published by the Investment Company Institute, an industry association. No performance informa-

tion. Updated annually.

Handbook for No-Load Fund Investors, by Sheldon Jacobs ($40; Irwin Professional Publishing, a division of McGraw Hill; 800-262-4729). Excellent guidance on choosing a fund, plus performance data on more than 1,800 funds. Updated annually. Available in libraries and bookstores.

Individual Investor's Guide to Low-Load Mutual Funds ($24.95; 625 N. Michigan Ave., Chicago, IL 60611; 800-428-2244). Comprehensive information on more than 900 no-load funds, compiled by the American Association of Individual Investors, whose members get the book free. Includes performance records, risk ratings and information on portfolio holdings. Updated annually.

Kiplinger's Mutual Funds ($5.95; 1729 H St., N.W., Washington, DC 20006; 888-547-5464). An annual guide to choosing the best funds with advice for novices and experienced investors alike. Presents performance data for more than 3,000 funds. Includes Kiplinger's picks for the 20 best funds in America, as well as top performers in 14 categories over one, three, five, ten and 20 years.

Morningstar Mutual Funds ($495; Morningstar Inc. 225 W. Wacker Drive, Chicago, IL 60606; 800-735-0700; www.morningstar.com). A compendium of mutual fund analysis updated every other week. Covers about 1,700 funds.

Value Line Mutual Fund Survey ($295; Value Line Publishing, 220 E. 42nd St., New York, NY 10017; 800-535-8760; www.valueline.com). A biweekly publication analyzing the performance of about 1,500 mutual funds.

remained in the top 25. The effect was more dramatic in one-year total returns. Funds with sales or redemption fees occupied 21 of the 25 top spots before charges were factored in, but only 12 afterward.

For bond funds the difference was even more striking. Load funds occupied 21 of the 25 top spots in the five-year ranking before commissions and redemption fees, and only 12 after. In one-year rankings, 21 load funds dominated the 25 top performers before loads and redemption fees, and five remained in the rankings after.

This isn't to say you should never consider investing in a load fund. Some do beat the pack consistently, just not so often as some salespeople would like you to believe. A number of such funds appear in the listings you'll find later in this chapter. If your knowledge of funds is minimal, relying on a broker or financial planner to recommend some that fit your goals makes sense.

If you go this route:

- **To give yourself time to earn back the sales commission,** plan to hang on to the fund for several years,
- **To avoid getting stuck with a losing load fund,** choose one that's part of a family. Once you've paid the initial load, many fund families will let you switch to different funds with similar commission structures without paying again.

Still, by following the advice in this book, you should be able to find several no-load funds that can meet your objectives.

WHAT IS THE FUND'S EXPENSE RATIO?

The expense ratio, which was discussed earlier in this chapter, shows how much of your potential earnings get eaten up by the costs of running the fund. Pay attention to this number, but don't fixate on it. The fund must subtract expenses (except for sales fees) before calculating its total return, and the total return is a much more important number.

For example, in a recent year, GAMerica Capital, an aggressive-growth fund, had a high expense ratio of 3.46% but delivered a total return of 37.28%. That same year, AIM Weingarten A fund, with similar objectives, reported an expense ratio of only

1.67%—less than one-half of GAMerica Capital's—but AIM Weingarten A had a total return of 25.956%. Clearly, an investor wouldn't complain about GAMerica Capital's expenses in this case. Expense ratios tend to affect relative payouts from bond funds more than payouts from stock funds, and they can make a critical difference in money-market funds.

WHAT SERVICE DOES THE FUND OFFER?

Some funds make it easier than others to open and close accounts, get information about net asset values, switch from one fund to another within a family, and so forth. A fund family is a series of funds run by the same company—Dreyfus, Fidelity, Oppenheimer, Putnam, T. Rowe Price or Vanguard, for example. Most families make it easy to switch from one family fund to another (they want to keep you in the family even though your objectives may change), by letting you do it over the telephone or, in some cases, by waiving or reducing sales fees. You can get information about special privileges offered by families from prospectuses and accompanying literature.

The Funds

THE GROUPINGS OF FUNDS ON THE FOLLOWING PAGES WILL help you zero in on candidates for further investigation. In each category, the funds selected have excellent long-term records in their groups, although we are not recommending that you buy any of them on that basis. Use the phone numbers to order prospectuses and other literature and review them carefully before investing. (Money-market funds were discussed in Chapter 3.)

FUNDS FOR LONG-TERM INVESTORS

This is by far the biggest category of funds that invest in stocks and bonds. Some are more volatile than others, but all should be considered long-term investments that you anticipate holding for a minimum of three to five years. (For listings of funds, see the table on page 134.)

GROWTH FUNDS. These seek long-range capital gains by investing in large, established companies whose stock prices are expected to rise faster than inflation. Growth-stock funds are best suited for investors who want steady growth over the long term but have little need for income in the meantime. Funds in this group generally carry average risk, with volatility rankings around 4 or 5 on Micropal's 9-point scale (see the discussion on page 125). Following are some growth funds that have done well over the past five years. Some funds listed as no-load may charge a redemption fee.

GROWTH-AND-INCOME FUNDS. Like growth funds, these invest in common stocks of well-established companies. But growth-and-income funds also seek current dividend income. Risk ratings tend to be low to average for this group. The goal of these funds is to provide long-term growth without much fluctuation in share price, even in declining markets.

BALANCED FUNDS. These funds own both stocks and bonds, usually in a fixed proportion. The top performers in this category tend to own more stocks than bonds.

INDEX FUNDS. The idea behind index funds is simple enough: It's tough to beat the market consistently, so why try? These funds don't try. Instead, they buy stocks that form the market index they seek to track—the S&P 500, the S&P 100 and the Dow Jones industrials are most popular—and hang on. Theoretically, this approach should yield a return that matches the index. In practice, portfolio managers of index funds can't resist doing some buying and selling to try to beat the index they're tracking. All come very close to achieving their goals, making index funds a conservative way to hitch a ride on the market. Risk, because it matches the market exactly, is average with these funds.

FLEXIBLE PORTFOLIO FUNDS. Unlike funds that carefully limit the kinds of investments they make, flexible funds can swing back and forth—from all stocks to all bonds or all cash, or any mixture of investments—depending on where the funds' managers think is the best place to be at the time. Some of these funds are also known as asset allocation funds. We don't believe that any of them

Funds for Long-Term Investors

FUND	MINIMUM PURCHASE	FRONT-END LOAD	PHONE
Growth Funds			
Alleghany/Montag & Caldwell Growth	$ 2,500	none	800-992-8151
American Century Growth	2,500	none	800-345-2021
Fidelity Blue Chip Growth	2,500	none	800-544-8888
Gabelli Value	1,000	5.50%	800-422-3554
Janus	2,500	none	800-525-8983
Legg Mason Value P	1,000	none	800-822-5544
USAA Growth	3,000	none	800-531-8181
Growth-and-Income Funds			
American Investment Co. of America	$ 250	5.75%	800-421-4120
Babson Value	1,000	none	800-422-2766
Dodge & Cox Stock	2,500	none	800-621-3979
Fidelity	2,500	none	800-544-8888
Janus Growth and Income	2,500	none	800-525-8983
Strong Growth and Income	2,500	none	800-368-1030
Balanced Funds			
Fidelity Balanced	$ 2,500	none	800-544-8888
Flag Value Builder A	2,000	4.50%	800-767-3524
Oppenheimer Quest Balanced A	1,000	5.75%	800-525-7048
T. Rowe Price Equity Income	2,500	none	800-638-5660
USAA Income Stock	3,000	none	800-531-8181
Index Funds			
Fidelity Spartan Market Index	$10,000	none	800-544-6666
Schwab International Index Inv.	1,000	none	800-266-5623
T. Rowe Price Equity Index 500	2,500	none	800-225-5132
Vanguard Extended Market Index	3,000	none	800-635-1511
Vanguard 500 Index	3,000	none	800-635-1511
Global Equity Funds			
Janus Worldwide	$ 2,500	none	800-525-8983
Pilgrim America World Growth A	2,000	5.25%	800-331-1080
International Equity Funds			
TIAA-CREF International Equity	$ 250	none	800-223-1200
T. Rowe Price International	2,500	none	800-638-5660
Scudder International Stock	2,500	none	800-225-2470
Templeton World A (Franklin)	1,000	5.75%	800-237-0738
Warburg Pincus Int'l Equity Common	2,500	none	800-888-6878
Socially Conscious Funds			
Calvert Social Investment A	$ 1,000	4.75%	800-368-2748
Domini Social Equity	1,000	none	800-762-6814
Dreyfus Third Century	2,500	none	800-782-6620
Parnassus	2,000	3.50%	800-999-3505
Pax World	250	none	800-767-1729

have built a long-term record strong enough to merit mention here. Proceed with caution.

GLOBAL EQUITY FUNDS. Investments of these funds don't stop at the border. They invest around the world, and at any time may have a majority of their portfolios in foreign stocks. Global funds and the next category, international funds, can make or lose money two ways: on the prices of the stocks they buy, and on the movements of currency values compared with the U.S. dollar. Because so many of these funds are relatively new and their records short, volatility rankings often aren't reliable indicators of risk. International and global funds should be chosen with special care.

INTERNATIONAL EQUITY FUNDS. These are global funds that invest most or all of their assets in companies located outside the U.S.

SOCIALLY CONSCIOUS FUNDS. Environmental awareness infuses the portfolio choices of some of these funds. Others take care to avoid investing in weapons manufacturers, nuclear-energy producers, cigarette makers, and so on. Many also look for companies known for enlightened personnel and operating policies. As a group, these funds tend to deliver a return that is competitive with funds that have similar investment objectives but do not impose social or political screens on their portfolio choices.

FUNDS FOR INCOME-ORIENTED INVESTORS

Funds designed primarily to generate income hold mostly bonds and will fluctuate in price more because of interest-rate changes than as because of stock-market gyrations. The following categories are suitable for the bond portion of your portfolio allocation but shouldn't be viewed as opportunities for long-term growth. Volatility rankings tend to be on the low side.

HIGH-QUALITY CORPORATE BONDS. These stick mostly to the bonds of top-rated companies with the best prospects for paying interest and principal on time. The average maturities of their holdings will vary, although some funds specialize in short- or intermediate-term issues of two to seven years. A few concen-

Funds for Income-Oriented Investors

FUND	MINIMUM PURCHASE	FRONT-END LOAD	PHONE
High-Quality Corporate Bonds			
Calvert Income A	$ 2,000	3.75%	800-368-2748
Harbor Bond	2,000	none	800-422-1050
Loomis Sayles Bond	25,000	none	800-633-3330
Stagecoach Lifepath Opportunity A	1,000	4.50%	800-222-8222
SteinRoe Intermediate Bond	1,000	none	800-338-2550
Strong Corporate Bond	2,500	none	800-368-1030
Global Bond Funds			
Merrill Lynch Global Invest & Retire B	$ 1,000	none	800-637-3863
Oppenheimer Strategic Income A	1,000	4.75%	800-525-7048
T. Rowe Price Int'l. Bond	2,500	none	800-638-5660
Scudder International Bond	2,500	none	800-225-2470
Strong International Bond	1,000	none	800-368-1030
U.S. Government Bond Funds			
American Century Target Maturities	$ 2,500	none	800-345-2021
Dreyfus U.S. Treasury Long-Term	2,500	none	800-782-6620
Fidelity Spartan Gov't. Income	25,000	none	800-544-8888
PIMCO Long U.S. Gov't.	varies	none	800-426-0107
Prudential Gov't. Short Intermediate	1,000	none	800-225-1852
Ginnie Mae Funds			
Dreyfus GNMA	$ 2,500	none	800-782-6620
Franklin Custodian U.S. Gov't. A	1,000	4.25%	800-342-5236
Lexington GNMA Income	1,000	none	800-526-0057
Vanguard GNMA	3,000	none	800-635-1511
Municipal Bond Funds			
Dreyfus Basic Municipal bond	$10,000	none	800-373-9387
Kemper Municipal Bond A	1,000	4.50%	800-621-1048
Nuveen Insured Muni Bond A	3,000	4.20%	800-752-8700
Safeco Municipal Bond	1,000	none	800-624-5711
Smith Barney Managed Muni A	1,000	4.00%	800-327-6748
SteinRoe Managed Municipals	2,500	none	800-338-2550
Strong Muni Bond	2,500	none	800-368-1030
United Muni A (Waddell & Reed)	500	4.25%	816-366-5465
Vanguard Intermediate Term	3,000	none	800-635-1511

trate on zero-coupon bonds, signaled by the words "target maturities" in the name.

GLOBAL BOND FUNDS. These funds buy bonds issued by foreign companies as well as U.S.-headquartered firms. If the value of the currency of a country rises in relation to the dollar, funds owning bonds from that country benefit from the exchange rate, which can give their portfolios an added boost. If the dollar rises, however, the fund suffers. If you understand the dynamics of such currency movements, it is appropriate to use global funds for a portion of your portfolio. They should not serve as a substitute for U.S.-oriented bond funds but as a supplement to them.

U.S. GOVERNMENT BOND FUNDS. As the name implies, these funds invest in IOUs issued by the Treasury and backed by the full faith and credit of the federal government. They may also invest in debt issued by federal agencies such as those described in Chapter 5, which don't carry the full government backing but are considered just as safe.

GINNIE MAE FUNDS. Ginnie Mae funds get their name from the acronym used for the Government National Mortgage Association. The funds load up on Ginnie Mae pass-through certificates (see Chapter 9), although they also buy other kinds of mortgage-backed securities. Their yields tend to reflect current mortgage rates. It is important point to remember that mortgage funds will be more volatile than bond funds when long-term interest rates are falling because homeowners tend to refinance, thus taking their higher-rate mortgages out of the pool.

MUNICIPAL BOND FUNDS. These funds buy tax-free bonds that are issued by state and local governments and their agencies. Some specialize in single states, but most buy from a broad range of issues around the country. The following funds stick to high-quality bonds.

FUNDS FOR AGGRESSIVE INVESTORS

These funds swing for the fences, going for profits by investing in risky stocks or bonds that, in the opinion of the funds' man-

Funds for Aggressive Investors

FUND	MINIMUM PURCHASE	FRONT-END LOAD	PHONE
Aggressive-Growth Funds			
American Century Ultra	$ 2,500	none	800-345-2021
Fidelity Fifty	2,500	3.00%	800-544-8888
Janus Mercury	2,500	none	800-525-8983
Spectra	1,000	none	800-711-6141
High-Yield Bond Funds			
Eaton Vance Income of Boston	$ 1,000	4.75%	800-225-6265
Fidelity High Income	2,500	none	800-544-8888
Invesco High Yield	1,000	none	800-525-8085
T. Rowe Price High Yield	2,500	none	800-638-5660
Vanguard High Yield Corp.	3,000	none	800-635-1511

agers, have a chance to hit it big. This is a high-risk environment suitable for only a small portion of the portfolios of experienced, knowledgeable investors.

AGGRESSIVE-GROWTH FUNDS. These seek maximum capital gains and don't care about dividends. They look for companies or industries that are down-and-out or for fledglings with good prospects but no track records. Many use options, short sales and other specialized techniques in an effort to boost return. (For an explanation of these techniques, see the glossary.)

HIGH-YIELD BOND FUNDS. "High-yield," of course, is the salesperson's name for junk. These funds come in both the corporate and municipal varieties and invest in bonds rated BBB and lower by Standard & Poor's rating service, or Baa and lower by Moody's. The yields are several points higher than those available from investment-grade bond funds, with typical holdings yielding 9% to 10% or more. The risks of default are higher as well. A number of junk-bond funds started rethinking their position after the big shakeout of the late 1980s (see Chapter 5) and have moved at least part of their portfolios out of junk bonds and into higher-quality issues. Such a fund could be a prudent risk for a small slice of your portfolio.

SINGLE-INDUSTRY FUNDS

If you have a special interest in a market niche—gold, biotechnology or health care companies, for example—there's probably a fund that can accommodate you. If the overused word "hot" could properly be applied to any segment of the mutual fund business in the past decade, it would be the so-called sector funds, led by the Fidelity group, which sponsors dozens of them.

Rather than assembling a diversified portfolio spanning a number of different industries, sector funds concentrate on a single industry. Thus, their fortunes rise and fall with that industry's fortunes, and their volatility rankings tend to be above average. A list of successful sector funds over the past several years reads like a list of the country's big-growth businesses (see page 140).

How Much Are You Making?

B Y CONSULTING THE PERFORMANCE RANKINGS OF MUTUAL FUNDS that appear regularly in *Kiplinger's Personal Finance Magazine* and other publications, you can get a pretty good idea of how well your fund is doing relative to other funds. But that doesn't necessarily tell you how well you're doing.

The mutual fund listings in newspapers report the net asset value (NAV) of fund shares. NAV is a fund's total assets divided by the number of shares outstanding. Relying on changes in the NAV of your fund would probably understate your return because the NAV doesn't tell you whether the fund has paid any dividends or distributed any capital gains over the period being measured.

Fixing on yield will also mislead you. Yields express dividends or interest as a percentage of the offering price; they don't reflect how the shares themselves may have risen or fallen in value.

TOTAL RETURN IS THE BEST MEASURE

What really counts is your fund's total return—the total wealth generated by your initial investment over the time period you're invested in that fund. That includes share appreciation as well as dividends, interest, and capital-gains distributions from securities the fund sells at a profit. A capital-gains payment actually acts to reduce the NAV because the fund pays out money that used to count as part of the value of its portfolio.

Single-Industry Funds

FUND	MINIMUM PURCHASE	FRONT-END LOAD	PHONE
Fidelity Select funds			
Biotechnology	$ 2,500	3.00%	800-544-8888
Computers	2,500	3.00	800-544-8888
Electronics	2,500	3.00	800-544-8888
Health Care	2,500	3.00	800-544-8888
Telecommunications	2,500	3.00	800-544-8888
Internet Fund	1,000	none	800-386-3999
Invesco Strategic funds			
Health Sciences	1,000	none	800-525-8085
Worldwide Communications	1,000	none	800-525-8085
T. Rowe Price Science & Tech.	2,500	none	800-638-5660
Seligman Communication & Info A	2,500	4.75%	800-221-7844
Vanguard Specialized funds			
Energy	3,000	none	800-662-7447

Your personal rate of return over a given period will be influenced by whether—and when—you purchased or redeemed shares, whether you took your dividends and capital gains in cash or reinvested them, and whether you paid a sales load (see the discussion earlier in this chapter).

Your quarterly and annual reports from the fund will stress total return, and you can approximate it in the meantime by using information that's typically included on your account statement, plus what you can glean from the newspaper listings (see page 128).

WHAT DID YOU DO WITH THE MONEY?

Your return will vary according to what you do with income you get from the fund, as this example will show:

You buy the Can't Miss fund, a no-load, at its net asset value of $10 a share. Six months later Can't Miss is riding high at $15 a share, at which time the fund decides to sell some stock, take some gains, and distribute $5 a share to you and its other shareholders. This restores the NAV to $10 and gives you the choice of taking the $5 in cash or reinvesting it in the fund—a choice we'll return to in a minute.

Can't Miss stays on its streak. A year after you buy it, it sports an NAV of $20—a 100% increase if you don't count the capital-gains distribution. But you must count it, because you received it. That $5 plus the $10 increase in the price of a share means that the $10 you invested a year ago has actually grown to $25— a total return of 150%.

The way the fund itself would calculate its total return would be to assume that the $5 distribution was reinvested in Can't Miss shares. That happened when shares were selling for $10, giving you 1½ shares for every one you started with. Each share is worth $20 at the end of the year, making 1½ shares worth $30—a 200% return on your original $10 investment!

As you can see, total return encompasses the total wealth generated from your initial purchase, not just changes in the market price of your shares.

Closed-Ends: Funds That Sell at a Discount

A S YOU GET MORE FAMILIAR WITH WHAT MUTUAL FUNDS ARE and how they work, you might want to consider investing in closed-end funds, many of which offer the opportunity to buy their assets at a discount.

Like an open-end mutual fund, a closed-end takes money from many investors and turns it over to a professional manager. But the similarities end there. In an open-end fund, shares are continually issued as people invest new cash and continually redeemed as investors withdraw money. A closed-end fund raises initial capital by issuing a fixed number of shares and no more, a procedure similar to selling a new stock issue. After the initial offering, the shares trade either on one of the stock exchanges or over the counter. You buy and sell the shares through a broker and prices are listed in the papers every day along with individual stock issues, mostly on the New York Stock Exchange.

Traditional wisdom dictated that you never bought a closed-end fund at its initial public offering. That's the only time that many brokers would try to sell you one, and small wonder:

Index Funds

Q: *Should I be buying index funds? I understand that they are stock funds that strive to match the performance of the S&P stock index. That seems defeatist to me. Do they have any advantages?*

A: Index funds attempt to match the performance of a given index by buying all the stocks (or a representative sampling of them) in the given index. Pure index funds aren't actively managed and thus aren't dragged down by management fees, brokerage commissions and other expenses. Indexing soared in popularity among both institutions and individuals in the 1980s as people realized that relatively few portfolio managers were capable of consistently beating the Standard & Poor's 500-stock index. Another thing that attracted investors was that, for most of the 1980s and the '90s, the strength of the stock market was in S&P-type stocks, meaning big companies. That situation could change, of course.

Roughly 6% of your investment usually went straight to the brokerage. When shares started trading on the open market, they almost always fell to reflect the diversion of 6% of their assets.

With the investing public increasingly wise to that trick, the companies that sponsor closed-end funds have taken another tack. While they still pay brokerages hefty fees to market funds, they don't take that money out of the hides of those who buy shares at the initial public offering. Instead, they get the money back gradually from all shareholders by charging much higher expense ratios.

For example, Van Kampen Municipal Opportunity II charges investors expenses of 1.94% annually. Such a high-cost fund tends to trade at a wider discount than other funds. The only silver lining to the new pricing method: Buying funds at initial public offerings is no longer an absolute no-no, although new funds often slip to discounts anyway.

Supply and demand determine the price at which a closed-end fund trades after the initial offering is sold out, and that's where the discounts—and premiums—come from. Closed-end funds provide a nearly unique opportunity to specialize in various investment areas, say, biotechnology stocks, stocks of emerging markets and the foreign stocks of a single country or region, and those markets tend to be volatile. When interest is strong, investors may be willing to pay a premium price for the fund.

When interest is moderate, the shares tend to sell at a discount. Several influences affect prices:

INVESTORS' ATTITUDES TOWARD CERTAIN KINDS OF ASSETS. Discounts on many closed-end funds specializing in high-quality bonds can be expected to shrink as investors bid up the price in the face of falling interest rates, for instance.

THE WAY SOME FUNDS ARE STRUCTURED. A fund may trade at a wide discount because it holds large unrealized capital gains that, if distributed to investors, could result in substantial tax liabilities for them.

INVESTOR SPECULATION. In 1996 and 1997 Russia had one of the best-performing stock markets in the world. Had you bought $10,000 worth of Morgan Stanley Russia and New Europe in October 1996 at 20¼ per share, the value of your holdings would have risen to nearly $15,555 less than a year later, when shares were trading at 31½. Unfortunately, by the first half of 1998 Russia's stock market was among the worst, and by April 1999 shares of Morgan Stanley Russia and New Europe had dropped to 10⅝₆.

FINDING THE RIGHT FUND

You choose a closed-end fund much as you would a regular mutual fund—by matching your investment goals and tolerance for risk to a fund with a compatible profile and a good investment record.

Ask the funds in which you are interested to send recent shareholder reports and, if available, offering prospectuses. Then look up the ratio of expenses to assets. A ratio greater than 1.56%— the average for open-end stock funds—indicates that operating costs may drag down the fund's return over the long run.

Closed-end bond funds contain a trap you don't have to worry about with open-end funds: Nothing prevents a fund from dipping into capital to maintain its dividend level and investor interest, even when earnings aren't sufficient to cover the payouts. Eventually the dividend will probably be cut, just as it would by an individual company.

Closed-End Funds

FUND	TYPE	PHONE
Adams Express	growth and income	800-638-2479
General American Investors	growth	800-436-8401
John Hancock Income	income	800-843-0090
Nuveen Municipal Income Tax-Free	income	800-227-4648
Scudder New Asia	Asian stocks	800-349-4281
Tri-Continental	growth and income	800-221-2450

LOOK FOR THE DISCOUNTS. Swings in discounts and premiums to NAV are crucial for short-term traders, less so for long-term investors. Still, if you're looking at several funds, all other things being equal, avoid funds selling at a premium to NAV and buy the one with the largest discount to NAV. But compare a fund's discount only with the discounts of other funds that have similar objectives and characteristics. Just as important, compare a fund's present discount with its historical range, and look for slightly wider than average discounts.

KEEP TRACK OF CHANGES. Because the possibility of changes in a fund's discount or premium adds some volatility to its price, timing of the purchase is more important for a closed-end fund than for an open-end fund. Thus, if you go this route, be sure to stay informed. Publications that regularly provide information about closed-end funds include the following (often available in public libraries):

- *Closed-End Fund Country Fund Report* ($225 annually; 202-783-7051), a newsletter that examines and makes recommendations from among single-country and regional funds.
- *Closed-End Fund Digest* ($169 annually; 805-884-1150; www.investools.com), a newsletter that offers analysis and commentary, as well as model portfolios of closed-end funds.
- *Investor's Guide to Closed-End Funds* (monthly; $85 for a two-month trial, $475 per year, $920 for two years; 800-854-3863; www.Herzfeld.com), a monthly newsletter that covers 20 to 40 funds representing a variety of objectives.
- *Morningstar Principia for Closed-End Funds* ($95 for one issue, $295

a year for quarterly updates, $495 a year for monthly updates; 800-735-0700; www.morningstar.net), software (IBM only) follows most closed-end funds and allows you to search for funds meeting your criteria.

- **The Thomas J. Herzfeld Encyclopedia of Closed-End Funds** ($125 plus $10 shipping; 800-854-3863; www.Herzfeld.com), a book that provides an introduction to closed-end funds, as well as detailed information on more than 480 funds.

A SLATE OF FUNDS

In the box on page 144 you'll find some closed-end funds that have been around long enough to compile decent performance records over at least three years. They must be purchased through a broker.

Unit Trusts: Funds With No Managers

JUST AS CLOSED-END FUNDS CAN STEP UP THE ACTION FOR INVESTORS willing to pool their money with others, unit investment trusts, or UITs, can slow things down. Unit trusts are sold by brokerage houses, which assemble portfolios, usually of bonds or mortgage-backed securities, and sell off pieces (called units) to investors. Like a mutual fund, a unit trust offers a slice of a diversified portfolio. Unlike a fund, a UIT isn't managed. Once assembled, it is left alone to generate interest or dividends, which are distributed to investors according to how many units they hold. Eventually the bonds in the trust mature or are called, at which time the trust pays out investors' principal and dissolves.

Units usually sell for about $1,000. A typical equity UIT has a 2.75% front load. after that the initial load is 1.75% on a rollover or a switch to another trust. Brokers also sell them in wrap accounts that charge an annual fee. (See Chapter 16 for a discusison of wrap accounts.) UITs are a very popular way to buy municipal bonds, which commonly require a minimum investment of $5,000. Because the trusts hold on to their bonds instead of trading them, you can expect to get a fixed dollar return that won't change much until the portfolio begins to mature some years down the road.

As with mutual funds, there are important differences among

UITs vs. Mutual Funds

Q: *My broker has suggested removing money from a tax-free mutual fund and putting it in a tax-free unit investment trust. What do you think about this idea?*
A: One of the major problems with unit trusts is that there's no central data base that measures their comparative performance. But here are a few points to keep in mind and a few questions to ask your broker:

Why is he recommending a UIT rather than a mutual fund or (if you have enough money to make it worthwhile) direct ownership of a diversified package of municipal bonds issued by your state?

What are the maturities of the bonds in the UIT's portfolio? The longer the maturities, the more you expose yourself to inflation and interest-rate risk. If interest rates rise because inflation accelerates at some point in the future, your returns will be eroded by higher inflation, even though you won't lose any principal if you hold the trust to maturity. On the other hand, if inflation stays under control for the duration of the UIT, you've presumably locked in attractive yields for quite a while.

What kinds of bonds will the unit trust own? You want to own decent-quality bonds that can stand on their own merits without the help of insurance.

What is the front-end commission and what annual fees will you have to pay? How do those expenses compare with what you're paying in the fund?

unit trusts that you overlook at your peril. Unfortunately, you often can't get more than a few details in advance because brokerage firms try to sell out their UITs quickly; this practice has the effect of encouraging you to sign up before you receive a prospectus. The broker can tell you the anticipated yield of the units, the sales charge and the credit ratings of the bonds in the portfolio.

You need to know more. Ask about the call provisions of the bonds in the portfolio. There is a chance that issuers of bonds with approaching call dates will redeem the bonds early if interest rates decline, leaving you with a new investment decision to make in the face of declining rates. You should also ask about the earliest maturity dates in the portfolio and the lowest-rated bonds. A maturity date, a called bond or a default on the part of an issuer would each serve to reduce your return from the trust. Of the three, a default in the portfolio is clearly the worst that could happen.

Check those details yourself when you receive the prospectus. If the trust isn't what you expected, if the broker misinformed you or you misunderstood the description, most brokerage firms will agree to cancel your order, especially if you tell the broker in advance that you need to inspect the prospectus before you can be sure.

What if you want out before the trust matures? The larger brokerage firms usually stand ready to buy back units from their customers. When that isn't the case, you can sell them through your broker, who will look for a buyer in the secondary market, at no commission charge to you.

CHAPTER 7

Foreign Stocks & Bonds: Think Globally

OUR INVESTMENT PORTFOLIO SHOULD CONSIST mostly of stocks and bonds of U.S. companies. But you should devote a portion of it to foreign stocks and bonds. Chapter 1 laid out the reason why: the promise of a growing global economy. This chapter will show you how to take advantage of that growth by investing in the countries and companies that stand to benefit from it the most.

Diversification is one good reason to go global: Interest rates, inflation, unemployment and other economic forces in other countries move at different tempos different from those in the U.S. These differences can create investment market upswings in Britain, Japan, Germany and other countries at the very time that U.S. markets are on the downswing.

This point of view is contrary to the popular notion that the world's financial markets are now so closely linked that they march in lockstep toward a common fate. According to that school of thought, when the U.S. market goes up or down, the European markets will follow quickly, then the Japanese market and so on around the world in one continuous loop.

The facts, though, are quite different. Studies show that less than 10% of the movement of Japan's stock market in the 1980s could be linked to moves in the U.S. market, and only about a fourth of the change in the Morgan Stanley Europe, Australasia and Far East (EAFE) index, a widely accepted gauge of foreign share performance, correlated with the action in U.S. share prices. This isn't to say that no links exist, especially during financial disasters: Virtually all stock markets plunged during the crash of 1987, and extreme movements either way in one market can be expected to reverberate in other markets. There is no question that the world's financial markets are linked more closely than ever before on a day-to-day basis, but over the longer run, they tend to be influenced most heavily by events in their own countries.

Of course, the most compelling reason to invest beyond our borders is to make money. As with all investments, you make money abroad sometimes but not all the time. For the five-year period ending in mid 1995, the EAFE index generated a total return averaging 17.5%, versus 14.7% for the Standard & Poor's 500-stock index. As a result, the list of top-ranked stock mutual funds over that time span was dominated by global and international funds. Foreign bond funds also performed well.

The situation in the second half of the '90s was reversed. The performance of the U.S. stock market blew away most of the rest of the world's. During the "Asian contagion" of 1997-98, the economic problems of Thailand, South Korea, Indonesia and other Pacific Rim nations brought their stock markets crashing down while U.S. stocks continued to reach record highs. By mid 1999, though, the Asian markets had come roaring back, restoring much of the value lost during the crisis and richly rewarding investors who had had the nerve to buy after these markets had crashed. The lesson in all this: To protect yourself from sudden collapses in any single country's market, for the bulk of your overseas investing, stick with international and global funds diversified across several countries. If you must buy a single country's stocks, try to do it after a major market decline and be prepared to hang on for a few years.

Sometimes the success of foreign investments is due in part to a decline in the value of the dollar against the world's other major currencies. A decline in the dollar boosts the U.S. value of shares denominated in foreign currencies because those currencies buy more dollars. We doubt thatß you can count on much in the way of a similar boost in the years ahead. Besides, outguessing the currency markets isn't something amateurs can do with much success. In fact, it's not something the pros have managed to do with much success, either.

Can foreign investments continue to pay off without the support of a declining dollar? Probably. The economies of many nations, particularly smaller ones, can reasonably be expected to grow at a much faster rate than the economy of a giant like the U.S., where billions of dollars in economic expansion add only a fraction of a percentage point to our multitrillion-dollar economy. Thriving economies in smaller countries can translate into faster-rising share prices.

If you wanted to diversify your portfolio in proportion to stock values around the world, you'd put 60% or more of your stock holdings overseas. We recommend a more modest level: about 10% to 15% of your stock holdings in foreign shares.

Three Ways to Go Global

INFORMATION ON FOREIGN STOCKS IS HARDER TO GET AND HARDER to evaluate than information on U.S. stocks. What's more, disclosure rules and accounting standards vary from country to country. Because you have limited time to spend investigating the unfamiliar, a good way to invest in foreign markets is to pick a pro to do the digging for you.

MUTUAL FUNDS

Funds constitute the simplest approach to global diversification and therefore perhaps the best. As explained in Chapter 6, they give you a slice of a professionally managed diversified portfolio. They are easy to buy, easy to keep tabs on and easy to sell. Several U.S.-based mutual funds have done an impressive job of picking foreign stocks and bonds.

Keep in mind the useful distinction between global funds, which invest in U.S. as well as foreign issues, and international funds, which put most or all of their assets in foreign stocks and bonds. You can often tell from the name of the fund which road it takes: Kemper Global Discovery and Scudder International, for instance. Sometimes, though, the emphasis isn't obvious from the name: Templeton Foreign is an international fund, for instance, and USAA World Growth is a global fund.

These distinctions are important, but they are not critical. What really counts is the fund's record compared with the records for similar funds, which you can find by consulting the references listed on page 130. Find out about the fund's future direction by studying its prospectus. A number of international and global funds with excellent records are listed in Chapter 6.

Because the net asset values of global and international stock funds are affected by fluctuations in the value of the dollar as well as fluctuations in foreign stock prices, those funds can be quite volatile in the short run. Thus, you should count on holding them for at least three to five years.

CLOSED-END FUNDS

These funds, which are described in detail in Chapter 6, sell a certain number of shares when they start and then generally no more. After the initial offering, the shares trade on one of the exchanges or in the over-the-counter market (see Chapter 4) and are bought and sold through brokers like any other stock.

Because share prices of closed-ends are determined by demand for the shares and not by the value of the stocks in the fund's portfolio, the price that investors pay is either higher (a *premium*) or lower (a *discount*) than the share's underlying net asset value. Money is gained or lost on changes in these discounts and premiums. The changes can be breathtaking, resulting in astonishing volatility for funds as they pass into and out of favor with investors.

So-called single-country funds, which concentrate exclusively on stocks of companies based in one country, are especially vulnerable to this volatility; even regional funds aren't immune under the right circumstances. When the so-called Asian flu began to spread through the Pacific Rim nations in the fall of 1997, the closed-end Korea Fund lost more than two-thirds of its market value in less than a year, taking until mid 1999 to achieve a shaky recovery. A similar fate struck the Asia Pacific Fund. Despite its broader base, it couldn't withstand the bad news indefinitely, losing more than half its value in 1998 before struggling back the following year. When the crisis eventually threatened currency values in Brazil in the summer of 1998, the Brazil Fund plunged more than 50% in the course of a couple of months.

Breathtaking dives like that seem astonishing to U.S.

investors, accustomed as we are to somewhat more sedate price movements. This situation underscores the fact that the action in single-country funds is often created by short-term traders and speculators rather than long-term investors. Thus, the cardinal rule for investing in single-country funds: Never buy a single-country fund at a premium price; buy only when the fund is selling at a discount from net asset value. The funds that are selling at a premium—especially a substantial premium—should be left to the traders and speculators.

Be sure to apply that rule when investigating the closed-end funds listed in Chapter 6 and other closed-ends that may be suggested by your broker. You can follow the prices of these funds in the daily stock listings. You can track premiums and discounts of closed-end funds weekly in *Barron's* and every Monday in the *Wall Street Journal*. *The Value Line Investment Survey* tracks 15 single-country closed ends, and Morningstar sells a service that follows hundreds of them.

AMERICAN DEPOSITARY RECEIPTS

Usually called ADRs, these are negotiable receipts, priced in dollars, for shares of a foreign stock being held in a U.S. bank. Owning one entitles you to everything a shareholder gets, including dividends. An ADR trades like a stock, and its price reflects both changes in the value of the underlying stock and shifts in the value of the company's home currency against the dollar. An ADR may represent one foreign share or multiple shares.

Hundreds of ADRs trade in the U.S., many on the exchanges or over the counter via Nasdaq (see Chapter 4). But prices for most of them can be obtained only from brokers who have access to the "pink sheets." These are literally pink sheets of paper, distributed daily, with listings of thousands of non-Nasdaq, over-the-counter stocks. Many companies' ADRs are listed only on the pink sheets because the companies are unwilling to meet the disclosure requirements of the U.S. stock markets, which are often considerably tougher than those of their own countries. Some brokerage firms follow the larger companies' ADRs, and the *Value Line Investment Survey* tracks about 50 of them. You may check numerous ADRs at J.P. Morgan's ADR site (www.adr.com) and the Bank of New York ADR site (www.bankofny.com/adr).

ADRs can give you access to shares in foreign companies that are household names in America—Honda, Toyota, Volvo, Sony, Hitachi, Pioneer, Canon, Fuji, Nestlé and others. ADRs can also be the route to companies you may not be familiar with but whose businesses you understand—telephone companies in Spain or Mexico, for example. But the difficulty of obtaining and interpreting financial information on such companies suggests that you're better off letting the pros do the work. If investing in American depositary receipts means acting with less information than you can get on American-based or exchange-listed stocks, don't do it. Instead, invest through mutual funds and closed-end funds, which are better equipped to obtain and interpret the financial information you need.

So, in sizing up ADRs, you should apply the same standards you'd use to gauge a U.S. company, as described in Chapter 4. If you can't get that information, don't make the investment.

Special Opportunities in European Stocks

IN 1992, LONG-ESTABLISHED TRADE BARRIERS HINDERING CROSS-border commerce among 12 European countries were essentially abolished. Belgium, Denmark, France, Germany, Britain, Greece, Ireland, Italy, Luxembourg, the Netherlands, Portugal and Spain became one big economic market. To put it in American terms, selling French dinnerware in Greece and vice versa was supposed to entail no more cross-border red tape than selling aspirin made in Indiana to a drugstore chain in California. In 1999, most of these countries agreed to benchmark their currencies to the euro, a bold step toward a common European currency that would make commerce across the Continent even simpler. By one estimate, the euro will eliminate $65 billion a year in currency exchange costs—a welcome injection of efficiency for all sorts of European trade.

All this may or may not succeed in spurring the growth of the sometimes-sleepy economies of Europe, but the cooperation demonstrated so far has planted a seed of hope for more jobs, lower consumer prices, and savings in business costs thanks to greater efficiencies, equitable taxation, new competition for government contracts and less regulatory confusion.

The European euphoria that followed the start of this process in 1992 has proved to be terribly premature. Still, a more-unified Europe should create remarkable new opportunities as the years go by. And further down the road, the opening up of the vast consumer markets of Russia and other countries of the former Soviet Union could be the most exciting economic development of the 21st century. Upper-tier companies equipped and prepared to compete should emerge with bigger world-market shares and brighter long-term prospects. Investors in those companies should prosper, too.

How can U.S. investors join in the party? By focusing on strong American and European companies in industries that figure to benefit most from the new opportunities. This could include airlines, ad agencies, makers of over-the-counter drugs, food and beverage companies, hotels and tourist industries, and trucking lines.

Many of the most promising European companies are available as ADRs, or their shares have found their way into U.S.-based mutual funds. It's not hard to spot the Europe funds because they tend to use the word in their names:

- **Fidelity Europe** (800-544-8888; www.fidelity.com)
- **Invesco European** (800-525-8085; www.invesco.com)
- **Merrill Lynch Eurofund** (800-637-3863; www.ml.com)
- **T. Rowe Price European Stock**
  (800-638-5660; www.troweprice.com)
- **Vanguard European Stock Index Fund**
  (800-662-7447; www.vanguard.com)

These funds delivered excellent returns for much of the latter half of the 1990s. Examine them just as you would any fund, using the criteria described in Chapter 6.

American Stocks with Global Connections

ACTUALLY, IT'S NOT ALWAYS NECESSARY TO INVEST IN FOREIGN companies to earn profits in foreign lands. In fact, if you restrict your quest for globalization to foreign-based companies, you'll miss a lot of good companies based right here at home. Plenty of U.S. brands and trademarks command large, profitable and growing niches in Europe and Asia. U.S.-based companies make parts and components for almost every car built in the world, even premium-priced European and Japanese imports. U.S. firms dominate the market for indispensable tools of the information age: entertainment and TV programming, cellular phone equipment, fiber optics, computers and software.

A lot of the names are household words all over the world: Cisco Systems, Coca-Cola, Walt Disney, Ford, General Electric, IBM, Intel, McDonald's and Microsoft. Here are a few more, with reasons to consider adding them to your global portfolio, provided they pass muster when you check them out. They aren't necessarily timely buys right now, and all should be considered long-term investments.

Bausch & Lomb. Sells contact lenses in dozens of countries; about a third of its revenues come from foreign sales.

Corning. Not just a glass company anymore, Corning may be America's joint-venture king. It is involved around the world in ventures with Samsung, Mitsubishi and more than a dozen smaller firms. It also builds and operates modern factories in eastern Europe.

H. J. Heinz Co. A high-profit, low-cost food producer, its name is found on labels in nearly 200 countries.

Hewlett-Packard. A computer hardware company that has more than half of its sales coming from 100 different markets outside the U.S.

Illinois Tool Works. Its plants in more than 30 countries make switches, fasteners, seat assemblies and other essentials for automobiles, airplanes and computers.

Medtronic. This Minneapolis-based manufacturer of medical instruments is best known for its heart pacemaker. It sells in more than 120 countries, generating 40% of sales and nearly 30% of profits outside the U.S.

Merck & Co. The bluest of blue chips, Merck, a pharmaceutical company, makes nearly half its sales in foreign countries, with 20% in Europe.

CHAPTER 8

Real Estate: How to Tell If It's for You

THE FIRST PIECE OF REAL ESTATE YOU BUY SHOULD BE the roof over your head. Although home prices in the 1990s haven't outrun inflation so dramatically as they did in the 1970s and 1980s, they have stayed a step or two ahead in most areas. Besides, homeownership provides much more than just a place to live. Because the down payment you make is only a fraction of the home's value, you get a degree of financial leverage hard to find elsewhere. Your mortgage payments buy a little more equity each month, giving you a forced savings plan that can grow to substantial proportions as the years go by. On top of that, a home remains one of the few tax shelters still available to people of ordinary means: The mortgage interest is tax-deductible, and up to $250,000 on the sale of a home is tax-free if you file an individual return ($500,000 if you file a joint return). The box on page 160 sums up the financial advantages of homeownership.

It seems clear that real estate in the foreseeable future won't be the path to riches that it once was. Commercial real estate—offices, stores, shopping centers—is especially risky for amateur investors. It took most of the '90s to work down the glut of commercial properties on the market. While excess office space is gone in most cities, it lingers in a few. In the 21st century, it seems safe to assume that there will be less demand for office space as companies downsize and more employees telecommute. Need for retail space is also expected to be low in the next few years. There will still be a need for industrial space, but many companies will move away from the cities and into suburbs and rural areas. In the meantime, taking advantage of opportunities in commercial real estate requires deep pockets and a specialized knowledge of local business prospects that few amateurs possess.

This chapter will describe investment techniques best suited to residential real estate: single- and multifamily houses, and condominium apartments. Several forms of indirect ownership of commercial real estate also are considered.

In light of the occasional distress in many residential markets, it may seem a little odd to suggest that real estate is a reasonable way to diversify the risks in a portfolio that consists mostly of stocks and bonds. In fact, many people probably shouldn't invest in real estate. Done wrong, it can be a pain in the neck with precious little reward to show for your trouble. But if you're patient and willing to work hard, the payoff from direct ownership of investment real estate can be substantial even in a period of sedate price appreciation, provided the property meets the following criteria:

THE PROPERTY PRODUCES A POSITIVE CASH FLOW. That is, you can charge enough rent to more than cover what you pay out each month in principal and interest on the mortgage, operating expenses and so forth.

YOU ACTIVELY MANAGE THE PROPERTY. This is a critical requirement that permits you to deduct the depreciation allowance (discussed later) from your other income, thus reducing your tax burden at the same time the value of your investment is growing.

RENTALS ARE IN DEMAND IN YOUR AREA. You have to pay the mortgage and maintenance costs even if you're not collecting any rent. Trouble finding tenants can be a disaster for the bottom line of your rental real estate investment.

PROSPECTS ARE GOOD FOR PRICE APPRECIATION. A couple of positive signs: The property is in a good neighborhood or in one that's on the way up, and the population of the area is growing.

YOU INVEST FOR THE LONG HAUL. That means you must be prepared to hold the property for several years. In some areas, it is still possible to buy a run-down property, fix it up and sell it within a few months for a profit. But those opportunities, often overrated in the best of times, are always hard to find. Real estate prices are cyclical, and you should be prepared to ride out the bad times so that you can sell in the good times.

Why Real Estate Is Unique

I F IT MEETS THE FOREGOING CONDITIONS, RESIDENTIAL REAL estate can be a good addition to a diversified portfolio. Besides generating income month after month and profit potential in the long run, well-selected real estate has some unique characteristics to recommend it. It is an ideal inflation hedge, for one thing. If unforeseen events lead to a spell of high inflation such as we experienced twice in the 1970s, owners of real estate can expect to prosper. Real estate also offers leverage, valuable tax benefits, and the chance to profit from local pockets of prosperity even if the national economy is struggling.

THE BENEFITS OF LEVERAGE

Leverage comes from using borrowed money to buy the property. The smaller your down payment, the more leverage you've got working for you. Without leverage, real estate investing wouldn't be worth the trouble. With it, the profits can sometimes be spectacular.

Consider Fred and Ed, two investors who buy identical three-bedroom condominium apartments in the same building on the same day. Each pays $100,000. Fred, feeling flush from a recent inheritance, pays cash. Ed puts $20,000 down and borrows the rest. Five years later, each investor sells his apartment for $125,000. For Fred, that's a 25% return on his $100,000 in five years; he could have done as well or better in a money-market mutual fund. But Ed, who had only $20,000 invested in the property, gets a return of 125%! (In reality the return would be a little bit less because the example doesn't take into account principal and interest payments Ed would have to make along the way. But Ed's investment would still far outperform Fred's.) That's how leverage works.

Of course, leverage can work against you, too. If the price of the condo had dropped $5,000 after five years, Fred's loss would

Why a Home Is Still a Good Investment

YOUR HOME IS one of the best investments you can make. Here's why:

IT FORCES YOU TO SAVE. When you pay the mortgage each month you pay both interest and principal. The principal repayments, plus any increase in home value, gradually build up your equity in the property—that's the difference between what you owe and what the home would sell for, and it's a valuable asset as years go by.

YOU GET ACCESS TO LEVERAGE. The long-term mortgage you use to finance your home lets you tap into a great wealth builder. You increase the earning power of your money when you borrow large sums using your home as collateral for the loan, as illustrated in this chapter.

TAX LAW SUBSIDIZES HOMEOWNERSHIP. You can deduct all the interest on up to $1 million you borrow to buy or build a home, plus the interest on up to $100,000 in home-equity loans. If you're in the 28% tax bracket, for every $1,000 of interest you pay on your principal residence, you get a $280 tax subsidy for homeownership. Local property taxes are also deductible in the year you pay them.

YOU GET ACCESS TO TAX-DEDUCTIBLE INTEREST. Home-equity loans are among the last remaining sources of credit with tax-deductible interest.

YOU CAN CLAIM MOST HOME-SALE PROFITS TAX-FREE. If you're single, the first $250,000 of profit on the sale of your principal residence will be excluded from taxable income. The exclusion rises to $500,000 if you're married and file a joint return. To qualify, you must have owned and lived in the house for two of the five years leading up to the sale. There's no age requirement for this break; you can use it as often as once every two years. However, if you sell your home for a good reason less than two years after you moved into it—"a good reason" defined by Congress as a move to a new job or for health reasons—you qualify for a partial exclusion. And even though this tax break is designed only for your principal residence, there's a way to legally squeeze tax-free profit out of a vacation home. After you sell your main home and cash in on the $250,000 (or $500,000), move into your vacation place and make it your home for at least two years. As soon as you meet the two-years-out-of-five requirement, the profit—including appreciation while it was your vacation home—qualifies for tax-free treatment.

have been 5% of his investment, but Ed's loss would have been a much more painful 25% of his original $20,000 investment. That's why having the ability to wait out bad markets is a key to making money in real estate. If you are forced to sell when the market is down, leverage can greatly magnify your losses.

TAX BENEFITS

The costs of owning investment real estate—interest on the mortgage, operating and maintenance costs, mileage you drive to inspect the property and so forth—are deductible in the year you pay them. And real estate offers a deduction for an expense you don't pay—depreciation. If your income is within certain limits and you meet other tests described later (see "A Rule That Limits Real Estate's Allure," page 166), depreciation can generate deductions that can be used to shelter up to $25,000 a year of income from other sources, even your salary. You'll have to pay back at least some of the depreciation deductions when you sell the property, but it can be a valuable tax break until then.

NATIONAL TRENDS VS. LOCAL MARKETS

The local nature of real estate markets offers another opportunity for profiting from well-selected properties. Stocks and bonds are bought and sold in a national marketplace, but real estate is strictly a local affair. Whatever the national trends, if you buy good properties in good locations, don't pay too much, and structure the deal so that rental income covers your out of pocket expenses, you can make nice profits in real estate over the long haul. But it will take a lot of work—much more work, in fact, than monitoring a portfolio of stocks and bonds. This chapter will describe that work in some detail. If it sounds like more than you're willing to undertake, then forget about owning investment real estate directly because you'll almost surely lose money doing it. Indirect ownership, described later in the chapter, would be a better idea.

Are You Cut Out to Be a Landlord?

IF YOU THINK YOU CAN MAKE MONEY AS A LANDLORD, YOU should be able to answer yes to every one of the questions that follow:

Do you have the analytical skills and patience needed to find and buy good investment properties? As a home buyer, you may be willing to pay a premium for an unusual house in a desirable neighborhood. But paying a premium price can be deadly for an investor. You'll need to spend time searching for properties and analyzing their income and appreciation potential.

Can you afford to tie up thousands of dollars for three to ten years?
Lenders typically require a 20% to 30% down payment from
investors buying a detached house, condo apartment, duplex or
small multifamily building. And your investment will be difficult
to sell on short notice.

Do you have the time and ability to manage the property? Somebody has
to find tenants, collect the rent, oversee the property, keep the
books, and perform necessary repairs and maintenance. You
could hire a management company to do the work, but you'd
still have to monitor the property manager, and you'd pay 5%
to 10% of your rental income for the service for a yearly rental
and 15% to 25% for management of week-to-week rentals in
resort locations.

Undeterred? Then, let's go shopping. As a potential landlord,
you're looking for three things: the right location, the right
building and the right price:

THE RIGHT LOCATION. Location is synonymous with success in real
estate. The property should be near public transportation, so
that renting is not dependent on owning a car. Depending on
whom you wish to rent to, good neighborhood schools, nearby
stores, parks and recreational facilities may be important. The
street shouldn't be too steep and the house shouldn't have too
many stairs because either condition could cause many renters to
look elsewhere.

THE RIGHT BUILDING. You want a place that's typical, not unique.
Remember, you're not going to live there; you want to rent it out.
Your chances of finding a tenant are best if the place appeals to
most people looking for something in that price range. The
structure should be in good condition and you should have
access to records that will permit you to make accurate estimates
of maintenance and repair costs.

THE RIGHT PRICE. Single-family detached homes and condominium apartments are often overpriced relative to the rent they can
command. That's because their prices are influenced by the
value buyers place on them as homes, which includes the

prospects for future price appreciation. But tenants are willing to pay only for current shelter value, which depends on such things as square footage, the number of bedrooms and distance to their workplace. If you keep in mind the features that make a place good to rent, as opposed to being a good place to own, you are more likely to pay the right price.

The Numbers You Need

WHETHER YOU WILL PROFIT FROM A REAL ESTATE DEAL depends on two things: cash and time. Your goal should be to part with as little cash as possible as slowly as possible, and to recoup your investment as quickly as possible. In that direction lies your profit.

You can't rely on appreciation alone to make your investment profitable. You should also evaluate a property on its ability to produce current income and on its potential to generate higher and higher rents as time goes by. For example, you may be able to charge more for a house in a sought-after neighborhood if there are few other rental homes nearby.

How much rent can you charge? You'll need to check what comparable properties in the area are going for, of course. A rule of thumb says that the annual rent should be at least 9% of the market value of the property. On a $100,000 home, that means $9,000 a year, or $750 a month. Another common gauge is something called the gross rent multiplier, or GRM, which approaches the question from the other side of the equation. Real estate experts recommend paying no more for a property than 90 to 110 times its gross monthly rent. By that measure, a house that rents for $750 a month and sells for $100,000 has a GRM of 123, and seems priced too high for the rent it can get.

As you can see, the rule-of-thumb approach has its limitations. What you really need is a property that, when rented, will produce a positive annual cash flow, however slight. Assuming continuous occupancy, rental income should cover mortgage payments, maintenance, taxes and insurance. If rents don't cover those costs, you'll experience negative cash flow—an operating loss. Not only must you dig into your pocket every month, but you'll also be forced to rely on future appreciation to offset the loss and provide a good return on your investment. You will have to hope for a pool of prospective buyers ready to purchase your property when you are ready to sell it (and willing to pay a price higher than would be justified by rents alone), as well as readily available and reasonably priced mortgages. The best way to avoid putting yourself at the mercy of the market forces is to buy properties only if they produce a positive cash flow right from the start.

The Tax Angles of Real Estate

R UNNING A REAL ESTATE INVESTMENT IS PARTLY COMMON sense, partly a matter of knowing some special tax rules. You've got two potential kinds of current and future income: rent and price appreciation. And you've got several kinds of tax-deductible expenses, led by interest on the mortgage and depreciation. The income sources are largely self-explanatory (later on, we'll show how to include them in a calculation of your return). The expense items require a little explanation.

MORTGAGE PAYMENTS

Only the interest is tax-deductible. If you hold the property for so many years that the interest portion of your mortgage payments shrinks into insignificance, it makes sense to seriously consider refinancing.

RENTAL EXPENSES

You can deduct the out-of-pocket costs of producing rental income. In addition to mortgage interest, the main out-of-pocket costs are as follows:

- **Property taxes;**
- **Insurance premiums** (including mortgage insurance);
- **Management-company fees;**
- **The cost of advertising** to attract tenants;
- **Legal and accounting costs** connected with drafting a lease or evicting a tenant;
- **Repair** and maintenance expenses;
- **Utilities,** if you pay them;

- **Money you pay others to care for the property**—for cleaning or gardening, for example, and
- **The cost of travel necessary to care for your property.** Typically this means a flat mileage deduction for driving, say, eight miles from your home to your rental apartment to unplug a drain. The considerable expense of visiting a distant rental property, including the cost of food and a hotel room, is also deductible, provided that the principal purpose of the trip is to inspect work on your property.

DEPRECIATION

This is the real estate investor's good-luck charm, the deduction that can turn a losing property into a winning one. Each year you get to write off a portion of the price you paid for the property (minus the value of the land, which you can't depreciate). The current annual depreciation allowance for residential rental property is 3.64% after the first year, a rate that reduces its cost "basis" to zero in exactly 27.5 years. (Commercial properties placed in service after May 12, 1993, such as stores and office buildings, get an annual allowance of 2.56% because they must be depreciated over a period of 39 years, and thus decline in value a little less each year. Older commercial properties get a 31.5-year schedule.) If you bought property and started renting it out when the depreciation schedule was more generous, you get to keep using that schedule.

The allowance has nothing to do with whether the property is actually depreciating in value. Even if its value is growing by leaps and bounds, you still get to claim depreciation. It is a crucial element in any real estate investment, especially if rental income doesn't cover expenses. The tax savings from depreciation could more than make up the difference.

For instance, say you're collecting $700 a month in rent on a condo but the mortgage payment, condo fees and other expenses amount to $800. At the end of the year you're $1,200 in the hole. That's tax-deductible, so in the 28% bracket you're actually $864 in the red—before depreciation. Say the apartment (not counting the land, which you can't depreciate) is worth $85,000. Applying the 3.64% depreciation allowance yields a tax deduction of $3,094 for the year. In the 28% tax bracket, that saves you $866. Thus, depreciation has turned your loss into a slight gain.

As alluring as that sounds, relying on depreciation to carry you while you hope for the value of the property to go up can be a shortsighted investment strategy. Uncle Sam's apparent generosity is really more like a loan than a gift: Every dollar of depreciation you claim (and you must claim it) serves to reduce the cost basis of your property. (The cost basis is just what it sounds like: the amount of your investment.) The effect is to increase the taxable profit when you sell, because that profit is the difference between the price you get and your cost basis. It's even conceivable that you could sell for less than you paid for the property and still owe taxes on a gain because the depreciation allowances have reduced the basis to below the selling price.

Here's an example of how depreciation can backfire on you if the value of your property fails to appreciate. Say you buy a rental house for $105,000 and hold it for five years. The building itself is worth $85,000 and you claim your depreciation allowance at the rate of $3,094 ($85,000 x 3.64%) per year for five years, a total of $15,470. That reduces your cost basis for the building to $69,530. Add in the value of the land and your total basis is $89,530. You sell the house and land for $95,000. Now, that's a loss of $10,000, since you paid $105,000 for the place. But for tax purposes, because you depreciated the basis of the property to $89,530, you'll owe taxes on a $5,470 ($95,000 – $89,530) capital gain. You can see that the depreciation allowance cuts both ways. The IRS giveth and the IRS taketh back.

Note: When Congress cut the top capital gains rate to 20% in 1997, it did not apply that rate to profit attributable to depreciation. Instead, it set a flat 25% rate for gain attributable to depreciation for periods after May 6, 1997.

You can increase the cost basis of your property by making improvements that add to its value. Installing thermal-pane windows, central air conditioning, a Jacuzzi in the bathroom and landscaping are enhancements that can be considered permanent improvements that raise the property's market value.

A Rule That Limits Real Estate's Allure

SO FAR, THE DISCUSSION OF DEPRECIATION HAS ASSUMED THAT you qualify to use the allowance to offset income from other sources. Most people do qualify, but if you don't, you should think long and hard before ever becoming a landlord.

Beginning in 1987, the tax laws divided income and losses into "active" and "passive" categories. (There's a third category, portfolio income, which crosses the lines. See Chapter 12.) Salaries are considered active income. Income and losses from real estate are considered passive. Your ability to mix active gains or losses with passive gains or losses is restricted to some degree, and for some investors it's seriously restricted.

Normally, unless you make your living from real estate, you simply are not permitted to use passive losses to offset active income on your tax return, a rule that would kill a major attraction of rental real estate if it weren't for a notable exception the law provides.

To qualify for the exception, you must "actively participate" in managing the property. If you do, and your adjusted gross income is under $100,000, you can deduct as much as $25,000 of rental losses against other income, including salary. The loss allowance is phased out at the rate of 50 cents for every dollar of adjusted gross income (which is your income before subtracting itemized deductions, exemptions and rental losses) above $100,000. Thus, it's gone at $150,000.

Passive losses you can't deduct in the year incurred aren't lost completely because you can use them to offset passive income you might generate in future years. Even if you have no passive income, you can use the excess to offset any kind of income in the year you sell the property.

What does it take to actively participate in the management of your property? You'll probably qualify as long as you're involved in approving tenants, setting rents, and approving repairs and capital improvements, even if you pay a management firm to handle the routine matters.

Figuring Your Gain—or Loss

THERE ARE SEVERAL COMMON METHODS OF CALCULATING YOUR return from a rental property. Let's examine a $120,000 house as an example. You put down 25% ($30,000) and finance the rest with a 30-year, 8%, fixed-rate mortgage. The lender requires you to pay three points (3% of the loan amount) to get the mortgage and another 1% for settlement expenses

Before-Tax Cash Flow

Purchase price	$120,000
Settlement costs (4% x $90,000)	+ 3,600
Total cost	**123,600**
Mortgage balance	– 90,000
Total cash invested	**$ 33,600**
Gross income	
Rent ($1,000 x 12 months)	$ 12,000
Expenses	
Mortgage payments ($660 x 12)	$ 7,920
Real estate taxes	1,500
Insurance	700
Maintenance	+ 900
Total Expenses	**$ 11,020**
Cash Flow Before Tax	$ 980
(Gross income minus expenses)	

such as loan appraisal, credit report, title insurance and attorney's fees.

Let's assume you sell the house after five years, and that the property appreciates 5% a year. For purposes of the illustration, we'll keep rents, property taxes and maintenance costs level for those five years. For simplicity's sake we'll also assume that the house stays rented the whole time, with no rent lost between tenants, that you actively manage the property yourself and that you are in the 28% tax bracket.

Before-tax cash flow is the simplest concept because before-tax cash flow is the cash left at the end of the year, after you have paid the mortgage, maintenance and other bills and collected all rents. Because this example covers the first year of ownership, the calculations include settlement costs.

Hmm—$980 profit. Not a lot, but a profit nevertheless. But let's see what happens when you take income taxes and depreciation into account—especially depreciation. First, you have to add something back in: The principal payment on the mortgage belonged in the previous calculation because it is a legitimate expense; you've got to pay it each month. But when figuring out your taxes, principal payment works the same as it does for your mortgage: It isn't deductible. So you have to add principal payments back in as an item of income.

There's a little twist to the depreciation allowance, too. In the first and last years of ownership, you don't get the full year's worth. Regardless of the day of the month you buy or sell the place, the IRS declares it to have been "placed in service" at the middle of the month of purchase. That complicates things a bit, but for the sake of simplicity let's say you bought the place on January 1, meaning you get 11.5 months of depreciation the first year. Even better! Depreciation has increased the gain to $1,329—still not great but definitely on the plus side. Now let's

Cash Flow After Tax

Cash flow before tax	$ 980	
plus principal payments	+ 682	
Operating income		$ 1,662
Deductible expenses		
points amortized over 30 years:		
2,700 ÷ 30 (3% of $90,000)		($90)
Depreciable portion of property		
Price paid		
(includes other closing costs;		
1% of $90,000)	$ 120,900	
minus value of land	− 40,000	
Depreciable portion	$ 80,900	
Depreciation allowance		
$80,900 ÷ 27.5	$ 2,942	
$2,942 ÷ 12	$ 245/mo.	
$245 x 11.5 months		($2,818)
Taxable income (or loss)		($1,246)
Tax savings in 28% bracket		
Tax loss x tax rate		
$1,246 x 28%	$ 349	
Cash flow before tax		$ 980
plus tax saving		+ 349
Cash Flow After Tax		$ 1,329

Net Sales Proceeds

Selling price of property		**$ 153,154**
minus sales expenses:		
6% commission	$9,189	
1% other sales expenses	$1,532	– 10,721
Gross sales proceeds		142,433
minus mortgage balance		– 85,652
NET SALES PROCEEDS		$ 56,781

see what happens after five years of rent collection and 5% price appreciation per year, after which you sell the place and count up your profits.

First, you've got to calculate what you net out of the sale (see table above). Assuming you're working with a broker, you'll need to subtract commissions and other sales-related costs and the balance of your mortgage.

Of course, net sales proceeds aren't the same as your profit. To figure that, you first need to calculate your "adjusted cost basis"—that is, the amount on which your taxable gain will be figured (see table below).

Now that you've got your adjusted cost basis figured out, you can calculate how you came out on this deal after five years (see table on following page).

Comment on this deal: An average annual after-tax return of 12.08% is quite good (on an annually compounded basis, you earned 9.9%—or almost 10%). You could have made that much or more in a good mutual growth fund without the trouble of buying, managing, keeping the books and selling a real estate investment. You'd probably want to earn a higher return than

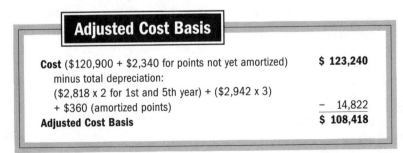

Adjusted Cost Basis

Cost ($120,900 + $2,340 for points not yet amortized)	**$ 123,240**
minus total depreciation:	
($2,818 x 2 for 1st and 5th year) + ($2,942 x 3)	
+ $360 (amortized points)	– 14,822
Adjusted Cost Basis	**$ 108,418**

Annual Average After-Tax Return

Gross sales proceeds	**$142,433**
minus adjusted cost	– 108,418
Taxable gain	34,015
Tax owed (28% bracket): 9,524	
Net sales proceeds	**$ 56,781**
minus tax on gain	– 9,524
Net sales proceeds after tax	**$ 47,257**
plus annual cash flows after tax	
($1,329 x 5)	+ 6,645
Total proceeds	**$ 53,902**
minus cash invested at start	– 33,600
Total Return	**$ 20,302**
% return on cash invested	**60.4%**
Annual average after-tax return	**12.08%**

that, through a higher positive cash flow each year or through higher annual appreciation, or both.

A Better Way to Judge Your Return

THE RETURN ON YOUR ORIGINAL INVESTMENT—WHICH IS actually the return on your down payment—is important to know, but it's not really a true picture of how you're doing year after year. If you've invested in a good piece of real estate, the value of the property should be increasing as time goes by. If your income from the property fails to keep up with the increased equity, your investment return is actually declining, whether you know it or not. You can check on how you're doing by calculating what's known as your return on equity.

Knowing your return on equity allows you to play "what if?" with your real estate investments: What if you sold the property and invested the proceeds elsewhere? Could you get a better return? Inattentive real estate investors are often surprised by the answer.

Return on equity is nothing more than your annual cash flow before taxes divided by your current equity in the property. (Current equity is the market value of the place minus the bal-

Return on Investment

	YEAR 1	YEAR 3	YEAR 5
Before-tax cash flow	$ 1,000	$ 1,210	$ 1,464
Investment	20,000	20,000	20,000
Return on investment	5%	6.05%	7.3%

ance you owe on the mortgage.) Say you buy a $100,000 rental property with a $20,000 down payment. The property produces a cash flow of $1,000 before taxes in the first year. After that, both the cash flow and the value of the property grow by 10% per year, and you pay off $400 on the mortgage each year. The table above shows what your return on your $20,000 investment would look like after the first, third and fifth year of ownership:

Because your return on investment is increasing each year, you may conclude that you're doing just wonderfully. But in fact, as your equity was rising, your return on that equity was declining, as the table below shows, assuming 10% equity and income growth per year.

Whenever equity in the property increases as fast as or faster than the income, as might happen in a market where prices were rising rapidly, return on equity will fall. Even if property values increase slowly and rents rise rapidly, return on equity is still likely to decline, although not so dramatically as in this example. What can you do about it?

One thing you can do is refinance, to pull some cash out of the property and put that cash to work in an investment that promises to produce a higher rate of return. You might use it, for example, to purchase stock or a mutual fund or to buy another

Return on Equity

	YEAR 1	YEAR 3	YEAR 5
Before-tax cash flow	$ 1,000	$ 1,210	$ 1,464
Property value	100,000	121,000	146,400
Loan balance	80,000	79,200	78,400
Equity	20,000	41,800	68,000
Return on equity	5%	2.9%	2.2%

piece of property. When the return on equity from that one diminishes sufficiently, repeat the process. Using the equity built up in one property to acquire another is the classic way for small real estate investors to accumulate substantial assets over time.

The Accidental Real Estate Investor

A LOT OF PEOPLE FIND THEMSELVES INVESTING IN REAL ESTATE almost by accident. This happens most commonly when you can't—or don't want to—sell your residence when you move, and so decide to convert it to a rental property instead.

The rules are the same as for other rental real estate except for two notable differences: First, the tax laws are much stingier when it comes to depreciation deductions; and second, converting probably means forfeiting the sweet, tax-free-profit deal now offered to homeowners.

THE SQUEEZE ON DEPRECIATION WRITE-OFFS

The value of the house for figuring depreciation deductions is your adjusted cost basis or the fair market value of the house, whichever is less. The basis is likely to be far less than what the house is worth when you convert it, particularly if you have pushed the basis down by rolling over profit from previous homes under the old tax rules.

Let's say your house is worth $150,000. You bought it for $100,000 several years ago and at that time rolled over $30,000 in profit from your previous home. If you convert the house to a rental property, your basis for depreciation purposes is a skimpy $70,000. Because you can't depreciate the value of the land, you must subtract its value to determine the amount on which to base your depreciation write-offs.

SAY GOOD-BYE TO TAX-FREE PROFITS

The new law that makes $250,000 of profit from the sale of a home tax-free ($500,000 if you file a joint tax return) applies only to the sale of your principal residence. If you convert that residence to a rental property, profit that would otherwise be tax-free will probably fall victim to the 20% capital gains tax when you do sell the place. We say probably because there are a couple of ways around it.

First, if you rent your home only temporarily—for example, between the time you move into your new home and the time you're able to unload the old one—you may still qualify for tax-free profit. To treat the house as your home, you must have owned and used it as your principal residence for at least two of the five years leading up to the sale. Thus, as long as you sell within three years of the time you move out of the house, you could qualify. (In this scenario, however, profit attributable to depreciation after May 6, 1997, would not be tax-free; rather, it would be taxed at a flat 25% rate unless you fall in the 15% tax bracket, in which case that rate would apply.)

Or, secondly, you could make the rental property your main home again and live in it for at least two years before selling. That way, you could requalify for the break. Although profit attributable to depreciation after May 6, 1997, would be taxable, the profit that built up before you converted the place and any profit due to appreciation during the time it was rented out could be tax-free—up to the $250,000 or $500,000 limit.

Indirect Ways to Invest in Real Estate

YOU DON'T HAVE TO OWN AND MANAGE YOUR OWN PROPERTIES to be a real estate investor. A much less bothersome route is to buy shares of publicly traded companies and mutual funds that own, develop or manage real estate.

REAL ESTATE INVESTMENT TRUSTS

A REIT (rhymes with street) is a pool of properties or loans, or a combination of both. You can buy shares in more than 300 commonly traded REITs the same way you'd buy any stock.

REITs can be high-yielding investments because they get special tax treatment. The income of most companies is taxed twice—once at the corporate level, and again at the shareholder level when shareholders report dividends as income. REITs are virtually exempt from corporate income taxes, provided they pay shareholders at least 95% of net income each year. As a result, REITs have more income to pay out.

Real estate investment trusts come in three general types:

Equity REITs invest in actual real estate, such as shopping centers and office buildings. Shareholders earn dividends from tenant rents and have a shot at capital gains when properties are sold.

Mortgage REITs put you in the loan business—you buy a piece of a real estate loan portfolio. These are volatile, high-yielding securities whose prices can suffer if interest rates (and thus investor yield expectations) rise or if mortgage rates drop and owners refinance. As a group, mortgage REITs are less attractive for long-term investors than equity REITs.

Hybrid REITs combine equity and mortgage holdings. Finite real estate investment trusts, called FREITS, have a limited life, usually about five to 15 years, after which time assets are sold and shareholders get the proceeds. Be wary of these. If a FREIT chooses its time to sell years in advance, it's betting that market conditions will be favorable at that time. If they aren't, the sales price will suffer.

In the early 1970s, high-yielding mortgage REITs heavily burdened with debt were almost entirely killed off by a collapse in commercial real estate prices. For 24 consecutive months starting in April 1973, REITs posted negative total returns.

During the early '80s, equity REITs outperformed the S&P 500, and with fewer gyrations. Investors returned to REITs and 33 new ones were started in 1985 alone. Performance was poor in the late '80s, picked up considerably in the early '90s only to take a nose-dive in 1998.

WHAT TO LOOK FOR. REITs with good performance records, such as New Plan Realty Trust (www.newplanexcel.com; 800-468-7526), Weingarten Realty Investors (www.weingarten.com; 800-550-4689), Federal Realty Investment Trust (ww.federalrealty.com; 800-658-8980) and Washington REIT (www.washreit.com; 800-565-9748) tend to share certain characteristics:

Sharp focus. They stick to a particular geographic area or type of development.

Strong cash flow. Cash flow—net income plus amounts written off for depreciation that require no cash outlay—determine dividends. Depreciation permits REITs to pay out more than 100% of net income in dividends.

Sustainable yields. Dividends of the strongest REITs tend to be relatively modest. Strong REITs deliver competitive total returns because their stock prices keep appreciating. Weak REITs with weak stock prices must offer a high dividend to be competitive, and often that dividend cannot be maintained.

Experienced management. Superior performance over at least five years is one of the surest signs of a solid operation. Experience is crucial in buying new properties at attractive prices and in tapping capital markets correctly. Good managers can add value to what they own by improving the tenant mix, adding space, marketing and generally upgrading their holdings. Managers who own what they manage have every reason to care about results. To get the share ownership figures for the trust's officers, ask the REIT to send its latest proxy statement and 10-K form. Ten percent or more insider ownership is a plus.

Boring but essential holdings. Among the projects that REIT analysts tend to like best are grungy, old, strip shopping centers. Successful REITs find ways to buy such properties at big discounts and rehab them into moneymakers. Such rehabs are recession-resistant, too, especially if they're anchored by a supermarket or a big discount store. A good mix might also include a high-volume drugstore, a dry cleaner, a liquor store, a discount shoe shop and an electronics store.

HOW TO BUY THEM. The standard advice is to buy REIT shares at a discount, meaning when the share price is less than the per-share value of assets. But that's easier said than done when times are booming. You can't appraise the assets yourself, and most brokers can't be of much help. A REIT may provide you with an appraisal, but it probably won't be current when you get it. And although many REITS trade at discounts, the best ones tend to sell at stubborn premiums. We suggest you buy REIT shares at discount whenever possible. You may find news or magazine articles or brokerage reports online that tell whether a particular REIT is trading at a discount. If you expect to buy and hold for five years or more, you can pay less attention to the discount.

Diversify your REIT holdings, just as you would stocks or bonds. Try to find a knowledgeable broker whose firm has at least one analyst covering several different REITs. For more information on REITs, check out the National Association of Real Estate Investment Trust's Web site at www.nareit.com.

STOCKS OF RELATED COMPANIES

Companies with big holdings of real estate assets include major homebuilders, some paper and forest-product companies, railroads, oil and mining companies, and certain insurance, manufacturing and retail companies. Only through careful study of their balance sheets and financial reports will you be able to determine how their real estate holdings might affect their stock prices and whether the property has any chance of being sold at a price high enough to significantly improve the company's profits.

MUTUAL FUNDS

Several mutual fund families offer real estate-oriented funds. Some of them are listed below:

- **American Century Real Estate Fund** (www.americancentury.com; 800-345-2021)
- **Fidelity Real Estate Investment Portfolio** (www.fidelity.com; 800-544-8888)
- **Van Kampen Real Estate Securities Fund** (www.van-kampen.com; 800-421-5666)
- **Templeton Global Real Estate** (www.franklin-templeton.com; 800-342-5236)
- **U.S. Global Investors Real Estate** (www.us-global.com; 800-873-8637)

The first three concentrate on the U.S. market. The last two have charters that permit them to invest globally. All five may own REIT shares. The Templeton fund charges a 5.75% sales fee, the Van Kampen fund charges 4.75% and the others are no-load.

Information for Real Estate Investors

Here are some Web sites that you may find useful if you're interested in investing in commercial real estate:

- **CommercialSource.com** (www.CommercialSource.com), is the National Association of Realtors' official commercial real estate Internet site.
- **InRealty: Internet Information for Institutional and Commercial Real Estate Investments** (www.inrealty.com), provides a multitude of links to sources of information on REITs, real estate mutual funds, sources of demographic and market data, books and more.
- **The National Association of Home Builders** (www.nahb.com), offers professional and consumer information and advice. Check out the online bookstore.

The Cohen & Steers Fund Family (www.cohenandsteers.com; 800-437-9912) sells funds that invest in REITs. In addition to selling closed-end funds that trade on the American Stock Exchange, it also sells load and no-load mutual funds.

REAL ESTATE LIMITED PARTNERSHIPS

We've yet to find a limited partnership we could like. They charge high fees, are illiquid, and have been marked by mediocre performance and failed expectations ever since they became popular in the early 1980s.

Investing in Raw Land

INVESTORS IN RAW LAND ARE TAKING A LONG SHOT AT SUCCESS. For one thing, vacant land doesn't produce any income while you're waiting for the price to go up. The methods available to finance its purchase aren't nearly so flexible as they are for property with a building on it. As mentioned earlier, you can't depreciate land. All these factors make small parcels of empty land very speculative ventures you should enter into only with the expectation of a very large reward.

The biggest challenge is to pick property that winds up on the high side of the wide price swings that are the hallmark of empty land. Then there's the very real chance of being ripped off if you're foolish enough to buy land without checking it out thoroughly. The third—and fairly new—challenge is to avoid running into environmental laws that could block your plans for the property or even cost you unforeseen thousands of dollars if you must remedy an existing problem.

PRICE VOLATILITY

Land values tend to go up and down in sync with a region's economic fortunes. Prime farmland in central Iowa fell from a peak of $3,500 per acre in 1982-83 to about $1,200 during the depth of the Farm Belt's troubles in 1986. In early 1999, farmland values declined in five Midwestern states for the first quarter since 1986 because of a textbook case of supply and demand: too much livestock, grain and soybeans, and not enough demand, particularly from weakened Asian economies. Volatility is also influenced by outside factors. Much of the building frenzy in Texas during the mid '80s—and the related run-up in land prices—was fueled by generous federal tax incentives. When tax reform removed most of those in 1986, investors fled, hastening the price collapse.

RIP-OFFS

Land scams are far from extinct. A North Carolina couple were arrested in 1998 for trying to sell a piece of land they didn't own. The swindlers altered the sign on property that had been advertised for sale in the newspaper. They asked prospective buyers, who visited the property, for $2,500 in cash to hold it. Nobody handed over any money, but the intended victims drove by the property again later and found a different name on the sign. Suspicious, they contacted the police and rescheduled a meeting with the swindlers. The "sellers" were arrested and found to be suspects in similar scams statewide.

ENVIRONMENTAL RESTRICTIONS

The law makes it risky to buy land without an environmental checkup. If you purchase a plot of wetlands, for instance, the

Deducting Investment Property Loss

Q: *I recently sold a vacant lot at a lake property development at a substantial loss. The property was held in title with two co-owners for more than 20 years. We've been told we can deduct the loss on our federal income-tax returns if we establish the fact that the property was an investment. How can we do that?*

A: There would be no question of your intent if you and your co-owners had drawn up a document, when you bought the property, saying that you never intended to build a personal residence and that you would sell when the value increased. Even without such proof, you have a strong case with the Internal Revenue Service for treating it as investment property because you never built on the land and you bought the property with other people.

government probably won't let you build on it without a great deal of difficulty and expense, if it lets you build at all. If land contains buried hazardous waste, you could be forced to pay thousands of dollars have those wastes removed, even though you had nothing to do with putting them there in the first place.

WETLANDS. These are loosely defined under the Clean Water Act as land that is sometimes wet or swampy or that supports certain kinds of vegetation and wildlife. No development is permitted on designated wetlands without permission from the U.S. Army Corps of Engineers and the Environmental Protection Agency. Unfortunately for some buyers, you can't always spot such property with the naked eye. In one case, unsuspecting investors bought vacation lots for $36,000 each, only to discover that they couldn't build on the lots because they are wetlands.

You can get wetlands maps from the U.S. Geological Survey's Earth Science Information Centers (888-ASK-USGS; www–nmd. usgs.gov/esic/esic.html;), with nine regional offices around the country. The maps cost $5 each, plus $3.50 for shipping and handling. Check also with county extension agents.

HAZARDOUS CHEMICALS. Under the 1980 Superfund law, you may be on the hook for cleanup costs of contaminated soil and water, even if you had nothing to do with creating the problem. For information on the Environmental Protection Agency's list of contaminated sites, you can call the EPA's hazardous waste hotline (800-424-9346; in Virginia, 703-412-9810). But you may have better luck asking around at the local level. Call the state's department of natural resources or environmental agency. Explain that you want to know whether your site is listed on the Comprehensive Environmental Response Compensation and Liability Information System, or CERCLIS, list. You may also search online at www.epa.gov/superfund/sites/query/basinstr.htm. The CERCLIS list contains more than 31,000 sites that have been called to the attention of the EPA or state agencies for possible contamination problems.

RADON. Radon is a naturally occurring, cancer-causing gas that emanates from certain rocks, such as granite. A high level of radon requires corrective steps, adding to the cost of building. For a reading on local levels, try the local health department, or call the National Safety Council's radon hotline (800-55RADON; www.nsc.org/ehc/indoor/radon.htm) for answers to specific questions about air quality and references to regional, state and local agencies. Local contacts can inform you about local radon levels and give you the names of contractors who can help you take corrective steps.

How to Get a Good Price

You can never be sure that the value of your property will grow fast enough to justify your investment. But you can get a good idea of its potential by studying the area's price trends, business and demographic projections, and development potential, as well as the local political climate.

You can get a good overview from *Emerging Trends in Real Estate*, an annual study by the Real Estate Research Corp., one of the nation's oldest real estate valuation and consulting firms (www.rerc.com). Copies of *Emerging Trends* are available by mail for $25 each from Pricewaterhouse Coopers (1301 Avenue of the Americas, New York, NY 10019; www.pwcglobal.com/us/) and from Lend Lease (787 Seventh Ave., New York, NY 10019, Attn: Emerging Trends; www.lendleaserei.com); portions of the study are available online.

When you find a location you like, check out the surrounding community. What businesses or civic activities are nearby, and would they draw people to the area? Is the economy diverse? What are the population projections? Local chambers of commerce, realty offices and bank loan officers are good sources for that kind of information. For a chamber of commerce near the area you are researching, you can search online at www.uschamber.org/chambers/index.html.

How to Check the Property

Be sure that the property is accessible and that the costs of owning it and building on it are reasonable. An unsuspecting buyer of waterfront land in Maine was stunned to discover that to build on his new lot he would have to pump sewage 400 feet uphill through solid rock—at a cost of about $30,000. In other developments, buyers faced bills of $20,000 to $30,000 just to bring in electricity.

If you are buying from a developer who operates across state lines and is selling 100 or more lots, most of what you need to know to protect yourself can be found in the property report that is required by the Office of Consumer and Regulatory Affairs, RESPA, Interstate Land Sales Division (ILSD), Room 9146, Washington, DC 20410; 202-708-1420; www.hud.gov.

If you're buying from an owner who isn't regulated by the agency, the ILSD report can still serve as a useful model. Current zoning restrictions and tax assessments on the property should be the first items to investigate.

The ILSD report also requires information about the following items:

TITLE. Find out whether there are any liens on the land and verify who owns the oil, gas, mineral and water rights. Conduct your own title search, or hire a firm to do it for you.

ROADS. Are they public? How good is the surface? Who's responsible for maintenance? In cold areas, is snow removal feasible and affordable?

UTILITIES AND FACILITIES. How will water and sewer lines, electricity, gas and phone service get to the property? How much will they cost and who will pay? Has the water quality been checked recently? Is the soil suitable for a septic system? Are there any drainage problems?

SERVICES. Where are the police and fire stations, school and hospital? Shopping centers? Offices where potential buyers of your property might work?

LOOK FOR UNIQUE PARCELS

Unless your parcel has some distinguishing feature, such as a waterfront location, be skeptical about its appreciation potential in a large resort or retirement community. In a new development, the developer's remaining inventory should be small, so that the company won't be competing with you in the resale market. Better yet, buy in the resale market, in which lots are often cheaper and problems have had time to surface.

COMPARE LOCAL PRICES

Before you agree to a price, check comparable properties in the area. Developers often advertise their lots in distant big cities, where potential buyers are accustomed to high land prices. This research is best done online at one of the real estate sites such as www.realtor.com and www.homes.com.

THE SAD NEWS ABOUT FINANCING RAW LAND

Banks willing to make loans on raw land typically require a large down payment—25% to 30% isn't unusual—and other assets for collateral. They also favor loans of five to ten years, which raises the monthly payments. Financing offered by a developer or an individual seller might be a better bet. An owner might be willing to finance the sale and might accept a ten-year note with 5% to 10% down. A good negotiator should be able to borrow at below bank rates.

If you're buying rural land, community banks might offer more competitive rates, or you might get good terms through a local farm credit bank. Call the Farm Credit Council (202-626-8710) for the number of a local farm credit lender, or check online at www.fccouncil.com for general information. Specifics are for subscribers.

MORE SAD NEWS—TAXES

Land deals don't have many tax advantages. As we emphasized earlier, land isn't depreciable, and the deductibility of interest on a loan used to buy it may be restricted. Check with your accountant or financial adviser for details.

CHAPTER 9

Mortgages: Meet Ginnie, Fannie & Freddie

OWNING REAL ESTATE DIRECTLY BY BUYING AND MAN-aging properties, and indirectly by buying shares of real estate investment trusts or mutual funds, offers a chance for capital gains in the future with an income stream along the way. But what if you want the income but don't want to take the risks inherent in trying for the capital gains? After all, mortgages often pay higher yields than bonds and other income-oriented investments. For investors in search of income, mortgages offer a tempting combination of relatively high interest payouts plus a high degree of safety of principal.

There are no risk-free ways to invest in mortgages, but some ways are riskier than others.

The riskiest way is to buy a mortgage from a lender who wants to get rid of it. Home sellers who "take back" a second mortgage from the buyer to facilitate the sale are often willing to sell it at a substantial discount so that they won't have to wait several years to get their money. They may offer these "secondary-market" second mortgages through advertisements in newspapers, or they may enlist a real estate broker to help them find investors willing to take the paper off their hands. Don't be one of them. Your claim on the underlying property comes after that of the lender on the first mortgage—probably a bank that knows how to protect itself. In addition, you are taking the risk that a home buyer you know little about (except that he or she needed a second mortgage in order to afford the home) will be able to pay you back. Yields that were once a dazzling 14% to 16% might have blinded you to the risk. Now that the yields on these mortgages are around 8.5% or so, it's just not worth the headaches.

A better way to invest in mortgages is through vehicles known as mortgage-backed securities. Owning them is a reasonably safe way to get above-average income. Understanding their risks requires understanding where they come from.

Meet Ginnie, Fannie and Freddie

MOST MORTGAGE-BACKED SECURITIES ORIGINATE WITH THREE federally connected agencies: the Government National Mortgage Association (Ginnie Mae); Fannie Mae (formerly the Federal National Mortgage Association); and Freddie Mac (formerly the Federal Home Loan Mortgage Corporation). Of the three, only Ginnie Mae is technically a full-blown federal government agency. The other two are government regulated but are private shareholder-owned companies with no government guarantee backing their securities.

The role of all three agencies is essentially the same—to buy up mortgage loans from lenders such as banks and savings and loan associations, package them into multimillion-dollar pools and sell off pieces of the pools to investors. The pieces, known as participation certificates or pass-through securities, often sell in minimum denominations of $25,000. Investors who buy them get the homeowners' principal and interest payments passed along to them as income.

This payment schedule is one major difference between bonds and mortgage-backed securities: Bonds pay interest semiannually; mortgage-backed securities pay interest and principal every month. The principal portion of the payment is tax-free; the interest is fully taxable. Another difference is that although the mortgages commonly mature in 30 years, the average life of a mortgage-backed security is thought to be about 12 years, because so many homeowners move or refinance and in the process pay off their mortgages early.

The three agencies work slightly different markets. Ginnie Mae restricts its buying and packaging activities to government-insured or -guaranteed FHA and VA mortgages, making the principal about as safe as it can be. Fannie Mae and Freddie Mac buy conventional mortgages, but their activities are regulated by the government and for practical purposes can be considered no riskier than Ginnie Maes.

What Could Go Wrong?

S ETTING ASIDE FOR A MINUTE THE $25,000 MINIMUM INVEST-ment, Ginnies, Fannies and Freddies appear at first glance to be the ideal combination of above-average returns and below-average risks. They are backed or regulated by the feder-al government, yet often yield a percentage point or two more than Treasury bonds of comparable maturity. So how could you possibly lose?

It's easy. Like any fixed-income investment, mortgage-backed securities operate under the influence of interest rates. If rates go up, the market value of your holdings goes down because newly issued securities pay more than yours, as explained in Chapter 5. In that respect, Ginnies, Fannies and Freddies act like bonds. But when rates go down, the value of bonds goes up, and that's not necessarily the case for mortgage-backed securi-ties. Homeowners tend to refinance to take advantage of lower rates, meaning they pay off their old mortgages. So as rates decline, the mortgage pool shrinks. You get your principal back early and have to find a place to reinvest it at a time when inter-est rates are low. You could move the money into newly issued mortgage-backed securities and comfort yourself with the thought that you're still earning a higher yield than you could get from other investments. But the fact remains that you were counting on an even higher payout.

As a response to the dilemma of prepayment, an increasing number of pass-through securities have 15- or even seven- or five-year maturities. While these shorter maturities are less risky, you can also expect from 0.25 to two percentage points less in yield, and you'll still have to look for another harbor for your money when the security matures.

What Can You Do?

H OW CAN YOU PROTECT YOURSELF AGAINST THE EARLY PAYOFF blues? You have three choices: mutual funds, collateral-ized mortgage obligations, and stock in the issuers.

MUTUAL FUNDS

You can cushion some of the blow—and sidestep the $25,000 minimum—by investing in one or more of the dozens of mutual funds that buy Ginnie Mae, Freddie Mac and Fannie Mae pass-throughs and participation certificates and parcel out shares in them for a typical minimum investment of $1,000. The principal portion of the mortgage payment the fund receives is automatically reinvested in the fund and the interest is passed along to shareholders each month. (If you wish, you can have your interest reinvested, too.)

Because a fund holds mortgages with a variety of maturities, it has some protection from the effects of interest-rate movements. However, funds have sometimes packed their portfolios with high-yielding mortgages in an effort to attract investors. If it has paid a premium for those certificates (meaning it paid more than face value to get the higher yield, as described in Chapter 5) it will be forced to write off that premium if the mortgages get paid off early; the higher the rate, the more likely that is to happen. When it does, the value of the fund declines and its investors lose money.

A mortgage fund that is yielding significantly more than most other funds of its type, or one that is yielding more than a percentage point or two above the current rate being charged by lenders for new 30-year mortgages, most likely paid a premium price for some of the mortgages in its portfolio. If so, its yield advantage will not last. Such funds are especially vulnerable when interest rates are declining, and should be approached with caution. If you avoid this trap and invest for the long run—three to five years, at least—a mortgage mutual fund can be a reliable way to earn high yields with virtually no risk of default. For a list of such mutual funds with good performance records, see Chapter 6.

COLLATERALIZED MORTGAGE OBLIGATIONS

Called CMOs, these mortgage-backed securities—along with their cousins, REMICS (real estate mortgage investment conduits)—were devised by brokerage firms to solve two problems: the erratic cash flow from Ginnie Mae-type investments stems from the unpredictability of principal paybacks, and the high $25,000 minimum investment that priced many investors out of the market.

A CMO takes the payments from a lot of mortgage-backed securities and splits them into groups of bonds with different maturities, called tranches—three years, five years and ten years, for example. The minimum denomination is $1,000. Most maturity classes get some interest from the mortgages, but principal repayments go first to the tranche with the shortest maturity. When those bonds are retired, the principal is channeled to the bonds with the next shortest maturity and so forth until all classes have been retired (when all the mortgages in the pool have been paid off). Thus, the longer the maturity of your tranche, the greater your protection against early principal payoffs.

CMOs have been created with as many as a dozen different tranches, but investors aren't shielded entirely from the prepayment risk inherent in mortgage-backed securities. Principal payback may actually come sooner or later than the date specified for the tranche. And because the CMO is returning principal throughout its life—not just at the end, like a bond—you get nothing back at maturity. Imagine your surprise if you've spent the principal, thinking it was all interest.

Uncertainties like that make investors demand a higher yield from a CMO than they would from, say, a U.S. Treasury note or a bond with the same maturity. So, CMOs typically yield about a percentage point more than Treasuries, sometimes higher.

A few more things to know about CMOs:

They don't necessarily contain government-backed mortgages. The issuer could also be a bank or even a homebuilder. The underlying collateral may be conventional, uninsured mortgages with the backing not of the government but of the financial services company, such as a brokerage firm, that packaged the deal. The safest CMOs, however, contain Ginnie Maes, Fannie Maes and Freddie Macs.

Count on holding them until maturity. Although there is a secondary market for CMOs, their steady erosion of value caused by the payback of principal make them a poor trading vehicle for small investors.

There's another problem with CMOs that should make you think twice before you sink any money into them: They are prime vehicles for the kind of notorious "derivative" transactions that plunged many a mortgage fund to double-digit losses in 1994 and 1995.

Because CMOs and CMO funds are crammed full of interest-only and principal-only instruments, they became favorite playgrounds for the creators of so-called *structured derivatives*—in effect, synthetic securities whose fate is determined by the movements of some other security. One of the most common of the structured derivatives, called an *inverse floater,* is designed to generate higher yields in a climate of declining interest rates. When they work, inverse floaters protect investors against loss; when they run up against unanticipated market movements one way or the other, they can cause astonishing losses in a very short time.

Derivatives have been around a long time in the form of puts and calls, stock-index futures and other fairly common instruments (see Chapter 11). The kind of structured derivatives for which CMOs became a natural magnet are a creation of the computer age. They get the blame for sinking not only a number of mortgage and bond funds in the mid '90s, but also a large federal credit union in Maryland that dabbled in CMOs.

Don't spend a lot of time trying to understand structured derivatives. Instead, scour prospectuses of any CMO or mortgage fund investment you might be considering for the following tip-offs to trouble: interest only (I/O), principal only (P/O), indexed securities, mortgage strips, structured notes and inverse floaters. If the prospectus authorizes such instruments, watch out.

STOCK IN THE ISSUERS

Both Fannie Mae and Freddie Mac sell common stock to the public on the New York Stock Exchange. (Ginnie Mae, which is a government agency, does not sell stock.) They make money by collecting fees for the pass-through and participation securities they package using mortgages they buy from thrifts and other lenders, and from interest on such mortgages that they hold for their own portfolios.

Although these stocks are classified as part of the banking industry, which is characterized by generally sedate stock-price movements, the stocks tend to be volatile, with higher highs and lower lows than the market as a whole. Investing in them offers reasonable prospects for avoiding the vagaries of interest-rate swings and early principal payouts while tapping into future profits from the anticipated long-term strength of the secondary mortgage market. But it is not a good way to invest for income. Yield on these issues averaged less than 1.5% in mid 1999 . If it's income you want, you'll have to stick with the mortgage-backed securities themselves, with all their uncertainties.

CHAPTER 10

P ·ecious Metals & Collectibles: All That Glitters Doesn't Grow

INCE GOLD PRICES PEAKED AT $850 AN OUNCE WAY back in 1980, the metal has failed miserably to live up to its ancient reputation as an inflation hedge. Even if you had bought gold in 1982 at the decade's low price of $325 and held it until 1996, when it reached a high of $416, your investment would have produced an annual appreciation rate of less than 2% during a period when the Standard & Poor's 500-stock index delivered better than 10% per year. By the summer of 1999, gold was selling for about $260 an ounce.

Gold's bragging rights as the world-champion hedge against disaster are also being seriously challenged. In the face of financial and geopolitical catastrophes that include the worst single-day stock-market crash in history (October 19, 1987), the disintegration of the Soviet Union and the outbreak of subsequent civil wars, unimaginable terrorist activities, a multinational war in the Middle East, the collapse of the Japanese stock market, and a multinational war in the Balkans, gold mostly slumbered—meandering between $400 and $500 an ounce and spiking only briefly and weakly when the news was at its worst. After that, it drifted down again.

In the aftermath of such a disappointing couple of decades for gold, has the time come to reject both of those claims and conclude that gold won't protect you against inflation and disaster? Or should you keep the faith, anticipating that the link is only temporarily broken? The risk of the first choice is that you could be wrong and your portfolio could be battered some day by unforeseen events. The risk of the second choice is that you forfeit other opportunities to make your money grow.

For most people, our advice is simple: Forget gold and invest your money elsewhere. Even the most fervent believers in the metal's right to a place in your portfolio don't recommend making it more than 5% to 10% of your assets. At that level, you'd need substantial assets before a little gold would make much difference, even if some unforeseeable event caused gold's price to double or triple.

If you do have a substantial investment portfolio—say, several hundred thousand dollars—the choice isn't so clear. The ups and downs of supply and demand for gold can create opportunities to profit even if neither disaster nor hyperinflation occurs in your lifetime. But buying and selling to take advantage of price changes would require paying close attention to market forces. Forgetting for a moment the irony of doing such a thing (gold investors often insist that a major attraction of gold is that you don't have to pay attention to the markets), it's important to know how gold and other so-called hard, or tangible, assets differ from stocks and bonds and other financial assets.

The Whys and Ways of Gold

GOLD WILL ALWAYS HAVE VALUE BECAUSE IT IS USEFUL, DURABLE and rare. If all the gold ever mined were gathered in one place, it would form a solid block only about the size of a ten-story office building. Because gold is virtually indestructible, metal mined 5,000 years ago could theoretically still be found somewhere in the world, or orbiting around it. Commercial uses for gold range from the everyday, such as in jewelry and camcorder parts, to the exotic, such as the components of satellites. Gold is also remarkably malleable: An ounce of it can be stretched into a wire 50 miles long.

The world has long recognized these intrinsic qualities of gold, and it still does. People manage to bribe their way out of locked-up countries by crossing the palms of officials with gold, the universal currency. And in times of crisis, many people still seek refuge in gold. When the stock market crashed in 1987, the U.S. Mint sold 198,000 ounces of American Eagle coins, compared with 63,500 ounces the month before.

How Can You Invest?

Gold comes in shapes and sizes ranging from 400-ounce bricks to tiny wafers weighing only a gram.

COINS. The most popular form of ownership is bullion coins: American Eagles, Australian Kangaroo Nuggets, British Britannias, Canadian Maple Leafs, Chinese Pandas, Austrian Philharmoniker and South African Krugerrands weighing from one-tenth of an ounce up to an ounce, with a couple of sizes in between. Coins sell for about 3% to 6% more than the value of their gold content on the day of the transaction.

If you own gold, you need a way to store it securely—say, in a safe-deposit box—and you should buy insurance for your holdings. Some dealers simplify the logistics of ownership by sponsoring "certificate" plans, under which they store the gold for you and issue a certificate entitling you to delivery of the metal if you want it. You can also find statement accounts at some dealers. These leave the gold in the dealer's name, with you as the "book entry" owner, something like stock held in street name (see Chapter 16). The chief advantage of this form of ownership is convenience: You can buy and sell your gold over the phone and not worry about storage. You pay commissions on purchases and sales, and a small charge for storage and insurance.

MINING STOCKS AND MUTUAL FUNDS. Stocks of companies that mine gold make wonderful conversation pieces because they have such interesting names: American Barrick, Battle Mountain, Placer Dome, Echo Bay, Homestake. Whether they make wonderful investments is another question.

Gold-mining stocks are affected by overall trends on Wall Street and by corporate decisions both good and bad that may have little to do with the price of gold itself. A company that institutes low-cost mining methods, strikes a rich lode or astutely hedges its sales through the futures market can experience solid earnings. A poorly managed company will surely sink no matter what happens to gold prices, but a well-managed company should soar if prices explode. The major full-service brokerage firms (see Chapter 16) follow gold-mining stocks and will be happy to offer their recommendations.

Gold-oriented mutual funds buy the shares of domestic and foreign companies that mine, explore for, process or sell gold. Some also own a bit of bullion. The funds are easy to find because almost all have the word "gold" in their names. The rewards for investing in them were a lot harder to find for most of the 1980s. Gold funds soared in 1993, only to weaken again and continue to be weak into 1999. They are highly risky but occasionally do reward investors with double-digit returns commensurate with those risks. Unfortunately, returns in the minus double-digits have been more common. Tread very carefully in gold funds. Be nimble and be quick.

You can also invest in gold via options or futures contracts—notoriously arcane devices that attempt to anticipate price changes of the metal (see Chapter 11). Leave this game to the mining companies.

Should You Invest in Gold at All?

To review the argument for gold: In normal times, your stocks, bonds and cash equivalents deliver a balanced overall return while gold does little or nothing. In bad times, however, gold is supposed to prosper when other investments do poorly because it offers a refuge from the storm. So having gold in your portfolio provides insurance protection, even though you hope that you never need it.

The problem is, gold isn't necessarily acting that way anymore, as we saw a couple of pages ago. Why not? Three factors have been at work in the past several years—factors that can reasonably be expected to affect prices in the future as well:

SUPPLY AND DEMAND. Record amounts of gold have come onto the market in recent years, much of it the result of modern mining techniques that can economically sift 50 tons of low-ore rock for an ounce of the yellow metal. Demand spurred by foreign buying and strong sales of gold jewelry sparked a price run-up in the early '90s, but sustained high mine output is forecast over the next several years.

TRADING TECHNIQUES. Gold-mining companies have become aggressive and sophisticated gold-market speculators, locking in their prices on the futures markets in a way that satisfies crisis-mentality demand that might otherwise drive prices much higher. Such trading programs, experts say, serve to restrain gold prices more than in the past.

INVESTMENT ALTERNATIVES. Today, big investors can avoid—or profit from—world crises by quickly moving their money into the most stable currencies, either directly or through international and global mutual funds or specialized currency funds.

In addition, there are less-exotic ways to hedge against inflation or global uncertainty. You could buy a U.S. Treasury bill and roll it over automatically every three months, or buy shares in a short-term T-bill mutual fund. Either gives you safety of principal plus relatively high current return and the opportunity to profit from the rising interest rates that would surely accompany a surge in inflation.

An Even Weaker Case for Silver

YOU CAN BUY A STAKE IN SILVER MUCH THE SAME WAY THAT you do in gold—in bars and coins of various sizes, via certificate programs, and by investing in companies that mine the metal. Perhaps because you perform these transactions across the very same counters where gold is bought and sold, many investors think of gold and silver as birds of a feather. They're not. Precious-metals merchants used to encourage such mistaken linkage by speaking of the ratio of gold prices to silver prices as if there were some magical relationship between the two that eventually would be restored. Don't count on it.

The price of silver is determined by demand that springs mostly from industrial usage. The biggest sources of demand are jewelry and silverware, followed by photography. Most of these areas have shown an increase in demand for silver in recent years. Industry continues to use silver in batteries, bearings, electronics, water purification, and medical and dental applications and more. Photography's share of silver usage continues to climb because of the greater silver demands of color film. The market for jewelry and silverware remains stable. When the price of silver rises, industrial users find ways to use less of it, either by substituting something else or stepping up efforts to reuse minute amounts that they would otherwise discard.

Meanwhile, the output from silver mines has grown steadily in recent decades, but so has demand in most years. Still, the yearly average price of silver has remained between $4.03 and $5.53 an ounce for the past ten years, a far cry from silver's average high of $20.65 in 1980, when a handful of rich investors appeared to have driven prices up artificially. That incident dampened enthusiasm for silver as an inflation hedge, perhaps permanently.

Because silver is primarily an industrial metal, the demand for it is subject to the fluctuations of economic conditions. It does have intrinsic value, but because of the relatively ample supply of silver compared with that of gold, investors have refused to assign it as treasured a place in their portfolios. The one time they tried—in 1980, when the price soared to its all-time high of $48 an ounce—the plunge that followed scared many investors away for good. Those who stuck around and bought more silver during the 1980s paid an average price of $11.25 an ounce, according to the Silver Institute. At the end of the 1990s, the price still stood at less than half that level.

Clearly, any opportunity to make money in silver belongs to those with great patience or great luck.

Why Collectibles Aren't Investments

ONE OF THE MOST MISUSED WORDS IN THE MARKETING OF luxury goods, whether new or antique, is "investment." Purrs the TV commercial for an expensive automobile: "It's not a car, it's an investment." "Invest in a fine fur," says the furrier. The same claims are made for art, antiques and other collectibles. Collectors of everything from baseball cards and limited-edition plates to Chinese ceramics and rare stamps are led to believe they are making an investment.

High-quality tangible goods—a fine car, jewelry, handcrafted furniture, a beautiful painting—have their own rewards of ownership, but inflation-adjusted appreciation usually isn't one of them. The best that can be said for most good collectibles is that they depreciate more slowly than lesser examples of their type. You wouldn't consider slow depreciation, or even just a holding of value, to be satisfactory in financial investments, would you? If a stockbroker tried to persuade you to buy shares of XYZ Corp. because the shares would probably decline in value, but not much, you would collapse in laughter.

As we have stated in different ways throughout the book, an investment is something you buy with a reasonable expectation of current income, future profit, or both. An investment should exhibit some or all of the following characteristics:

LIQUIDITY. You can convert it to cash fairly quickly if you have to. This requires a large, well-organized market of buyers and sellers who are easy to contact.

LOW TRANSACTION COSTS. You can sell it easily for something close to retail value; that is, you pay a low sales commission. Sellers of homes have to pay about 6% of the sales price as commission; stockbrokers normally charge commissions between 1% and 5% (though online brokers may charge even less).

LOW COST OF OWNERSHIP. Ideally, after the initial purchase, you shouldn't have to put more money into your investment for storage and insurance.

CURRENT INCOME. You probably want at least a little income, such as interest, dividends or rent, while you're waiting for the asset to rise in value.

A TRACK RECORD OF APPRECIATION. There's no guarantee that anything you buy will rise in value—stocks and bonds included—but a real investment has a track record of at least holding its value against inflation, and, ideally, exceeding inflation.

Tangible assets, whatever their quality of craftsmanship or rarity, fail those litmus tests of a true investment.

The biggest problem with collectibles as investments is liquidity. They are very difficult to sell at all, let alone for a price approaching or exceeding what you paid for them. Until recently, it wasn't simply a matter of picking up the phone and getting a price quote for your rare porcelain doll or Federal-period sofa, let alone selling it in the same call, as you can with stocks and mutual funds. But, as it has with so many other things in life, the Internet is changing this situation somewhat. Whether it's in informal chat rooms or the somewhat more formal auction Web sites such as eBay, you can get an idea of how much other collectors are willing to pay for your cherished collectibles. The Internet gives collectors of unusual items access to a much wider network of prospective buyers and sellers. In fact, eBay's founder, Pierre Omidyar, got the idea for his company when his fiancée was having trouble finding trading partners for Pez™ dispensers. You can, of course, also add to your collections this way, although you are less assured of authentication than when buying from recognized dealers. Aside from the Internet, unless you are an advanced collector who knows other collectors who will pay you retail (or close to it) on short notice, you must sell your goods to the same dealers you bought from originally, or wait for the next auction of your specialty and take your chances.

Transaction costs are very high for collectibles. To cover their business expenses—financing inventory, advertising, paying for travel, meeting the rent, exhibiting at shows—dealers try for at least a 100% markup. To put it another way, they will usually pay a collector only 50% of the price they'll try to get when they resell an item. As a collector, you are usually buying at retail and selling at wholesale, so the retail price has to double before you can get back just your original cash outlay, which will have been eroded by inflation in the meantime. (Some dealers will guarantee in writing to "buy back" at full price anything they sold—but not in cash, only as credit against the purchase of something else in their inventory.)

Selling at auction will enable you to keep more of the sale price: the high bid minus a commission of at least 20%. But you never know what might be bid for your item on the day of the auction; the price could be disappointingly low. Before the auction you may be able to set a "reserve"—a price below which your item won't be auctioned off—but if no one offers at least the reserve price, you have to take it back and try to sell it some other day, or some other way. You may well owe a listing fee regardless and incur out-of-pocket expenses, such as for freight.

During your ownership of a collectible, you're getting no

income from tying up your money. And you have costs of ownership, too—appraisals, insurance, maintenance, storage, security. There is also the problem of authenticity, a result of the tendency of unscrupulous people to alter antiques and produce convincing fakes whenever the price of some category of collectible begins to soar.

PROFITS AND PATIENCE

We all hear and read stories about fabulous profits in art, coins, antiques and other collectibles, but the stories tend to spotlight unusual windfalls that don't mirror the broad market experience. The gains are typically one of two kinds: a quick profit in a hot market, which is high-risk speculation, not investing; or the opposite, strong appreciation achieved after many years of patient ownership, during which the collector received no income and took a chance on changing fads and tastes. And the big profits are rung up by the finest examples of their type, rare items that usually cost a lot of money in the first place.

If you do have collectibles to sell, you might wish to consult the following resources:

Official Price Guide to Collectibles, by Harry L. Rinker ($19.95, House of Collectibles; www.rinker.com)

Kovels' Antiques and Collectibles Price List ($14.95, Three Rivers Press; www.kovel.com), which include resources and retail prices for thousands of collectibles.

Maloney's Antiques and Collectibles Resource Directory ($28.95; Antique Trader). Go to www.maloneysonline.com to see sections of this available online.

In the 1970s and early 1980s, high-quality collectibles enjoyed strong collector demand, and many items did experience a sharp rise in their retail price (which, as we've noted, is usually much higher than what the owner can realize by selling). But this boom blinded many collectors to the historical fact of long periods in which most of the same items languished, out of style and flat in value.

Booms and Busts

There have been booms and busts in every kind of collectible—furniture, jewelry, baseball cards, rare photographs, Tiffany lamps, you name it. One of the earliest antiques manias was during the 1920s, when rich collectors paid astronomical prices for the fine pieces of 18th-century American furniture. Then prices fell and flattened through the following three decades, before beginning to recover in the 1960s and skyrocketing in the '70s and '80s.

On an inflation-adjusted basis, the record prices paid for some antiques in the late '20s were not even approached until the million-dollar barrier was broken with the sale of a fine Philadelphia tea table in 1986. Then, in January 1987, a Chippendale wing armchair was sold for $2,750,000, setting a world record at that time for furniture. In January 1996, a carved kneehole desk brought $3.6 million.

At the legendary auction of the Reifsnyder collection in 1929, for example, a superb Philadelphia Chippendale highboy sold for $44,000, a great fortune at a time when the annual earnings of the typical American worker were just $1,400. If that magnificent chest of drawers came on the market today, it might well sell for more than $3 million. But even at such a fabulous price, the highboy would have earned just 7% a year compounded since 1929, an investment return that was easily exceeded by the 10% average annual return on high-quality stocks over the past 60 years. Of course, a collector who might have bought that highboy at a much lower price during the dark days of the '40s or '50s, when antiques were out of favor, would have achieved a much higher annual rate of return.

During the 1920s, newspaper publisher William Randolph Hearst avidly collected Staffordshire dinnerware with transfer-printed scenes of America. In 1925, he paid $1,100 for a beautiful dark-blue-and-white platter with a view of New York City on it, made around 1830. At the dispersal of his collection in 1938, the same platter sold for $370—quite a slide in value in 13 years. If that $370 platter had managed to double in value every 10 years (roughly a 7% compounded annual rate of appreciation), it would be worth almost $23,000 today. But platters of this type can be bought for about $5,000 today. That's still a good deal of money for a piece of china, but proportionately much less than

Stomping on the Stamp Market

Q: *Can you tell me what happened to the market in rare, investment-grade postage stamps? Several years ago it was going great, but today you don't hear anything about it.*

A: Following years of speculation during which stamp prices climbed, the stamp market went bust in the '80s. It has returned to being a collector's—rather than an investor's—market, and all but the rarest stamps are appreciating slowly. To determine your collection's value, have it appraised by a dealer who specializes in the type of stamps you collect.

To locate a dealer in your area or for information on appraisals, contact:

- **The American Stamp Dealers Association** (3 School St., Glen Cove, N.Y. 11542-2548; 516-759-7000; www.asdaonline.com). To receive a printout of local dealers, send a self-addressed, stamped envelope or check the Association's searchable listings online.

- **The American Philatelic Society** (814-237-3803; www.west.net/~stamps1/dealer.html). The Society also provides for online search of its membership listing.

- **You can also check your library** for the current Scott Standard Postage Stamp Catalog or the Scott Specialized Catalog of United States Stamps, both of which list current retail prices for stamps.

its price many years before. In short, that lovely piece of English ceramics wasn't such a hot investment, underperforming a money-market mutual fund account.

There have been several boom-and-bust cycles recently, too, with a variety of objects. In the late 1980s, for example, baseball card prices rose enormously high and then the bubble burst and prices plummeted. Cards from that time period are now some of the least valuable of all cards. By the late '90s it looked as if the same thing was happening with Beanie Babies.

LOVE NOT PROFIT

The odds are very good that after the millenium, art, antiques and collectibles being bought at record-high prices today will not enjoy the real rate of return of carefully selected financial assets. Having said that, let's not forget that collecting is wonderful fun, and that high-quality tangibles are a joy to own. They can be a decent store of value, too, when compared not with financial assets but with other utilitarian and decorative goods.

Antique furniture, for example, is the only kind of household goods that give you current utility plus some degree of retained value. Knowledgeable collectors with a fine eye for quality have a reasonable chance of making a little money, too. They buy for love, not profit, which means they are guided in their purchases by their own tastes, not the fads of hot markets. If the things they love were shunned by other collectors at the time of purchase, they were able to buy low, giving them the opportunity to sell high a few years later—assuming that other collectors had come around to their tastes in the meantime. This has been the experience of many trailblazing collectors of such things as folk art, '60s "muscle cars" (such as the Pontiac GTO) Victorian furniture and other categories that once were ignored.

In that direction, not in the direction of the crowd, lies the best hope for actually making money in collectibles. Good luck, but don't include collectibles in your long-range plans for financial security. That would be confusing a hobby with an investment strategy.

Investments You Can Live Without

ROKERS HAVE A LONG LIST OF GOOD INVESTMENT products to sell, without which there would be no need for books like this one. When it comes to stocks and bonds and such, the question is not whether you should invest, the question is which to choose and when. This chapter is about investments that, in our opinion, flunk the "whether" question. For reasons of high cost, lack of liquidity, size of the risk involved or amount of effort required compared with potential reward, we think you're better off without them.

Put and Call Options

THE APPEAL OF PUTS AND CALLS IS LEVERAGE: YOU CAN CONtrol 100 or more shares of stock for a fraction of their market price. The problem with puts and calls is that they turn investors, who need a long-term frame of mind, into traders with a short-term frame of mind.

A put gives you the right to sell 100 shares of the stock at a fixed price—called the striking price— within a specified period of time, usually a few months but sometimes as long as three years. If the share price does fall before the deadline passes, your puts will be worth more than you paid for them. Because these options are bought and sold on stock markets, just like their underlying stocks, you could then sell them at the higher price and pocket the profit, or you could exercise your right to sell the stock for more than its current market value. Neat trick.

A call gives you the right to buy 100 shares of the stock at or near its current price. If the price goes up, you could buy the shares if you wanted to, then quickly sell them at the higher price, or you could simply sell your call contracts at a higher price than you paid for them.

The degree of leverage you get with puts and calls depends on how long it is before the option expires and how far away the option price is from the current price of the stock. For example, at a time when Microsoft was selling for about $85 a share, you could buy a put with a striking price of $80 for about $2 a share ($200 for the minimum 100-share contract) with an expiration date about 60 days away. A contract with the same striking price but about 90 days away from expiration was selling for $2.75 per share. The price is called a premium, and in general, the closer you get to the expiration date of the option, the smaller the premium. If the deadline passes without the put or call being exercised, the option simply expires.

What's called writing covered calls, a relatively conservative way of playing the options game, takes advantage of this expiration feature—in fact, it depends on it. The technique entails selling a call option on a stock you own. Say you own 100 shares of AT&T and the stock's price is $50. In February you sell to another investor (through your broker) the right to buy your 100 shares for, say, $55 before the end of June. You have written a covered call.

Why would you want to do such a thing? Because you collect extra income, the premium, for selling the option. A range of $2 to $12 per share is possible, in 100-share minimums. For your covered call on AT&T, you collect about $200, which you keep, no matter what happens to the price of the stock.

The technique works beautifully if the stock price remains unchanged or at least stays under the strike price. In that case the option expires worthless, and you wind up with more income from your stocks than you would have collected otherwise. If the price rises a lot—which is what the call buyer was betting on—the buyer will certainly exercise the option, denying you the benefit of any gain above the strike price. If the stock plunges, you can comfort yourself with the premium you collected.

Chances are good that the covered calls you write will expire worthless. So what's wrong with the technique?

First, the risks may be modest, but the amount of your time and energy involved is not. Writing covered calls is hardly worth the trouble unless you do it regularly, with the aim of making 10% to 15% on your holdings. Achieving that profit entails a lot of calendar watching. What's more, if someone is willing to buy your covered call, that investor presumably has reason to think the price of your stock is going to go up more than you think it's going to go up. You'd better take the time to find out why.

Second, commissions on options are proportionately higher than on other kinds of transactions because of the relatively modest sums involved. At a full-service broker, commissions can range from 4% of your premium to 10% or more, depending on the size of the transaction. Online brokers may be cheaper, but their commission schedules tend to follow the same pattern: Options cost more to trade per dollar invested.

Third, writing a covered call means putting 100 shares of your carefully selected stock at risk of being snatched out of your portfolio on the basis of a temporary spike in the price. That kind of speculation is inconsistent with a long-term investment program, and that is the main argument against writing covered calls.

You can also buy and sell puts and calls on the major stock market indexes, specialized indexes and even foreign currencies. For investment managers responsible for hedging tens of millions of dollars' worth of stocks and armed with lightning-fast computers, dealing in such options leads to what's called program trading (see the Glossary). For individual investors, it leads to lunacy.

Commodities Futures

THE IDEA OF SPECULATING ON THE FUTURE PRICE OF SOYBEANS, corn, cocoa, crude oil and other commodities may strike you as so absurd that it is hardly worthy of comment. But an amazing number of investors who wouldn't dream of getting involved in something so arcane allow themselves to get talked into paying someone else to do the speculating for them. But first things first.

What you trade in the futures markets is not a product but a standard agreement to buy or sell a product at some later date—usually within six months or so—at the price set when the contract is purchased. You need to put up as little as 2% to 10% of the value of the underlying commodity contract to get in on the action.

This sort of leverage can lead to fantastic profits if prices move the right way: Say you buy a futures contract that commits you to take delivery of 100 ounces of gold at $400 an ounce on a specified date six months from now. That's $40,000 worth of gold, but the margin is 5%, so you pay only $2,000 for the contract. If the price goes to $440 an ounce—10% above your contract price—you make a profit of $40 an ounce when the contract is fulfilled. On 100 ounces, that's a $4,000 return on your $2,000 investment. You've doubled your money on a 10% increase in the price of gold.

The dark side, of course, lies in the direction of a price decline. Unlike an option, which gives you the right to buy or sell the underlying stock, a futures contract is an obligation to buy or sell the underlying commodity. (In practice, investors can offset a contract to buy at a particular price with a contract to sell at about the same time at the same price. That way, only money changes hands, saving commodities investors from having to cope with unwanted truckloads of live cattle or pork bellies.)

Nevertheless, if the price moves against you, you can't just let the contract expire, as you could with an option. You'll have to deliver on the contract and cover your leveraged losses. Suppose that in the foregoing example the price had sunk 10% instead of rising. Your contract would obligate you to pay $40,000 for 100 ounces of gold worth only $36,000. In that case, you'd be buying at $40,000 and selling at $36,000 (unless you wanted to take delivery of the gold, which would be your choice). Because you could close the deal via contracts with a 5% margin, your loss would be the $2,000 you originally invested in the $40,000 contract to buy, plus the $1,800 you'd have to spend to offset it with the $36,000 contract to sell.

To review: Your original futures contract cost $2,000 and it's a total loss. You must cover that obligation with a second contract, which costs you $1,800 (5% of $36,000). Actual loss on your

$2,000 investment: $3,800. That's the dark side of leveraged speculating in commodities futures. Unless you're a farmer, a food processor or a manufacturer who needs to lock in the price of a physical commodity to protect your business, this particular speculation is best left alone.

Commodity Funds

C OMMODITY FUNDS OFFER THE SAME POTENTIAL ADVANTAGES as mutual funds: professional management, the ability to diversify, and, often, access to up-to-date information and high-quality research. Funds are usually limited partnerships, in which money put up by individuals is used by a professional trader to speculate in futures. The organizer, a company or an individual, becomes the general partner, overseeing operations and hiring the trading adviser, or manager. The other investors are limited partners; their responsibility for losses is limited to the amount they invest. Partnership units usually cost $1,000, and investors as a rule must buy at least two to five units. They are bought and sold through brokers.

There is surely something to be said for professional management, and some commodity funds have delivered truly breathtaking returns. Commissions are typically lower than they are for real estate partnerships, but management fees may be higher. What you gain in professional management, however, you lose in liquidity. There is virtually no secondary market for these investments; units usually can be redeemed only by selling them back to the general partner. Because fund values can fluctuate sharply, when you get into a fund and when you get out can play the key role in whether or not you end up a winner.

Hybrid Funds

S OME BROKERAGE FIRMS OFFER THE CHANCE TO TAKE A TOE-IN-the-water approach to the commodities markets through hybrid instruments that combine a commodities investment with a safe one. These are also called guaranteed funds because most guarantee your funds back at the end of a certain time period, usually three to five years. Such hybrids may promise you your money back if you stay the course, plus a shot at making big money in the commodities market.

Say that you invest $10,000. A hybrid fund may take $6,000 of that to buy U.S. Treasury zero-coupon bonds that return $10,000 in five years at maturity. This means that you're fairly well assured of getting your original investment back if you hold your shares for five years. Your remaining $4,000 goes to a smart commodities manager who may just get you a nice additional profit.

The problem with these funds is that they are expensive. One popular offering collects a fee of 6% per year on total net assets—even on funds just sitting there, invested in Treasury zeros. As noted in the fine print in the prospectus, that's equivalent to a 15% annual fee on the $4,000 you have invested in commodities. You could do a lot better on your own by finding a less risky speculation and buying your own T-zero.

Contractual Mutual Funds

THE MAJOR DIFFERENCES BETWEEN CONTRACTUAL FUNDS AND the rest of the mutual fund universe are these:

You agree up front to invest a fixed sum of money each month for ten to 15 years. There's some leeway—you can make several contributions in advance or skip payments for up to a year without having your plan terminated. Despite the word "contractual," the obligation to invest is not legally enforceable.

You plunge into a fee structure that swallows as much as half of your first year's investment. Over the life of a contract, as much as 9.5% of the money you put in goes not to buy shares but to compensate the broker, financial planner or insurance agent who sold you on the idea, or to the operators of the fund. As a group, these are the costliest mutual funds.

You may have 45 days to change your mind. After that, if you want out of the fund before the contract is up, you may lose as much as 40% of what you've invested. Sales charges are bunched in the first year of your investment plan. And after the first 18 months these charges are totally nonrefundable to the investor.

Contractual plans justify the large front-loaded charges by saying that they are an inducement for people to stick with a plan, because the longer you stay with it, the more you amortize the initial fees. But a commitment to invest regularly is one thing, and a commitment to stick with one fund for as long as 15 years is quite another. Your goals in life may change—you marry, become a parent or need to tap your investments for, say, the down payment on a home. Your fund can change, too. Portfolio managers come and go.

The irrefutable argument advanced by contractual funds for putting money into them is that regular, long-term investing is smart. You benefit from dollar-cost averaging—by investing the same amount of money each month, you buy more shares when the price is down and fewer when it is up, and that usually means your average cost per share is lower than it would be otherwise. Also, by taking the long-term approach and reinvesting your gains, you benefit from compounding—the shares you bought with dividends last month generate more dividends the next time, and so on.

But you can invest small amounts regularly for long periods in any of hundreds of mutual funds, and you can do it a lot more cheaply than in contractuals. The alternatives for building wealth slowly and steadily are almost innumerable. The contractual fund seems suited for that very small percentage of people who feel so lacking in willpower that they can save only with a gun to their head.

A FEW FUNDS

Fidelity Destiny Plan I (http://fiis.fidelity.com/destiny/; 800-752-2347), the largest of this breed, shows contractual plans in their best light because it has done an excellent job of managing its assets. But investors in Destiny had fewer dollars working for them in the early years than they would have had in practically any other fund, meaning that Destiny's performance had to outstrip similar noncontractual funds just to stay even. It did quite well, as have other contractual plans with similar fee structures. They are:

Fidelity Destiny Plan II (as above), a clone of its successful namesake has enjoyed high returns also.

AIM Summit Fund (www.aimfunds.com; also sold by brokers) part of the Houston-based AIM family of funds.

Penny Stocks and Microcap Stocks

D ESPITE THE NAME, AN ISSUE NEEDN'T COST MERE PENNIES TO qualify as a penny stock. The North American Securities Administrators Association (NASAA) defines penny stocks as certain issues selling from a penny to $5 a share. The Securities and Exchange Commission defines a penny stock as any stock traded over the counter that sells for less than $5 a share. For many people the term "microcap stock" has replaced the term "penny stock." Microcap stocks have not officially been defined by the SEC, but the agency offers investor educational material on its Web site (www.sec.gov). Often the sellers of micro-cap stocks have priced them a bit higher per share than penny stocks in order to avoid the penny-stock rules. The same cautions that apply to penny stocks apply to microcaps.

A lot of investors figure that it's bound to be easier to score big with a minipriced issue than with a high-priced one. It stands to reason that even in a powerful bull market it will take several years for a giant like Microsoft or Colgate-Palmolive to double or triple in price. But a $5 stock? Better yet, a $1.25 stock? They have been known to double in less than a week. Any list of top percentage gainers—for a day, a month or a year—is likely to be dominated by stocks selling in or near single digits. By the same token, the biggest percentage losers also tend to be low-priced stocks.

Another attraction is that cheap issues allow investors to buy 100-share lots with small outlays. Buying "even lots" like that can be psychologically soothing and, in many cases, can give you a break on commissions.

Some investors even believe that cheapness is an indication of good value. That belief completely misconstrues what makes for bargains—stocks that are priced low in relation to earnings per share, cash flow per share, book value per share and other basic measures described in Chapter 4. All else being equal, a $1 stock of a company that earns 10 cents a share is no better value than the $100 stock of a company that earns $10 a share.

THE BIG RISKS IN LITTLE STOCKS

Companies with low share prices are usually small, young or both. Such companies simply have a harder time making a go of it than larger, more-established concerns.

The spread between bid and asked price—meaning the broker's commission—is likely to be high in relation to the stock prices, because many of these stocks are not actively traded. If you pay $5.50 a share for a stock with a bid price of $5 and an asked price of $5.50, the stock must rise 10% just for you to break even—and that doesn't include additional commissions beyond the spread. A spread of 12½ or 25 cents for a $70 stock is inconsequential.

Low-priced stocks are more volatile. Think about it: The minimum move for a stock is one-eighth of a point up or down, called a "tick." That means a $2 stock moves 6% on each tick.

Companies with very low share prices are often in severe financial trouble. In other words, low-priced stocks often deserve to be cheap.

SCAMS IN PENNY AND MICROCAP STOCKS

Penny-stock swindles are estimated to bilk U.S. investors out of billions of dollars a year. NASAA figures that fraud, combined with the high risks that accompany investing in tiny firms, makes the odds of breaking even, let alone making money, about 1 in 10.

Among the most common practices in the netherworld of penny stocks are inflated markups by brokers who buy shares for a nickel and sell them for a dime—a commission of 100%. NASAA also found instances of manipulation of share prices by brokers and their cohorts, and of high-pressure sales spiels targeting unsophisticated customers for whom such risky investments are unsuitable.

Microcap stocks are often involved in "pump and dump"

Complaining About a Broker

Q: *I invested in some microcap stocks that have fallen in value more than 70% since I purchased them less than a year ago. How can I find out whether my broker has engaged in illegal activity, and what can I do about it?*

A: If you suspect that your broker is not on the up-and-up and you would like to file a complaint, you have a few options.

You can alert your state's division of securities regulation or, on the national level, contact the National Association of Securities Dealers (NASD), which regulates individual brokers. Call their public disclosure number (800-289-9999) for the address of the office near you that deals with complaints, or visit the NASD's Web site (www.nasdr.com).

NASD investigates all customer complaints and censures members if rules have been violated. It does not recover monetary damages, but it does provide arbitration facilities for customers with disputes involving $5,000 or less. This is a quick and inexpensive alternative to court proceedings, and NASD member brokers are required to participate.

If you wish, you can file a complaint with the Securities and Exchange Commission (Enforcement Complaint Division, Mail Stop 2-2, 450 Fifth St., N.W., Washington, DC 20549-0202).

The SEC also publishes a free brochure for investors, *Microcap Stock: A Guide to Investors* (www.sec.gov/consumer/online.htm; 800-732-0330).

scams that typically involve fraudulent sales information—including exaggerated claims (pump) about a particular company. Promoters of these companies usually own large amounts of stock and profit when the price rises as a result of their promotional efforts. When the price rises, the promoters dump their stock and take their profit, leaving investors with greatly devalued securities. Other fraudulent practices include unauthorized trading and "churning," in which excessive trading of customer accounts is used to generate commissions for the broker.

To avoid scams, take these precautions:

Don't buy anything on the basis of an unsolicited phone call or e-mail from a broker affiliated with an unfamiliar firm who promises big and fast profits from a low-priced stock. As one regulator put it: Why should someone you've never even heard of want to make you the deal of a lifetime?

Be extra vigilant before investing in a low-priced stock that's not listed on an exchange or on the computerized Nasdaq market. Prices for thousands of these non-Nasdaq over-the-counter issues can be found only on the "pink sheets"—printed lists that are updated just once daily and are generally available only to brokers. Pink-sheet penny stocks and microcaps are especially ripe for abuse because investors cannot get up-to-the-moment price quotes easily and because the companies don't have to issue regular financial reports, as do Nasdaq- and exchange-listed companies.

The SEC has a "cold-calling" rule designed to protect investors from high-pressure sales tactics involving pink-sheet stocks. Before a broker unfamiliar to you can sell you penny stocks over the phone, you must sign a suitability statement, plus a purchase agreement, the first three times you buy shares covered by the rule. You can request a copy of the rule (and other consumer information) from the Securities and Exchange Commission (Publications, 450 Fifth St., N.W., Washington, DC 20549; 202-942-7040; www.sec.gov).

If you have ever been tempted to buy a penny stock over the phone, try this: Send for the SEC rules. Then, the next time a penny stockbroker calls, starting reading the rules aloud. You won't have to hang up; the broker will hang up on you.

Be equally cautious about investing contacts you make online; you can get information about online stock fraud (and report suspicious activities) at the SEC's Web site (www.sec.gov). Its Office of Internet Enforcement fields 200 to 300 messages a day from the public concerning potential scams. The most common complaint involves "spam"—junk e-mail sent to individuals, usually touting a small-company stock.

In a classic "pump and dump" fraud, a company pays individuals or newsletters to talk up its stock price. When the price of the stock rises, the scam artists—company officers and whoever else is in on the scam—sell or "dump" their numerous shares all at once. The scam artists make a big profit when they sell. Flooding the market with shares causes the price of the shares to drop drastically, and the investor loses big time. The SEC recently accused 44 companies and individuals of illegally touting small-company stocks over the Internet.

Also on the rise are "cybersmears," in which scam artists make money by selling a stock short (a strategy to profit from declining prices; see the Glossary) and distributing false information to depress its price.

Internet scams can elude investigators because the people behind them can put up a site one day and take it down the next, and do it cheaply and efficiently.

To report possible fraud, forward questionable messages or Web-site addresses (along with your home state) to:

- **the SEC** at enforcement@sec.gov
- **the North American Securities Administrators Association** at cyberfraud@nasaa.org
- **your state** securities department

CHAPTER 12

How Taxes Affect Your Investments

HE ART OF TAXATION CONSISTS IN SO PLUCKING THE goose as to obtain the largest possible amount of feathers with the least possible amount of hissing." That's how Jean Baptiste Colbert, who was finance minister to Louis XIV, summed things up in the 1600s. As an investor at the dawn of the new millennium, you must be aware that how you invest your money is crucial to determining how much of your earnings and profits will be plucked away by the Internal Revenue Service.

Different kinds of investments are treated differently by the IRS. Less than 20 years ago, earnings from some investments ran head-on into a 70% federal tax rate, while earnings from other investments were taxed at the gentlest of all rates: 0%. Today, the official rates run from 0% to 39.6%. Almost all states demand to share in your investment success, too.

Understanding the rules can pay off handsomely, but keeping up with them is not easy. Congress is always tinkering, a tendency epitomized by the issue of capital gains. Capital gains are profits from stocks, bonds, real estate and other investments. Whether all or just part of such profits should be taxed is the subject of a never-ending battle in Washington. Not so long ago, 60% of capital gains were tax-free; now, 100% are taxed. The Taxpayer Relief Act of 1997 did bring some welcome relief to investors by lowering the maximum tax rate on long-term capital gains—defined as profit on investments owned more than one year before selling—from 28% to 20%. For someone in the top (39.6%) bracket, that's almost the same as making 50% of the profit tax-free.

Your investment success is going to depend in part on keeping your eye on the true bottom line: your after-tax return. That is what you get to keep after the government claims its share. And what you get to keep depends on where you put your money.

Savings Accounts and Certificates

THE BASIC RULES ARE MERCIFULLY SIMPLE. INTEREST YOU EARN in a savings account is fully taxable in the year you earn it. It doesn't matter whether you withdraw the money or let it compound inside the account.

On certificates of deposit, the IRS also usually demands its share as the interest is earned. An exception lets you postpone the tax bill temporarily if you put your savings into a CD that matures in a year or less. In that case, the interest is taxed in the year the certificate matures. If you invest in a six-month CD in September, for example, the interest earned on it during the current year won't be taxed until the following year, when the certificate matures. For deposits with longer maturities, the interest is taxed in the year it is credited to your account.

Your bank, credit union, or savings and loan will send you a notice each year showing how much interest to report to the IRS. (The IRS gets a copy, too.) The institution will also report as income to you the value of any inducement it gave you to get your business. The extra tax on such "income" isn't worth worrying about if all you got was a toaster or a videotape. But an expensive incentive could create a noticeable tax.

If you withdraw funds from a CD before it matures and have to pay an early-withdrawal penalty, the IRS will subsidize your loss. You can deduct such a penalty whether or not you itemize other deductions on your tax return.

COMPLICATIONS FOR CHILDREN'S ACCOUNTS

The same rules generally apply to interest earned inside a custodial account set up for your children, but there's a complication: the so-called kiddie tax. It was created because Congress worried that parents were stashing funds in kids' accounts so that the interest would be taxed in the child's low tax bracket rather than in the parents' higher one. To prevent such lamentable maneuvers, Congress declared that if a child under age 14 has unearned income over a certain amount, the excess is to be taxed at the parents' top rate. (Unearned income is basically earnings from investments, while earned income is earnings from a job.)

As explained in Chapter 13, the kiddie tax applies the parents' tax rate to a child's income when unearned income passes $1,400. For a child under 14, the first $700 of investment income is tax-free, and the next $700 is taxed at the child's rate, probably 15%. Only unearned income above $1,400 is taxed at the parents' rate, which is probably 28% or 31%. (The triggering point for the kiddie tax is indexed to rise with inflation, but it will remain at $1,400 for 2000.)

Although the kiddie tax was designed to prevent families from shifting income to children as a tax-saving strategy, it doesn't entirely eliminate the opportunities. In an account earning 8%, for example, the balance in your child's name could exceed $15,000 before the earnings would be threatened by the kiddie tax. Assuming $1,400 in interest is the child's only income, the first $700 would be tax-free, and the 15% tax on the remaining $700 would be about $105. If that same money were invested in the parents' name, and the earnings taxed in the 31% bracket, the tax bill would be $434. That $329 savings is available year after year.

Remember that the kiddie-tax threat disappears on a child's 14th birthday. If your son or daughter turns 14 any time during the year, even on New Year's Eve, the kiddie tax does not apply to any income received during the year.

U.S. Savings Bonds

AS NOTED IN CHAPTER 5, TODAY'S SAVINGS BONDS CAN STILL BE attractive, despite the elimination of the guaranteed minimum interest rate in 1995. The key attractions are the rate's flexibility and the bonds' taxability.

EE bonds have three special tax appeals:

NO STATE OR LOCAL TAX. The interest is free of state or local tax. That hikes your effective return. If your state tax rate is around 7%, for example, avoiding that tax adds about 0.5% to the taxable-equivalent yield.

DEFERRED FEDERAL TAX. Federal tax on the interest is deferred until you redeem the bond. This allows money that would otherwise go to the IRS to remain invested for further growth. (Series HH bonds, also described in Chapter 5, are free from state tax but the interest is paid out in semiannual installments and taxed in the year received.)

The tax-deferral feature makes series EE bonds popular for college savings plans. Because tax is deferred until the bonds are cashed, bonds purchased in a child's name (as they often are at birth or for other special occasions in the child's life) can escape the kiddie tax described earlier. Assuming that the bonds are not cashed until the child is 14 or older, the interest will be taxed in the child's bracket. (If the parent is a co-owner, however, the parent will be stuck with the tax bill.)

Sometimes it makes sense to forgo this tax deferral, though, and report the interest each year as it is earned. For a child with little or no other income, reporting the interest year by year could render part or all of it completely tax-free, because the child's total income is so low that no tax would be due.

To report interest annually, file a tax return for the child showing the amount of interest earned by the bonds during the first year. Banks have tables showing how much that will be. Or you can track it yourself with *Savings Bond Wizard* software available free at www.publicdebt.treas.gov/sav/savwizar.htm. File the return even if no tax is due, to show intent to report bond interest annually. Then you don't have to file another return for the child until his or her income is high enough to require it.

TAX-FREE INTEREST FOR COLLEGE. The third advantage of EE bonds is that you can make them tax-free without going through the annual-reporting rigmarole. Interest on bonds purchased by parents is tax-free if the money is used to pay a child's college bills. Freedom from both state and federal tax really boosts the true return on this investment. At 4% interest, the double-tax-free virtue gives the bonds a taxable-equivalent yield of between 6.2% and 7.2% in most states, depending on your income.

To qualify, the bonds must be purchased and owned by the parents, who must be at least 24 years old when the bonds are purchased. (Bonds purchased before 1990 don't qualify.)

For qualifying bonds, the interest is tax-free if, in the year the parents redeem the bonds, they also pay qualifying educational expenses—basically, tuition and fees for a dependent child—equal to the value of the bonds. If you pay $10,000 in tuition and fees and redeem bonds worth $10,000 or less, all interest would be tax-free. If you cash in $10,000 worth of bonds and pay $7,500 for a child's qualifying expenses, only 75% of the interest would be tax-free. Parents must also meet certain income tests. See Chapter 13 for more information on using EE bonds as part of a college savings plan.

The Basics of Basis

W HEN YOU MOVE BEYOND SAVINGS TO STOCKS, MUTUAL FUNDS and other investments that give you the potential for greater rewards in exchange for the risk of losing part or all of your money, your tax life becomes more complicated. On the bright side, the complications are generally beneficial if you know what the rules are and understand how to take advantage of them.

The beginning point is an understanding of tax basis. Your basis is essentially the amount of your investment in a piece of property such as a share of stock, a bond, or a mutual fund share—in other words, the amount you compare with what you get when you sell the property to determine whether you have a profit or a loss.

Sounds simple enough, but it's not, really. Not only is the basis affected by how you acquire an investment, but the basis of different investments can change while you own them. You must keep track of the basis of every investment you own, and that means keeping good records. Your basis depends in part on how you obtained the property in the first place.

IF YOU BOUGHT IT, you've got the simplest job of figuring your basis. When you buy a stock, bond or mutual fund share, for example, your basis begins as what you pay, including any commissions. If

Figuring the Basis on Inherited Stock

Q: My sisters, brother and I each received a gift of stock from our parents. The shares were purchased in small amounts over a long period of time; some are a result of stock splits and some were inherited by them from their parents as long ago as 1935. How do we figure the basis?

A: If your parents don't have good records, you'll have to spend some time in the library with old newspapers looking up stock prices for the dates the shares were purchased. If you do not know the exact dates of the purchases, you could check the high and low for the year and use the midpoint.

The basis for shares that your parents gave you is their purchase price plus the commission. If you plan to sell all the shares, the effect of stock splits doesn't matter. Once you've reconstructed what your parents paid for the shares they purchased, you need to pinpoint the basis of those they inherited—that's the stock's value on the date of death of the previous owner. If you sell for a gain, adding the basis of the stocks your parents purchased to the basis of those they inherited gives you your basis. If you sell the stock at a loss, however, the basis is either the amount just figured or the value of the stock at the time of the gift, whichever is lower.

you buy 100 shares of SureThing Inc. for $40 a share and pay a $100 commission, your tax basis in each share is $41—the full $4,100 acquisition cost divided by the number of shares purchased. Keep the purchase confirmation form in your files.

IF YOU GOT IT AS A GIFT, the basis depends in part on whether you eventually sell it for a gain or a loss. If you sell for a profit, your basis is the same as the basis of the previous owner—he or she passes on the basis along with the property. But if the sale results in a loss, the basis is either the previous owner's basis or the value at the time of the gift, whichever is lower. In other words, you don't get to deduct any decline in value that occurred before you got the gift.

IF AT THE TIME OF THE GIFT THE PROPERTY IS WORTH MORE THAN THE BENE-FACTOR'S BASIS, all you need in your records is his or her basis. It becomes your basis. But if the property has declined in value, your records will need to show both the previous owner's basis and the value at the time of the gift. Say that a rich and generous uncle gives you 200 shares of stock for which he paid $10,000 but which are worth just $8,000 at the time of the gift. If the stock rises in price so that you eventually sell it for $12,000, your basis for determining gain is $10,000—your uncle's basis. If the share value continues to fall and you sell for less than $8,000, however, the basis for figuring your loss is the $8,000 value of the stock at the time of the gift. If you sell for an amount between $8,000 and $10,000, you have neither a gain nor a loss.

One additional complication: If the gift is large enough to trigger the federal gift tax, which generally applies to gifts over $10,000 and is owed by the donor, your basis is increased by part of the tax the donor incurs.

IF YOU INHERITED IT, your basis is "stepped up" to the value of the asset on the date of death. (When large estates are involved, the value on a date within six months after death is sometimes used.) This rule means that the tax on any profit that built up during the previous owner's lifetime is forgiven. You'll be taxed only on income and capital gains that accrue after you inherit the asset. If its value falls and then you sell, you can deduct the loss. This rule also applies if you become the sole owner of property after the death of a joint owner. When a husband and wife jointly own stock and one spouse dies, for example, the survivor's basis becomes his or her half of the original basis plus half of the stock's value at the time the joint owner died. If you inherit property, be sure to pinpoint the stepped-up basis to hold down your tax bill.

While the step-up in basis applies to assets such as stocks, bonds, mutual funds and real estate, it doesn't apply to retirement plans—like 401(k)s and IRAs—or annuities. The person who inherits a retirement plan or annuity will be taxed on appreciation during the previous owner's lifetime just as he or she would have been taxed. Such gains are treated as ordinary income—not capital gains—and taxed in your top tax bracket.

Capital Gains and Losses

IN ADDITION TO TRACKING THE BASIS OF YOUR INVESTMENTS, YOU also have to keep an eye on the calendar so as to figure gains, deduct losses, and avoid the wash-sale trap.

FIGURING GAINS

The law segregates investment profits into two classes: short-term and long-term capital gains. Assets owned one year or less produce short-term gains or losses; those held over 12 months get long-term treatment. The distinction is very important.

The maximum tax rate for long-term capital gains is now 20%. (If you're in the 15% tax bracket, tax on long-term gains is just 10%. If the capital gain itself pushed you from the 15% bracket to the 28% or higher bracket, the amount of the profit that would fall in the 15% bracket gets the 10% rate; the rest is taxed at 20%). Short-term gains are still taxed in your top tax bracket, which can be as high as 39.6%.

Investment real estate doesn't get the full advantage of the 20% rate. Instead, a 25% tax rate applies to profits that result from depreciation deductions. (Because each dollar of depreciation reduces your basis by $1, it adds $1 to your profit when you sell.) The 20% rate also doesn't apply to profit from collectibles, such as stamps, antiques and coins. A top rate of 28% applies to profits from the sale of collectibles owned more than one year.

DEDUCTING LOSSES

If your investments produce a loss, the government will help absorb it—up to a limit. Losses can be used to offset any amount of capital gains each year, but no more than $3,000 of losses beyond that can be deducted against other income, such as your salary. Leftover losses, though, can be carried forward and deducted in future years.

Say that during the year your investments produce $10,000 of capital gains and $14,000 of capital losses. The losses would offset all the gains, so you'd owe no tax on the profits. But only $3,000 of the excess $4,000 in losses could be deducted against other income. In the 28% bracket, that would save you $840 in taxes. The leftover $1,000 loss could carry over to the next year.

The deductibility of capital losses makes your portfolio fertile ground for tax maneuvering, especially at year-end. Although you should not let the tax tail wag the investment dog by allowing tax factors to control buy or hold decisions, neither should you ignore the possibility of converting a paper loss to a real one to offset gains or other income.

Avoiding the Wash-Sale Trap

Say you own stock showing a big paper loss. You expect the shares to recover, but you could use a tax deduction this year. So you sell the stock to take the loss, then buy it right back. Result: You get the tax deduction you sought and you still own the stock.

Pretty clever—provided you waited more than 30 days after the sale before you bought back the shares. Buy them back any sooner and the IRS will deny the tax loss. It considers the deal a wash, because you wind up with the same stock in your portfolio.

You trigger the wash-sale rule if you buy "substantially identical" securities within 30 days—before or after—the sale of securities showing a loss. There's no precise definition of substantially identical, but it definitely covers shares in the same company whose shares you just sold.

With mutual funds you can skirt the wash-sale rules fairly easily by using funds with similar objectives but different portfolios. You could sell a Scudder growth fund at a loss and immediately buy a Twentieth Century growth fund to position yourself for an anticipated market upturn.

Stocks

UNLIKE INTEREST ON SAVINGS, WHICH IS GENERALLY TAXED AS it is earned, profits from stocks are shielded from the IRS until you sell. As a result, you gain important flexibility. Postponing a sale from December to January, for example, allows you to delay reporting the profit by a full year. Accelerating a sale, on the other hand, might allow you to use a loss in a year when it would be most beneficial.

Making the most of this advantage requires keeping careful records so that you can calculate your basis correctly and pinpoint the profit or loss from a potential sale.

As noted earlier, the basis can change while you own an investment. If a company in which you have invested declares a stock split, for example, your basis in each share will drop because your original basis will be spread over both the old and the new shares. Assume you own 100 shares, each with a $40 basis, and the company declares a two-for-one split. That split suddenly makes you the owner of 200 shares. Your original $4,000 investment does not change, however, so your basis in each share drops to $20 ($4,000 ÷ 200). The holding period for the shares you received in the split is the same as that for the original shares. If you have owned the shares for more than 12 months at the time of the split, the new shares immediately qualify for long-term treatment.

When you buy additional shares through a dividend reinvestment plan (see Chapter 4), the basis of those shares is their actual cost to you. If you reinvest $300 in dividends and you get 25 shares, for example, your basis in each share would be $12 ($300 ÷ 25). The holding period for the newly purchased shares begins on the day after they are purchased.

CONTROLLING THE SHARES YOU SELL

Keeping track of the basis sounds like a hassle, but it's essential for successful tax planning. It's particularly important when you buy the stock of the same company at different times and prices. When you decide to sell some of the shares, being able to identify which ones to part with permits you to control the tax consequences of the deal.

Let's say you bought 100 shares of XYZ stock in January 1997 for $2,400, giving you a basis of $24 per share. In January 1998, you purchased 100 more shares, this time for $2,800. Your basis in each share is $28. In January 1999, you purchased another 100 shares for $3,000, giving each share a basis of $30.

When the stock hits $40 a share in May, 2000, you decide to sell 100 shares. If you simply tell your broker to sell 100 shares, the IRS FIFO rule—first in, first out—comes into play. It's assumed that the first shares you purchased—the 1997 group with the $24 basis—are the first ones sold. That would create a long-term taxable profit of $16 a share or $1,600. At the 20% tax rate, that would cost you $320.

Here's a better idea: Tell your broker to sell the shares purchased in 1999, with a $30 basis. The taxable profit will be just $10 a share, or $1,000. The 20% capital gain rate will cost you $200.

In either case you'd get $4,000 from the sale, but your tax bill would be quite different. In most cases, you'll want to structure the sale to produce the smallest taxable profit. It's possible, though, that circumstances will warrant selling the asset with the lowest basis first—if, for example, you have sufficient losses to offset the larger gain. Also be careful to watch the calendar to guarantee preferential long-term-gain treatment if you can.

CONTROLLING THE TAX BITE ON DIVIDENDS

Dividends you receive from stock you own are usually fully taxable. And, odd as it sounds, sometimes you owe tax on dividends you never see. For instance, dividends invested through a dividend reinvestment plan (see Chapter 4) count as taxable income even though you never lay hands on the money. What's more, if the plan allows you to buy shares at a discount from market value, the discount counts as taxable income, too. It is also added to your cost basis for those shares. Thus the basis of the new shares would be what you actually paid for them plus the amount of the discount you had to pay tax on.

When companies pay dividends in shares of stock instead of cash, the value of the stock dividends is generally not taxable that year. Instead, the new shares dilute your basis in the shares. Say you have 100 shares of stock with a basis of $2,500, or $25 a share, and you get a stock dividend of ten shares. The $2,500 basis is then spread over the 110 shares, giving each one a basis of $22.73. The effect is that you'll pay tax on the value of the stock dividend when you sell the shares because you report a higher profit as a result of the reduced basis.

If the company gives you the choice of taking a dividend in stock or in cash, the dividend is taxable in the year you receive it even if you take the shares. The market value of the shares counts as income, but the basis of your original shares stays the same.

From time to time, shareholders receive payments that don't come out of company earnings but are actually a return of part of their original investment. These payments, which will be labeled "capital distributions" by the company, aren't taxable. But they do reduce your basis in the stock, which will increase your profit or reduce your loss when you sell.

Bonds

INVESTING IN BONDS CAN BRING YOU STEADY INCOME AND, IF you're not careful, steady tax headaches. Corporate bonds generally pay interest every six months and it is taxable in the year you receive it. If you buy a bond at face value and hold it to maturity, tax on the interest is all you owe. But as discussed in Chapter 5, you can buy bonds at a premium (more than face value) or at a discount (below face value). Either situation complicates your taxes, particularly when it comes to keeping track of your basis.

BONDS BOUGHT BETWEEN INTEREST PAYMENTS. The price of bonds sold between semiannual interest dates includes the interest accrued since the last payment date. For the seller, that part of the price is interest income and should be reported as such rather than being counted as part of the price of the bond when determining gain or loss on the sale. For the buyer, the "purchased interest" is not part of the basis. Rather, when you receive your first interest payment on the bond, part of it is considered a nontaxable return of part of your investment rather than taxable interest.

Say you purchase a $10,000, 8% bond midway between semiannual $400 interest payments and you pay $10,200 for the bond and the $200 of accrued interest. When you get the first $400 interest payment, half of it is considered return of your investment. (You report the full amount on your tax return, though, then subtract $200 as "accrued interest." If you forget the subtraction, you'll overpay your tax.) Your basis in the bond is $10,000.

DISCOUNTED BONDS. When you buy bonds at a discount from face value, the tax rules that apply depend on the type of discount involved and the date the bond was issued.

Original-issue discount (OID) bonds are, as the name suggests, issued for less than face value. This basically means that part of the interest will be paid when the bond is redeemed for more than its original price, rather than in regular payments over the life of the bond. You have to wait for your money, but the IRS does not want to wait for its share of it. Each year that you own the bond, you have to report as interest income a portion of the original discount amount. (The method you must use to calculate how much to report depends on when the bond was issued, but each year the issuer should send you a 1099-OID form showing the taxable amount.) Good records are critical here. The portion of the original-issue discount you report as income each year increases your basis in the bond. If you fail to keep track, you could wind up paying tax on the same income twice—once as original-issue discount interest and later as part of the profit on the bond.

Market-discount bonds usually sell at a discount because interest rates have risen since they were issued, or because the safety-rating agencies have downgraded the issuing company's rating (see Chapter 5). For bonds issued after July 18, 1984, the difference between the price you pay for a market-discount bond and its redemption value is considered to be interest that will accrue between the time you buy the bond and the time it matures. You can wait until you dispose of the bond via sale or redemption to report that interest income, or you can figure how much interest accrues each year and report it annually. If you opt to report a portion of the market discount annually, your basis in the bond increases by the amount reported as interest income. You're probably better off waiting.

Zero-coupon bonds, as discussed in Chapter 5, pay no interest until maturity. Issuers compensate investors for their patience by issuing zeros at steep discounts from their redemption value. A new 30-year zero with a face value of $10,000 and a yield to maturity of 8%, for example, would sell for about $950 today.

Because a zero-coupon bond is really nothing more than the OID idea carried to its extreme, the OID rules apply. Even though you don't see the money, interest is taxed as it accrues, so each year you must report and pay tax on the interest your investment is assumed to have earned that year. The bond issuer or your broker should send you a notice showing how much to report.

This "imputed" interest hikes your basis in the bonds and, again, it's up to you to keep track. Consider this example: You buy zeros for $7,000 that are called (redeemed early by the issuer) three years later for $8,600. During the intervening years, you report $2,000 of imputed interest. That raises your basis to $9,000, so that even though the bonds are called for $1,600 more than you originally paid, you actually have a $400 loss. (On zero-coupon municipal bonds, accruing interest raises your basis even though the imputed interest is not taxable.)

PREMIUM-PRICED BONDS. When you buy a taxable bond for more than its face value, as you might do to capture above-market rates, the IRS gives you a choice of how to deal with the premium. You can spread it over the life of the bond, offsetting part of the taxable interest income each year. Or you can wait until you sell or redeem the bond to crank the premium into your tax calculations.

(One problem with amortizing the premium is that you have to figure out how much to deduct each year. Exactly how you do that depends on when the bond was issued. Basically, for bonds issued before September 27, 1985, the annual deduction can be determined by dividing the premium by the number of years to maturity. A more complicated method—explained in IRS publication 550, *Investment Income and Expenses*—applies to more recently issued bonds.)

If you do amortize the premium, your basis in the bond decreases by the amount of the deductions you claim. (If you buy a tax-exempt bond at a premium, you must amortize the premium. Amortizing doesn't generate any tax deductions, but it does reduce your basis.)

A simpler alternative to amortizing the premium is to wait until you sell or redeem the bond and report the premium all at once. If you redeem the bond at face value, you can claim a capital loss equal to the size of the premium. Although this route is easier, it might be less valuable if the loss offsets capital gains that otherwise would be taxed at 20%, while the amortization would offset interest income taxed in your top bracket—perhaps as high as 39.6%.

U.S. GOVERNMENT BONDS. When you invest in U.S. government obligations, you get a break compared with corporate bonds: The interest on Treasury bills, notes and bonds is exempt from state and local income taxes. You have to take this benefit into account when comparing yields.

Assume that you live in a state with an 8% state tax rate and can choose between investing $10,000 in a corporate bond yielding 8% or a $10,000 Treasury bond yielding the same. Either investment will generate $800 of interest annually and will cost you $224 in federal taxes if you are in the 28% bracket. On the T-bond, that's all you'd have to pay, leaving you with $576. With the corporate bond, however, your state would want its 8%, or $64. Because the state tax is deductible on your federal return, you get back 28% of that $64, so that the actual extra cost would be $46.08. Still, you'd wind up with just $529.92. The after-tax yield of the Treasury bond works out to 5.76%, compared with 5.3% on the corporate bond.

Treasury bills, which are issued with 13-week, 26-week and 52-week maturities, offer the chance to defer income from one year to the next. The bills are issued at a discount, with the interest paid when they are redeemed at face value. The tax isn't due until the year the bill matures. If you sell a T-bill before maturity, part of the sales price is accrued interest and must be reported as interest income rather than being counted in the capital gain or loss.

The interest on Treasury notes and bonds, which is paid every six months, is taxable in the year you receive it. When T-bonds and notes are purchased at a market discount or premium price, the same basic rules apply as for corporate bonds.

GINNIE MAES. If you invest in bonds guaranteed by the Government National Mortgage Association (GNMA), part of each payment you receive will be totally tax-free. As discussed in Chapter 9, Ginnie Maes represent an investment in a pool of home mortgages. As homeowners make their monthly payments, you get your share of the interest and principal. The principal portion is a return of your investment and is therefore tax-free. You should get a statement showing a breakdown between taxable interest and nontaxable return of principal.

MUNICIPAL BONDS. Municipal bonds are discussed in detail in Chapter 5. These are the investments that enjoy the best of all federal tax rates: 0%. Although you must report municipal-bond interest to the IRS each year, it is almost never taxed. (One exception allows the IRS to tax interest from "private-activity" bonds owned by a taxpayer who is subject to the alternative minimum tax, also described in Chapter 5.)

Although the interest on these bonds is tax-free, the IRS

wants its cut if you sell municipal bonds for a profit: Capital gains are fully taxable. By the same token, if you sell a municipal bond for less than your basis, the loss is deductible.

Cost basis is usually figured the same way as with taxable bonds. However, if you buy a tax-exempt bond at a premium, you must amortize the premium over the period you own the bond. Amortizing gradually shrinks your basis in the bond but you can't deduct the amortized amount, as you can with taxable bonds. If you buy a bond originally issued at a discount—including a zero-coupon municipal—you increase your basis each year by the amount of the interest accruing on the bond, but you don't have to report that amount as income. When you buy a municipal bond at a market discount, however, different rules apply. Your basis doesn't change. When you redeem the bond at face value, the difference between your purchase price and the face value is a taxable capital gain.

BOND SWAPS

Bond swapping is a maneuver that may allow bond investors to generate a tax loss without affecting the income stream from their fixed-income investments. What's involved is selling bonds that have fallen in value—because of rising market interest rates—and reinvesting the proceeds in other bonds. Consider this example:

Assume you own $100,000 face value of AA-rated bonds with a 7% coupon yield, a maturity date in 2016 and a current market value of $84,750. You bought the bonds at par, so selling at the current price would produce a $15,250 capital loss. Suppose, too, that you can buy $100,000 face value of AAA-rated bonds with a 7% coupon and a 2015 maturity, for $83,612.

Consider the result if you decide to sell one set of bonds and buy the other: Since they have the same par value and coupon rate, your annual income remains the same. Your bond rating increases from AA to AAA. You pull $1,138 out of the investment—the difference between what you got for the old bonds and what you paid for the new ones. And you can claim a $15,250 tax loss. If it offsets gains that otherwise would have been taxed at 28%, you save $4,270.

If you have bonds that show a paper loss, your broker should be able to help you find attractive candidates for swapping that won't run afoul of the wash-sale rule that were discussed earlier in the chapter.

Taxes and Your Mutual Funds

T HE PROFESSIONAL MANAGEMENT YOU GET WHEN YOU INVEST in mutual funds handles some of the tax work for you. The fund worries about the fluctuating basis of the stocks or bonds it owns. That spares you the hassle of amortizing bond premiums, for example, or of adjusting your basis to account for stock splits. But funds don't spare you all the tax-related work.

Except for money-market funds, the price of mutual fund shares fluctuates just as the price of individual stocks and bonds does. When you redeem shares, you need to know your tax basis in order to calculate your taxable gain or loss. You also need to know how long you've owned the shares to know whether you have long- or short-term gains or losses.

To protect yourself from overpaying your taxes on fund income, set up a separate file for each fund you own and faithfully keep it up to date.

Your basis in shares begins as what you pay for them. When you invest in a no-load fund, your basis is the share's net asset value on the day you buy. If you buy into a load fund, include the commission in your basis.

HANDLING UNDISTRIBUTED CAPITAL GAINS

From time to time, funds declare capital gains but retain the profits and pay tax on them rather than distributing the profit to shareholders. Such undistributed capital gains increase your basis in the shares. Even though you don't get a dime, you have to report the gain as income. You also get to claim a credit for the amount of tax paid by the fund on your behalf. Finally, you raise your basis in the shares by the difference between the undistributed gain and the credit you claim. If all this sounds like a lot of trouble for nothing, take comfort in the fact that claiming the tax credit cuts your tax bill now, and raising the basis reduces your tax bill when you sell.

HANDLING NONTAXABLE DISTRIBUTIONS

Funds occasionally make a payment that doesn't come out of earnings or profits. Such "return of capital" distributions are sometimes called tax-free dividends or nontaxable distributions, but they do reduce your basis in the shares, thus increasing the gain or diminishing the loss when you sell.

KEEPING TRACK OF REINVESTED DIVIDENDS

Mutual fund investments demand especially careful attention because you will probably be buying shares at different times and at different prices. If you have your dividends reinvested in additional shares, you'll be buying new shares monthly or however often the fund distributes income. Your basis in the new shares is their cost at the time of purchase. Thus, if $72.75 in dividends buys you 5.89 shares, for example, the basis of each share is $12.35 ($72.75 ÷ 5.89).

It's important to keep careful track of all this. If you don't, here's the potential threat: Say you invest $5,000 in a fund and each year have $500 of dividends reinvested in additional shares. After five years, you redeem all your shares for $10,000. What's your gain? An investor who simply compared the redemption amount with the original investment would pay twice as much tax as necessary. Because the $2,500 of reinvested dividends raised your basis by that amount, the gain is just $2,500, not $5,000.

HANDLING PARTIAL SALES

Good record-keeping habits really pay off when you sell only part of your fund holdings. In deciding which shares to sell, you can pick the ones that will produce the best tax result.

Redeeming shares with the highest basis will produce the lowest taxable gain. But since your shares are pooled in a single account by the mutual fund, who knows which ones got sold? You do, if you've kept good records. If you direct the fund to sell specific shares, the basis of those shares determines the tax consequences of the sale. (Keep records of your sale order, including a copy of a letter to the fund identifying the shares to be sold by the date of purchase and price paid, and a copy of the fund's confirmation of the sale. If you order the sale by phone, keep a copy of a letter to the fund confirming your instructions.)

If you just tell the fund to sell a certain number of shares without specifying which ones, the FIFO rule will govern which ones those are. FIFO assumes that the first shares you bought are the first ones sold. If the shares have been appreciating gradually, that ensures that those with the lowest basis are assumed to be sold—and that leaves you with the highest taxable profit.

If you prefer, you can use the average basis method for figuring gain or loss on the sale of your shares. There are actually two average basis methods: single- and double-category. With the former, you find the total basis of all the shares you own of a fund, then divide it by the number of shares and arrive at the average basis. The double-category method is similar, but you divide the shares according to whether you have owned them long term (more than one year) or short term (one year or less). To use the short-term average basis, you must have written confirmation that you advised the fund at the time of the trade that you were redeeming shares from the short-term group. Otherwise you use the long-term average basis.

The specific-identification method gives you the most flexibility but if you normally use the FIFO method, you should check whether the average-basis method can work to your benefit. However, once you start using average basis, you must use it for all future redemptions from the fund.

SWITCHING FUNDS

Switching from one fund to another, even within the same family, creates what the tax people like to call a "taxable event." To switch, you must sell the shares in the fund you're leaving. Unless you're moving out of a money-market fund, the switch is likely to produce a taxable capital gain or a deductible loss.

ACCOUNTING FOR ANNUAL FUND INCOME

Knowing how the IRS treats fund income can save you both trouble and money.

INCOME FROM MONEY-MARKET AND TAXABLE BOND FUNDS is considered dividend income for tax purposes, even though the source of the income is interest. If you accidentally report such income as interest, you'll probably hear from the IRS, which has been told by the fund that it paid you dividends.

INTEREST FROM A TAX-FREE MUNICIPAL BOND FUND escapes federal income tax. It may or may not be taxed by your state. Most states spare interest on bonds issued within the state's borders. The fund statement should show what percentage of the income you received was attributed to homegrown issues. That statement should also alert you if the fund owned any so-called private-activity bonds that might be subject to the alternative minimum tax.

INCOME FROM A FUND THAT INVESTS IN U.S. GOVERNMENT SECURITIES may escape some state tax. The interest would be free of state tax if you owned the obligations directly, and most states allow it to retain its tax-free status when it comes from a fund. Check with your state tax department.

ORDINARY DIVIDENDS are taxable in the year paid, whether you take them in cash or have them reinvested in new shares. Knowing when a stock fund declares dividends—its ex-dividend date—is important. When the dividend is declared, the share value drops by about the same amount. If you invest in the fund just before the ex-dividend date, the dividend you get amounts to a refund of part of your purchase price. But you'll also owe taxes on it. Better to buy after the ex-dividend date. The price of the shares will be lower by the amount of the dividend, and you won't owe taxes on the dividend.

CAPITAL-GAINS DISTRIBUTIONS—your share of long-term profits from portfolio trades during the year—are considered long-term gains regardless of how long you have owned the fund. Investors in tax-free bond funds are sometimes confused by capital-gains distributions. Such payouts are taxable because they represent your share of the profits realized when bonds within the portfolio were sold.

IF YOU OWN SHARES IN A FUND HOLDING FOREIGN SECURITIES, you may be in line for a foreign tax credit. Your year-end statement from the fund will show the amount of foreign tax paid on your behalf. You must include that amount in your taxable income for the year, but you can either write it off as an itemized deduction or claim a foreign tax credit. The credit is almost always the better deal.

Life Insurance and Annuities

CASH-VALUE LIFE INSURANCE, INCLUDING WHOLE-LIFE AND universal-life policies, is often promoted more as an investment than as insurance. Sometimes a very substantial part of the premiums is used by the company to pay not for insurance but for investments that build cash value. Policyowners may be able to invest their cash value in a choice of stock and bond mutual funds and other investments. The key tax break is that earnings within the policy are allowed to grow tax-free. Taxes aren't due until you cash in the policy, and you owe taxes only on the amount by which the cash value exceeds your premiums.

Annuities are another insurance product with tax advantages. When you invest in an annuity, the contract serves as an impenetrable wrapper that keeps the tax collector's hands off your earnings. No tax is due until you withdraw your funds, presumably in retirement. In exchange for that tax break, you agree to leave your money invested until you reach age 59½. Pull the money out early and the earnings are not only taxed but also subject to a 10% penalty. The penalty doesn't apply to taxpayers who are disabled, nor to any payment that is part of a series of periodic payments based on your life expectancy.

The penalty is designed to dissuade investors from trying to use annuities as short-term tax shelters. If you are at least 59½, you don't have to worry about the tax penalty. Note, though, that insurance companies generally apply stiff penalties of their own if annuity buyers withdraw funds during the early years of a contract. See Chapter 14 for more on annuities.

Deductible Investment Expenses

IF YOU BORROW MONEY TO MAKE AN INVESTMENT, THE INTEREST on the loan is usually deductible if the purpose of the investment is to generate taxable income. But if you borrow in order to invest in tax-free bonds, the interest is not deductible. Nor do you get the deduction if you borrow to buy a single-premium life insurance policy or an annuity. The gov-

Combining Rollover Accounts

Q: *Later this year, my company's pension plan and 401(k) plan will be terminated. Because I will not yet be 59½, I plan to roll the funds over into an IRA. Can I put both payouts into a single IRA?*

A: Yes, you can combine your payouts and roll them over into a single IRA within 60 days of termination, as long as all your contributions were made from pretax earnings. If you made any after-tax contributions, they cannot be rolled over. But because you've already paid taxes on them, you can invest or spend that amount however you like. Be careful to have the company make any rollovers directly to the IRA sponsor. If you take receipt of the money, the IRS will want 20% withheld for income taxes—even if you won't owe tax thanks to the rollover.

ernment does not want to subsidize loans used to purchase tax shelters. Interest on money borrowed to invest in a passive investment activity, such as a real estate limited partnership, is an expense of the passive activity and therefore deductible only to the extent of passive income.

The deduction for investment interest you pay is limited to the amount of investment income you report. If your investment income for the year is $5,000, your investment interest deduction cannot exceed that amount. For this test, investment income includes interest and dividends but not capital gains. Any interest you are unable to deduct because of the cap can be carried forward to future years and deducted when you have sufficient investment income.

Other expenses of investing that may be tax-deductible in whole or in part include the following:

Rental fees for a safe-deposit box used to store taxable securities.

Investment counseling or management fees.

Subscriptions to investment-advisory newsletters.

Cost of books (including this one) and magazines purchased for investment advice.

State and local transfer taxes on the sale of securities.

Fees paid to a broker or other agent to collect bond interest or stock dividends. (Commissions paid to brokers when you purchase stock aren't deductible. They are added to the basis of the shares.)

Cost of travel to see your broker to discuss investments. If you drive your own car, deduct the actual cost or the IRS standard rate, which was 32.5 cents per mile for the first three months of 1999 and 31 cents a mile from April 1 on. In either case, you can add in what you pay for parking or tolls.

Although all of the above expenses are deductible, it's not easy to get a tax benefit from any of them. All have been branded as "miscellaneous" expenses, and you can deduct them only to the extent that all of your miscellaneous expenses exceed 2% of your adjusted gross income (that is, your gross income after "adjustments," such as IRA contributions, but before itemized deductions). If your AGI is $50,000, for example, the first $1,000 of your miscellaneous expenses don't count.

PART THREE

Achieve Your Financial Goals

College: Investing for Your Child

A T THE BEGINNING OF ANY DISCUSSION OF COLLEGE costs and ways to meet them, it is obligatory to recite the figures. In this way parents can grasp the breathtaking magnitude of the task confronting them. Ready?

The average cost of four years of tuition, room and board, books, travel and so forth at a private college or university now tops $90,000. Reasonable assumptions about the pace of future increases would put that price tag at about $118,000 in five years, $151,000 in ten years and $193,000 in 15 years. The picture is less depressing at public colleges, where the tab is running at somewhat less than half those levels. The figures assume a 5% annual increase in college costs.

There are indications that the college cost escalator may be slowing down as we make the turn into the 21st century. Still, the idea of saving and investing enough money to handle bills anything like that puts many parents into a deep funk. But you probably won't have to come up with all of it—in fact, the vast majority of parents don't. A survey by the U.S. Department of Education found that parents pay the full cost less than 10% of the time. Most students' college bills are paid from a combination of sources that includes students' own savings and earnings, plus financial aid. It would be unwise to expect financial aid to bail you out, however. The bigger your income and other assets, the smaller your chances of qualifying for college aid programs, most of which are based on need.

If you can save half the cost of college, you can probably cover the rest through home-equity or other loans and your son's or daughter's savings from working during the high school and college years. Still, even half the cost is a very big number, and the sooner you start accumulating it the better. You can draw on many of the investment products and techniques described in this book. This chapter will suggest ways to construct a college savings plan that takes advantage of a number of options that have been created with college in mind, or that fit especially well into a college savings and investment program. In addition, certain tax breaks discussed later in this chapter will help alleviate this burden.

If your child's freshman year is close at hand, you should try to minimize the risks in your plan by sticking mostly with money-market funds and certificates of deposit timed to mature when the bills fall due. If you have three or four years to go, short-term bond mutual funds and conservative growth-and-income funds can be used to jack up the return without increasing the risk very much. If college is more than five years away, your choices are wider. In addition to portfolios of stocks and bonds and mutual funds that you assemble yourself, you can find plenty of customized college savings plans offered by banks, brokerages and mutual funds. Keep in mind that the word "college" on the label doesn't necessarily make a plan superior for the purpose. To have the best chance to succeed, your plan should have these characteristics:

IT SHOULD BE EASY AND ECONOMICAL TO CONTRIBUTE TO REGULARLY. Mutual funds with high front-end loads and high minimum investments would not be suitable for a college savings plan, nor would real estate (except home-equity buildup, which you can draw on for loans with tax-deductible interest). No-load mutual funds and savings bonds would be more appropriate.

IT SHOULD INCLUDE A BALANCED MIX OF LONG- AND SHORT-TERM INVESTMENTS. This is a commonsense rule for all investment plans because it acknowledges that the interplay of stock-market prices and interest rates makes some financial markets a better place to be than others at any given time. Having a variety of time horizons in your plan helps to smooth out the ups and downs and minimize the risks.

IT SHOULD BE AIMED AT A SPECIFIC GOAL. You don't know exactly how much college is going to cost, but the numbers just recited give you a pretty good idea. Pick a goal—$25,000? $50,000?—and a time frame—ten years? 15 years? Choice of a specific goal and time lets you make reasonable estimates of how much you need to put aside each month to achieve the goal, based on assumptions about investment return.

You can use the tables in the Appendix for this purpose. They show how fast different levels of regular contributions will grow at various rates of return. They can also provide a useful reality check for your expectations.

Say your child is ten years away from freshman year. You can set aside $100 a month. How much would you have to earn on the money to have $50,000 in ten years? Take a peek and you'll see that the earnings would be off the chart. If fact, you'd have to earn better than 16% per year—a possibility, but not a probability—and a return that high would require taking large risks. To reach your goal, you must step up your contributions. Doubling them to $200 a month would cut the necessary return to about 9%. If you invested $150 a month, you'd need to earn about 12.6% to reach your goal.

The time you have left before the college bills start to arrive and the amount of money you can regularly set aside should influence the investment choices you make. If you have ten years or more to raise the money, you can afford to take more risks than if college is only a few years away. At some point you may conclude that you can't possibly accumulate enough money to pay all the bills for college while funding your retirement plan and tending to other investment goals at the same time. In fact, most people can't do it, and that is why scholarships, loans and grants play such an important part in the college plans of many families.

But don't throw in the towel yet. One or more of the plans described on the following pages may make the difference.

Savings Bonds for College

U.S. SAVINGS BONDS ARE ABOUT AS SAFE AND CONVENIENT AS investments come. As described in Chapter 5, all savings-bond interest is exempt from state and local income taxes, and you can defer the federal tax on the earnings until you cash the bonds in, creating a tax-sheltered plan that's hard to beat. Interest rates are competitive: Bonds have earned 4% to 6% in recent years as rates have floated up and down with the market.

When used for college savings, bonds have a special kicker: Interest on series EE bonds redeemed to pay college tuition and fees for your children can escape federal income tax entirely if you meet certain tests. (Bonds purchased before 1990 don't qualify.)

The rules are actually fairly simple. The bonds must be purchased in the parent's name, not the child's. You must buy them after your 24th birthday or your spouse's 24th birthday and redeem them in the year you pay qualifying tuition and fees for the child attending a college, university, technical institute or vocational school. It's not a requirement that the child be born yet when you purchase the bonds, just that you pay your child's qualifying expenses in the year the bonds are redeemed.

The tax break gets phased out starting at adjusted gross incomes above about $79,650 on a joint return; it disappears at about $109,650. The take-back is in proportion to the amount your income exceeds the low end of the range. A couple making, say, $94,650 is halfway between the low and high ends and thus could escape taxes on about half the interest. For a single parent, the tax saving is phased out starting at about $53,100, and disappears entirely at about $68,100.

Those were the income ceilings in effect in 1999. They're indexed to inflation, so for a medium- or long-term savings plan, current levels aren't very meaningful. Assuming a 4% annual inflation rate, in 18 years—when today's newborn heads to college—the phaseout range on joint returns would begin at more than $161,000. That makes EE bonds an attractive college savings plan even for parents with very high incomes.

You don't have to keep burdensome records to prove your eligibility for the tax forgiveness when the time comes. But you should keep those earmarked bonds separate from others you might own. Record the serial numbers, face amounts, and issue and redemption dates. When you redeem the bonds, record the total proceeds—interest and principal—along with the name of the institution to which you paid tuition and fees (room and board doesn't count). If your bond interest exceeds the qualifying expenses, you escape taxes on the portion of the interest accounted for by the expenses.

You can buy savings bonds with no sales fees at most financial institutions, such as banks, or through your employer, with no transaction cost, in face-value denominations of $50, $75, $100, $200, $500, $1,000, $5,000 and $10,000. (The $50 and $75 denominations aren't available through payroll savings plans.) You pay half the bond's face amount and can figure to collect the face value within 17 years at the most, although maturity will probably occur sooner, depending on interest rates along the way. You continue to earn interest for 30 years. For more details, see Chapter 5.

Zero-Coupon Bonds

ZERO-COUPON BONDS ARE SO NAMED BECAUSE PAY NO INTEREST at all until maturity, although you do owe tax on the "imputed" interest year by year.

Zeros are described in detail in Chapter 5. As a college savings tool, zeros can be employed to best advantage in a long-range plan, although they can be useful in the relatively short range as well. Zeros sell at a discount from face value; the further away from maturity, the steeper the discount. A $1,000 zero yielding 6% and maturing in five years would sell for $740. A bond with the same denomination earning the same rate and maturing in ten years would cost $550. With a maturity of 18 years, the bond costs just $340.

If parents—or grandparents, uncles or aunts—socked a total of about $13,000 worth of such bonds into a newborn's account, it would grow to $38,000 by the time the college bills started to arrive. Along the way, the market value of the zeros will be more volatile than that of conventional bonds, but by buying zeros that mature during your child's college years, you can safely ignore their ups and downs in the meantime.

TAX ANGLES

Zeros don't pay interest each year, but the Internal Revenue Service insists that you act as if they do. As the interest accrues, it must be reported to the IRS, and the person receiving the interest owes tax on it. The situation gets muddled by what's called the "kiddie tax," which forces children under age 14 to pay tax on this kind of income above a certain amount at their parent's tax rate.

Properly handled, though, much of the income can be tax-free or be taxed in the child's low bracket. To hold the tax bill to the minimum, buy zero-coupon bonds in the child's name so that the income will be taxable to the child. Your broker can set up a free or low-cost custodial account.

The first $700 of investment income received by a child is tax-free. (That's the tax-free level in 1999 and 2000. The amount is indexed to inflation and could rise as the years go by.) For children under age 14, the next $700 is taxed at his or her own rate, probably 15%, and investment income in excess of $1,400 is taxed at the parent's rate—probably 28% or 31%.

The way the IRS says zero-coupon bond interest must be reported works to your advantage. Take a 6.5% zero that grows for 18 years from $322 to about $1,000. You don't simply report one-eighteenth of the difference, $38, each year. Instead you report interest as it actually accrues. The first year, a $322 investment earning 6.5% compounded semiannually earns about $21. The second year, your principal would be $343 ($322 + $21), and $23 of interest would accrue. The third year you'd earn $25, and so forth. (You'll get a notice each year from the issuer or your broker showing how much interest to report.)

Because the interest builds up much more quickly as the bonds near maturity—and after the child is 14—most of the interest earned on the bonds dodges the kiddie tax.

What if you invested $19,320 to buy 60 of those bonds for your child, so that you'd have $60,000 when they matured in 18 years? Here's the tax status of the roughly $40,680 of interest that accrues over the years, assuming the child has no other investment income, and allowing for no increase in the $700 per year tax-free allowance:

Tax-free: $12,600 ($700 a year).

Taxed at child's rate: $21,111 ($700 or less for each of the child's first 13 years; all of the income after the child turns 14).

Taxed at parents' rate: $6,969 (interest in excess of $1,400 for each of the child's first 13 years; none after that).

You can see that paying the tax as you go isn't so bad when financing college with zeros bought in a child's name. The first $700 of interest income each year is tax-free to the child, assuming that he or she doesn't have other investment income. By reporting the interest each year, you get to use that break 18 times; if the interest were reported all at once, you'd enjoy it only once, and it would stop at $700.

TREASURY ZEROS

For safety of principal while you're waiting for the bonds to mature, stick to zeros issued by the U.S. Treasury.

Issued in face values of $1,000, Treasuries are exempt from state and local taxes. They can always be counted on to pay a little more than savings bonds. However, Treasury zeros—called stripped Treasuries—aren't so convenient to buy in small lots, and whether your broker will be willing to take the trouble to hunt them down for an accumulation plan will depend on your relationship with the broker. You cannot buy zeros directly from the Treasury. Besides a broker, your only alternative is a zero-coupon mutual fund.

The biggest such fund is American Century Target Maturities Trust, formerly known as the Benham Target Maturity Trust (800-472-3389; www.americancentury.com), which offers Treasury zeros maturing every five years through 2020. American Century Target Maturities Trust does not charge a sales fee, requires small minimum investments ($1,000 initially for custodial accounts, $2,500 for regular accounts) and has an accumulation plan that allows you to purchase shares automatically each month via a bank draft ($50 minimum purchase).

TAX-FREE ZEROS

Interest from zero-coupon municipal bonds is free of federal tax and usually escapes income taxes in the states where they are issued. One problem with such bonds is their relative scarcity, a situation that has abated to a degree in recent years but still exists. Many municipal issues can be called, or redeemed, before maturity by the issuer if rates go down.

You buy muni zeros through a broker, at discounts to face

amounts of $1,000 and $5,000. To minimize risk, limit your choice of zero-coupon munis to those rated AAA or AA. It's not always easy to find such bonds that mature when you want them to, especially from your home state.

State College Savings Plans

W HAT COULD BE MORE APPEALING THAN THE CHANCE TO PAY tuition at today's rates in exchange for a guarantee that your child's actual tuition, no matter how far off or how large, will be covered by the government of your state? Such guaranteed-tuition plans are now offered in 34 states. Although it is widely believed that state-sponsored plans restrict your choices to in-state public schools, most allow you to take your savings to any accredited institution in the U.S., private or public, without penalty.

If your child decides to skip college, you're hit with a penalty, often 10% or 15% of your accumulated earnings or 1% of the account balance. The harshest penalties are levied by Alabama and Florida, which return only your contributions, with *no* earnings. But even if your child decides not to go to college, you may avoid the penalty by transferring the account to another family member or by deferring use of the money in case the beneficiary attends college up to ten years later.

The main drawback to prepayment plans is that they are treated more severely than one's personal savings and investments under federal financial aid formulas. Prepaid plans are considered a "resource" that reduces a family's aid eligibility dollar for dollar. Savings and investments are treated as a parental asset, of which only 5.6% is considered to cover college costs each year.

There is also the tax bill to pay. Even though parents need not pay taxes on imputed interest while the tuition money is accumulating, taxes are due—at the student's tax rate—on the difference between the original investment and its end value when you withdraw the money.

The plans vary widely, so it is important to check the return on investment, choice of in- or out-of-state college, fees, and rules regarding contributions. For example, if you miss your scheduled payments, some plans may cancel your account and return your money, minus a penalty.

For descriptions of various state plans check Kiplinger's Web site at www.kiplinger.com (click on "Personal Finances"). For links to state sites, go to the College Savings Plan Network site at www.collegesavings.org.

Life Insurance as College Savings

SHOULD YOU USE A FORM OF PERMANENT LIFE INSURANCE AS A college savings vehicle? One possible advantage is that earnings in such policies build up tax-deferred. But it's hard to assess how much college money a policy will provide in comparison with other savings alternatives. Commissions hold down your returns the first several years. Perhaps the biggest advantages of life insurance are that it forces you to save regularly and that the policy proceeds will cover your child's college costs if you die.

Variable universal life is probably your best bet if you do buy life insurance as a long-term savings vehicle. VUL policies, as they are known, allow you to invest the "savings" portion of your premium in a variety of mutual fund accounts, including stock funds. Other forms of cash-value insurance—whole life and universal—essentially invest your money in bonds and similar investments, so there isn't the potential for high returns.

Variable universal life insurance is worth considering for college savings if you need the insurance and if your time horizon is long enough to allow you to amortize the commission costs of the policy and average out the ups and downs of the investment markets. This means that an insurance-based college savings or investment plan makes most sense if your future college student hasn't yet celebrated his or her tenth birthday.

Two Plans for Putting It All Together

EACH OF THE FOLLOWING SUGGESTED COLLEGE SAVINGS PLANS is relatively simple and straightforward, and each sets an ambitious goal: accumulating the future cost of college for an infant. Paying the estimated $223,027 four-year price will require a nest egg of about $207,000 by the start of freshman year.

Both plans start when baby is born and assume 18 years until the first year of college. The first plan, a mix of stock and bond-oriented mutual funds, assumes steady contributions of $310 a month. The second plan relies on savings bonds, CDs and money-market mutual funds. The safety and tax advantages (for savings bonds) of these investments provide their appeal, but the trade-off is a lower rate of return. For that plan, monthly contributions are $600.

Most likely your child isn't an infant, but that doesn't mean you can't use either of these plans. In both, the critical juncture is age 13, when college is five years away. In Plan One, that's the time to throttle back on risk and start preserving gains via bonds and money-market funds. In Plan Two, age 13 is critical because savings bonds need to be held for at least five years in order to qualify for the floating maximum interest rates.

Thus, in both a risk-oriented portfolio and a safety-oriented portfolio—whether they are the ones suggested here or others of your own choosing—five years from the freshman year is the critical juncture for assessing where you are and how your plan is doing. If it's lagging, you have two choices: You can step up your contribution or you can take bigger risks in hopes of a bigger payoff. The closer you get to the freshman year, the less sense it makes to choose the second option.

PLAN ONE: MUTUAL FUNDS

With 18 years to go, you can afford to take some risks. Look for funds with good long-term records (ten-year average annual total return of 12% to 15% or better), no up-front sales fees, plus low minimum and subsequent investment requirements. Some suggestions (not recommendations) to get you started:

Fasciano Fund (800-848-6050; www.fascianofunds.com; $1,000 minimum)

Fidelity Fund (800-544-8888; www.fidelity.com; $2,500 minimum for a custodial account)

Montag & Caldwell Growth (800-992-8151; www.alleghanyfunds.com;

$500 minimum deposit for regular custodial accounts, $50 minimum initial deposit if you will make subsequent automatic deposits)

Tweedy Browne Global Value (800-432-4789; www.tweedy.com; $2,500 minimum for custodial accounts)

Rather than anticipate that your funds will return 15%, count on something more modest—say, 11%. You improve your odds by opening accounts with two or more funds for from $1,000 to $2,500 (depending on the funds' minimum requirements) rather than putting all your chips in one. Each month thereafter, put $145 into additional shares in each fund. At an 11% compounded rate of return, your holdings will total more than $100,000 when your child is in the eighth grade at age 13. (Your after-tax return will depend on your bracket and on the pattern of the earnings over the years. For simplicity, these examples ignore taxes. You won't be able to do that.)

With five years to go before college, start hedging your risks. At some point when the stock market is tending to head up rather than down, sell your shares in the equity funds and purchase shares in two well-run, no-load bond funds. From these, expect an annual total return of 8%. Keep sending $145 a month to each fund for more shares. Suggested funds (you can find more using the resources listed in Chapter 6):

Babson Value (800-782-6620; www.jbfunds.com; $1,000 minimum)

Harbor Bond (800-422-1050; $500 minimum for custodial accounts)

T. Rowe Price Dividend Growth (800-638-5660; www.troweprice.com; $500 minimum for custodial accounts)

Royce Premier (800-221-4268; www.roycefunds.com; $2,000 minimum initial investment, $500 initially if followed by automatic deposits)

When your child turns 18, if you have averaged 11% a year you should have more than $193,000. Now sell the bond-fund shares and consolidate the proceeds in a money-market fund or CDs earning at least 5%. The $193,000, earning money-market

Minors and Money Markets

Q: *My grandson is 18 years old. He wanted to invest in a money-market mutual fund, but he was told that he had to be 21 years old or have a guardian. What gives?*
A: Actually, your grandson is old enough to invest in a mutual fund, unless he lives in Alabama, Nebraska or Wyoming, where the age of majority is 19. (The age is 18 in the other 47 states and the District of Columbia.) It is illegal for minors to trade securities such as stocks, bonds or mutual fund shares, including money-market funds. Instead, parents can authorize purchases of shares for their children and hold them in a custodial account under the Uniform Gifts to Minors Act or the Uniform Transfers to Minors Act. For a minor who wants to invest his or her own money, there are more-complicated options, such as a limited guardianship or a revocable trust, that require the minor to give control of the money to an adult.

interest rates, should get you to graduation day.

As mentioned, earnings are taxed all along. But the tax bill starts low, and because you're investing a fixed sum over a span of years in which your earning power can reasonably be expected to grow, the increases in your income can go toward satisfying the tax bill. If the taxes and the risks in this plan worry you, the next plan may be more to your liking.

PLAN TWO: FIXED-INCOME INVESTMENTS

Start by investing $1,000 in EE bonds, CDs, Treasury bond funds, or money-market mutual funds. Invest another $300 each month and increase that amount by $50 each year of the plan. By year 13, you will be putting in $900 a month, and assuming an average interest rate of 5%, you will have built a nest egg of more than $122,000. Because you'll earn only short-term rates on EE bonds redeemed within five years of purchase (see Chapter 5), stop buying bonds when your child is 13, but don't redeem any for another five years.

Instead, pick one of the other investments and direct your monthly savings that way. Assuming you average at least 5% over the 18 years, your college fund will hold about $193,000.

The key to minimizing taxes in a plan such as this is knowing the rules, as explained earlier in this chapter.

Should You Save in the Child's Name?

PUTTING YOUR COLLEGE SAVINGS IN A CHILD'S NAME CAN SAVE on taxes as the years go by, but there are some potential drawbacks.

CUSTODIAL ACCOUNTS

Income generated by a so-called custodial account set up under the Uniform Transfers to Minors Act (or the Uniform Gifts to Minors Act in some states) is tax-free up to $700 a year, an amount that is indexed to inflation and thus will increase over the years. The next $700 is taxed at the child's rate, probably 15%. Anything above that is taxed at your rate until the child reaches age 14. You and your spouse can put up to $10,000 each into such an account without triggering any gift or estate taxes. These trusts are easy to set up. You can get a standard form from your bank or broker, and you'll pay no legal fees.

At 8% interest, characteristic of a good bond mutual fund, an account containing $13,500 would generate $1,080 in the first year, only $3,800 of which would be taxable to the child, assuming he or she had no other income. If the account were in your name, you'd owe tax on the entire amount. If you're in the 28% bracket and the child is in the 15% bracket, that's the difference between a tax bill of $57 and one of more than $300. Because of compounding within the account, the tax difference wouldn't stay the same over the years, but you can see that the savings can be substantial. But before you rush off to set up such an account, note the following:

ASSETS IN THE CHILD'S NAME COULD HURT YOUR CHANCES FOR FINANCIAL AID. The standard methodology used by colleges counts 35% of the child's assets as available to pay for college, but only 5.65% of parents' assets. Thus, $10,000 in the child's name will count as $3,500; the same amount in the parents' name would count as only about $560.

YOU HAVE NO ACCESS TO THE MONEY. If you need the money in a custodial account before your child turns 18 (or 21, depending on state law), you may be able to borrow from the account, but only if the money is used for the child's benefit.

YOU HAVE NO CONTROL OVER HOW THE MONEY IS USED. Once your child reaches the age of majority, he or she can use the money for anything. It doesn't have to be used for college.

TRUSTS

If you have at least $50,000 to put in a child's name, it could be worth the administrative costs to set up a minor's trust, called a 2503(c), or a similar kind of trust called a Crummey Trust.

You'll have to pay legal fees of several hundred dollars and file an annual tax return, but the first several thousand dollars of income earned by a properly established trust of this type is taxed at only 15%, even if the child is under 14. In a minor's trust, your child must have access to the assets at 18 or 21, when the trust terminates. A Crummey Trust can last beyond 21 but allows your child to withdraw contributions in the year that they're made. Consult a lawyer if you're interested in setting up something like that.

College Savings Help From the Feds

THE TAX LAW GIVES SOME VALUABLE RELIEF TO PARENTS OF college-age kids through two tax credits, the Education IRA, and other incentives.

THE HOPE CREDIT

The Hope scholarship credit is the more valuable of the two college credits. It's worth 100% of the first $1,000 paid for tuition and fees and 50% of the next $1,000. Unless your child goes to a very inexpensive school or gets a ton of scholarship money, you'll get the full $1,500 credit. You can claim Hope credits for each child who qualifies, but only for the freshman and sophomore years. So, if you have triplets attending college, you'll get three credits of $1,500 each for both their freshman and sophomore years, saving you a total of $9,000!

THE LIFETIME LEARNING CREDIT

For additional schooling for your children—or for yourself or your spouse—you can call on the "lifetime learning credit." It's worth 20% of the first $5,000 of college costs, for a maximum credit of $1,000. (When adding up qualifying costs for either credit, count tuition and fees but do not include room and board.) Unfortunately for those triplets, you can claim only one lifetime learning credit each year, regardless of how many qualifying students you're supporting.

PHASEOUT ZONES

The Hope and the lifetime learning credits begin to disappear as adjusted gross income rises between $40,000 and $50,000 on an individual return and between $80,000 and $100,000 on a joint return. If you otherwise qualify for a Hope credit for one student and a lifetime learning credit for another—totaling $2,500—but your AGI is $90,000 on a joint return (halfway through the phase-out zone) your credits would be limited to $1,250 (half the full amount).

Note this: Since academic years cross over two tax years, careful timing of tuition payments can ensure that you earn five credits for the four years your son or daughter is in college—or six credits if, as is true of so many students these days, it takes your child five years to get his or her degree.

THE EDUCATION IRA

In another move to encourage taxpayers to send their kids to college, Congress also created a kind of individual retirement account (IRA) that has nothing whatsoever to do with retirement. It also has so many restrictions that it may be more trouble than it is worth. The education IRA allows you to set aside up to $500 a year for a child's education. There's no deduction for the contribution, but money in the account grows tax-deferred, and withdrawals are tax-free if used to pay college bills. Anyone whose AGI is under $150,000 on a joint return or $95,000 on an individual return can use this education IRA. But you can set aside no more than $500 a year per child. Also, you are prohibited from funding an educational IRA in the same year that you contribute to a state-sponsored prepaid tuition program (see the discussion earlier in this chapter). Another twist: Parents are forbidden to claim a Hope or a lifetime learning credit for a child in the same year that tax-free money comes out of an education IRA to pay college bills for that child.

IRA WITHDRAWALS

The law also allows penalty-free withdrawals from regular IRAs to pay college bills for yourself, your spouse, your children or your grandchildren. But don't get too excited. Although Congress will waive the 10% penalty on education funds pulled out of an IRA before age 59½, you'll still owe tax on the withdrawal.

You should definitely consider a Roth IRA for college savings. You can contribute up to $2,000 a year. Contributions aren't tax-deductible, but once the account has been open for five years and you are 59½ or older, you can withdraw as much as you want, tax- and penalty- free. Younger parents can withdraw IRA *contributions* tax- and penalty-free for college expenses (or any other purpose), and leave the *earnings* in the account until retirement. If they dip into earnings early, that amount will be taxed. At any age, if one withdraws the money to use for college bills, there will be no penalty for early withdrawal.

STUDENT LOANS

If your adjusted gross income is below $40,000 on an individual return or under $60,000 on a joint return, you can deduct up to $1,500 of interest paid on student loans in 1999, even if you don't itemize deductions. The limit will rise to $2,500 a year in 2001. The right to this break disappears between $40,000 and $55,000 of income on individual returns, and between $60,000 and $75,000 on joint returns. You take this deduction as an adjustment to income, not as an itemized deduction, and it's available only for interest paid in the first 60 months after repayment begins.

EDUCATIONAL BENEFITS

As an employee, you can receive up to $5,250 of educational benefits from your employer as a tax-free fringe benefit, through May 2000, but only for undergraduate classes.

Retirement: Investing for Yourself, for Your Future

HE DREAM OF A SECURE AND COMFORTABLE RETIRE-
ment is the motivating force behind many invest-
ment plans—maybe even most of them. The
politicians in Congress know this very well, and
over the years have showered retirement-minded savers with
valuable tax shelters in which to store their dollars: individual
retirement accounts, Keogh plans, 401(k) plans and more. Wall
Street has responded with a vast collection of investment packages tailor-made to fit into those shelters. As a result, the key to
a successful investment plan for your retirement lies not only in
choosing the right investments but also in choosing the right
place to keep them. This chapter will examine those places and
help you choose the ones best suited to your circumstances.

Retirement planning is a complex, fluid thing subject to
adjustment as your circumstances change. But the basics don't
change. A financially secure retirement is the result of understanding and managing the interplay of four essential elements:
how much money you'll need when you get there, where the
money will come from, how much time you have, and how much
risk you're prepared to take to achieve your goal. Together, those
four elements will determine what you do and how you do it.

How Much Income Will You Need?

A USEFUL (THOUGH NOT ENTIRELY RELIABLE) RULE OF THUMB holds that you'll need 70% to 80% of your preretirement income to maintain a similar lifestyle in retirement. Aim at the higher percentage. Thus, if you're making $70,000 a year on the day you retire, figure that you'll need $56,000 afterward.

If retirement is some years down the road, figure that your income will grow and inflation will devour a good deal of its purchasing power in the meantime. It's possible to anticipate both contingencies by consulting the table below. For long-term planning purposes, a conservative estimate is that inflation will average about 4% annually between now and the time you retire. (That's the figure the government uses to project the long-term effects of inflation on social security.) If you expect raises and promotions to boost your income beyond the cost of living, add that figure to your inflation estimate.

For example, say you anticipate that your salary increases will

What Your Money Will Be Worth in the Future

THIS TABLE SHOWS how much your current savings and investments will be worth in the future, assuming various annual rates of return. It can also be used to calculate how inflation will affect your living expenses. Say you plan to retire in 20 years, and expect your investments to grow 10% a year between now and then. Find 20 years in the first column on the left and 10% on the horizontal scale across the top. The place where those two columns intersect shows a multiplier of 6.73. That tells you that $1,000 in your retirement account today will grow to $6,730 in 20 years, assuming a 10% annual return (6.73 x $1,000 = $6,730).

To use this table to calculate how much inflation will affect your living expenses, first, make an assumption about inflation; 4% is a reasonable estimate for the next 20 years. Where the 4% column intersects with 20 years, the multiplier is 2.19. That means that you'll need $2,190 in 20 years to match the purchasing power of $1,000 today. (For a wider range of interest rates, see the tables in the Appendix.)

				ANNUAL RATES OF RETURN					
YEAR	4%	5%	6%	7%	8%	9%	10%	11%	12%
				Future-Value Multiplier					
10	1.48	1.63	1.79	1.97	2.16	2.37	2.59	2.84	3.11
15	1.80	2.08	2.40	2.76	3.17	3.64	4.18	4.78	5.47
20	2.19	2.65	3.21	3.87	4.66	5.60	6.73	8.06	9.65
25	2.67	3.39	4.29	5.43	6.85	8.62	10.82	13.59	17.00

average one percentage point more than inflation. Add this figure to your inflation expectations for a total annual increase of 5% in this example. Say retirement is 20 years away. Now look at the table. Where 5% and 20 years intersect, the multiplier is 2.65. Hence, today's $70,000 salary will be $185,500 ($70,000 x 2.65) in 20 years. If you're shooting for 80% of preretirement income, your target retirement income goal is about $148,000.

Where Will the Money Come From?

WHERE WILL YOU GET THAT KIND OF MONEY—ESPECIALLY IF an early retirement is part of your dream? The worksheet on the following page will show you. Luckily, you probably won't have to provide all of the money yourself. In fact, before you can devise an investment plan to achieve the goal of a comfortable retirement, you need to calculate the portion of retirement income that your own investments must provide. And to make this calculation, you need a pretty good estimate of what you can reasonably expect from pension plans and social security. (More on that subject in a moment.)

One of the obstacles to retiring before age 62 is that you can't count on all your long-term savings and investments to kick in with income right from the start. The worksheet reflects the fact that employer pension benefits are rarely available before age 55, that social security benefits can't start before age 62 and that IRA funds are generally tied up until age 59½.

In the "Anticipated Resources" section, multiplying each of your various assets by 0.08 assumes you will be able to earn 8% a year on those assets, and lets you see whether you can live on the investment income without depleting your capital. (The 8% assumption about earnings reflects the fact that once you are retired, you'll want to keep your money in lower-risk investments that produce a high level of income.) Odds are that you'll have to dip into capital on some regular basis. You can use the "How Much Money You'll Need" table in the Appendix to test various pay-down schedules.

Now begin to plug in your numbers:

YOUR GOAL. The first step in using the worksheet is to state your goal: 80% of preretirement income.

Where Will the Money Come From?

Your Goal: Current income x Multiplier from Table, page 260 x 0.80 = $_____

Anticipated resources at crucial ages

RESOURCE	CURRENT VALUE x MULTIPLIER FROM TABLE, PAGE 260	50-54	AGE 55-59½	60-62	62+
Investments	$_____ x 0.08 = $_____	$_____	$_____	$_____	$_____
Equity in home	$_____ x 0.08 =		_____	_____	_____
IRAs	$_____ x 0.08 =	XXXXXX	XXXXXX	_____	_____
KEOGHs	$_____ x 0.08 =	XXXXXX		_____	_____
Other resources	$_____ x 0.08 =	XXXXXX		_____	_____
Pensions		XXXXXX		_____	_____
Social Security		XXXXXX	XXXXXX	XXXXXX	_____
Totals		$_____	$_____	$_____	$_____
Shortfall (your goal minus your total resources)		$_____	$_____	$_____	$_____

EMPLOYER PENSION BENEFITS. A trip to your company's personnel or benefits office should give you the answers you need about future pension payments.

Defined-benefit plans rarely provide benefits before age 55. Your personnel office should be able to estimate what you can expect when you plan to retire. You can probably count on your benefits to increase for each year that you delay retirement past age 55, provided you stay with the same employer. If you leave that company, your pension will almost certainly be frozen at the level you had earned before leaving. If you have a defined-contribution pension plan, the value of your account would probably keep growing after you left because you or the company would keep it invested.

SOCIAL SECURITY BENEFITS. A phone call to the Social Security Administration (800-772-1213), or a check of its Web site at www.ssa.gov, will get you a form called the "Request for Earnings and Benefit Estimate Statement." (Beginning in 2000, the SSA will send a copy of this statement annually to everyone age 25 years and older.) Fill it out to get an estimate of your future benefits.

Social security retirement benefits can't begin until age 62, and at that age, checks are reduced to 80% of what you'd get if you waited until 65 to start collecting. The age for receiving full benefits and the reduction for early retirement will increase gradually beginning in the year 2000.

SAVINGS AND INVESTMENTS. Begin with what you have in your retirement fund today and use a future-value multiplier from the table on page 260 to see what it will be worth in the future. If you have $50,000 now, plan to retire in 15 years, and expect your savings and investments to yield 6% a year after taxes, you should multiply $50,000 by 2.40—the figure where the 15 years and 6% columns intersect. That's $120,000. If that nest egg generates 8% a year, you can count on it for $9,600 ($120,000 x .08) toward your annual retirement needs.

EQUITY IN YOUR HOME. This line assumes that you will use your home equity as a source of income—either by selling your home and renting or by "buying down" to a smaller place and investing the freed-up equity to generate income. Begin with the current value of your house and apply a future-value multiplier from the table on page 260 to estimate its value when you'll sell it. If you can't guess which way values are headed where you live, use the current value. Subtract any mortgage you'll still have outstanding at that time and enter the result. (Because Congress has declared that the first $250,000 of profit from the sale of a home is tax-free—$500,000, if you file a joint return—it's highly unlikely that taxes will cut into your profit.) Multiply it by 8% to see how much annual income you can expect if you choose to use this source of income in retirement.

INDIVIDUAL RETIREMENT ACCOUNTS. Consider IRA money tied up until you reach 59½, although there are exceptions, as discussed later in this chapter. For this line, apply a future-value multiplier from the table on page 260 to the current value of your IRAs.

KEOGH ACCOUNTS. You can tap a Keogh without penalty starting at age 55.

401(K) AND PROFIT-SHARING PLANS. Money in 401(k) and other profit-sharing plans can be withdrawn without tax penalty as early as age 55 if you leave the job. If you roll over a distribution

How Much You'll Need to Get $100 a Month

THIS TABLE SHOWS the amount of money you'll need to yield $100 a month for the period indicated in the first column on the left, assuming various rates of return on the money. Other amounts can be figured as multiples of $100. For instance, say you need to draw $750 a month for 10 years from an amount of capital yielding 8%. First,

find where the 10-year and 8% columns intersect. That amount—$8,242—will yield $100 a month. Multiplying $8,242 by 7.5 shows that you'd need $61,815 earning 8% in order to collect $750 a month for 10 years. At the end of the period, the fund will be depleted. (For a wider range of interest rates, see the tables in the Appendix.)

YEAR	8%	9%	10%	11%	12%
			ANNUAL RATES OF RETURN		
			Amount Needed to Yield $100 a Month		
10	$8,242	$7,894	$7,567	$7,260	$6,970
15	10,464	9,860	9,306	8,798	8,332
20	11,955	11,114	10,362	9,688	9,082
25	12,956	11,916	11,005	10,203	9,495

into an IRA—to avoid paying all the tax at once—the money is controlled by the IRA rules.

Facing Up to a Shortfall

THE WORKSHEET ON PAGE 262 ALMOST CERTAINLY DELIVERS bad news: a shortfall that paints retirement as a swan dive into poverty. But take heart. In a sense, the exercise is stacked against you because it is based only on the growth of what you've accumulated so far and does not take into account any future savings.

Say you're hoping to retire in 20 years, and you face an annual shortfall of $24,000, or $2,000 a month. Use the table above to calculate the size of the nest egg you'll need in order to generate that much income for a given length of time. If you'll need the extra $2,000 a month for 30 years, for example, your additional nest egg must total $272,560, assuming it will be earning 8% a year after you retire. That means you'll have to invest enough over the next 20 years to have an additional $272,560 when you retire.

(A mathematical footnote: $272,560 may not seem to be enough to generate an income of $2,000 a month if it earns 8%, because 8% of $272,560 is only $21,804, which amounts to $1,817 per month. The apparent discrepancy is explained by two factors: First, the unexpended portion of the nest egg continues to earn interest, so that drawing out $2,000 per month in effect depletes the fund by something less than $2,000. Second, the schedule assumes that you will exhaust the fund in 30 years, so it's okay to nick the principal a little each month.)

How Much Time and Risk?

THE TABLE BELOW SHOWS HOW MUCH EXTRA YOU NEED TO start saving each month to accumulate your retirement fund. Assuming a 10% annual yield, you can see that $100 a month invested over 20 years will build a nest egg of $76,570. (Ten dollars a month invested for 20 years at 10% = $7,657 x 10 = $76,570.) Dividing the amount you need—$272,560—by that figure gives you 3.6. Multiply that by 100 and you can see that you need to sock away $360 a month over the next 20 years to meet your goal, assuming a 10% return per year.

Fortunately, that's not necessarily an extra $360 a month. Part of it may be covered by money you are already putting away in IRAs and other plans, plus future contributions by your employer to a job-related account. Also, the amount you need to come up with yourself probably drops as the years go by and other retirement income kicks in. If you needed the extra $2,000 a month for five years instead of 30—to tide you over for the years between an

How $10 a Month Will Grow

THIS TABLE SHOWS how much you'll have at the end of the period indicated if you save or invest $10 a month, assuming various annual rates of return. Results for other amounts can be calculated as multiples of $10. (For a more comprehensive version of this table, see the Appendix.)

YEAR	8%	9%	ANNUAL RATES OF RETURN 10%	11%	12%
			Amount Accumulated at End of Period		
10	$1,842	$1,950	$2,066	$2,190	$2,323
15	3,483	3,812	4,179	4,589	5,046
20	5,929	6,729	7,657	8,736	9,991
25	9,574	11,295	13,379	15,906	18,976

early retirement at 50 and age 55, perhaps—the monthly savings required over 20 years would drop from $360 to $129.

A Time-Appropriate Portfolio

WHAT KINDS OF INVESTMENTS OFFER THE BEST HOPE OF achieving your retirement goals? As described in Chapter 2, a core portfolio of stocks, bonds and mutual funds is ideal for a long-term goal such as retirement. Other chapters in this book describe how the investments differ and how you should go about selecting the best according to the time you have and your tolerance for risk. In general, the more time you have, the more risk you can take.

20 YEARS TO GO. With 20 years to go, for instance, an aggressive-growth mutual fund such as one of those listed in Chapter 6 would be appropriate for a portion of a portfolio dominated by growth stocks (or funds that specialize in them); zero-coupon bonds (especially zeros sheltered in IRAs and other retirement plans described later); well-selected real estate (provided it meets the criteria spelled out in Chapter 8); and other long-term investments.

10 YEARS TO GO. With ten years left, there's still plenty of time to recover from market reversals, but it's also time to think more conservatively. Market peaks present opportunities to move money out of risky aggressive stocks and into dividend-paying growth stocks with reinvestment plans (see Chapter 4). You can give your mutual fund portfolio a less risky profile by moving into growth-and-income funds, bonds, bond funds and long-term Treasuries. At this point in your life, consider keeping about 10% to 20% of your portfolio in cash, meaning money-market funds, certificates of deposit with staggered maturities, and Treasury bills.

5 YEARS TO GO. When you get to within five years of retirement, it's important to be conservative, but it's also important to remain diversified. Hang on to some growth stocks or growth-stock funds, especially those that pay good dividends. If interest rates look high, load up on bonds; if rates decline, you'll have the choice of selling them at a profit (see Chapter 5) or keeping them for the high income they provide. If you own rental real estate that has appreciated in value, look for opportunities to take the gain so that you can move the money into a more liquid investment that will produce more income in retirement.

The Investor's Catch-22

THIS DISCUSSION OF INVESTING FOR RETIREMENT UNDERSCORES what might be called the investor's Catch-22: The more time you have to achieve your goal, the more risk you can take in pursuit of it—but as a glance at the table of investment returns will show, the more years you have to go, the less risk you need to take to make your money grow. As you get closer to retirement, you may be tempted to increase your risk in hopes of achieving the higher return you need to accumulate the necessary funds. Don't do it. That's exactly the time when you should be reducing risk to conserve the capital you have.

You could—and should—consider working for a few more years, to collect the salary, increase your pension benefit and give your less-risky investments more time to grow. You could plan to work part-time in retirement. Probably you'll decide on some combination of strategies, cursing yourself for not starting a serious investment plan years earlier than you did.

The remainder of this chapter will explore the kinds of repositories for investments that have been created especially with retirement in mind.

Individual Retirement Accounts

HOORAY FOR THE IRA—THE INDIVIDUAL RETIREMENT account. It's a perpetual-motion money machine with a single goal—encouraging you to sock away retirement money that will grow unfettered by any taxes. The power of tax-free growth inside this tax shelter makes this simple tool a potent financial force over the long term. And part of the genius behind how it accomplishes its goal is the way it keeps you at arm's length from the money until you get close to retirement. No raiding the piggy bank for expensive toys along the way.

Rolling Over Profit-Sharing Money

Q: *I'm getting a lump-sum distribution from a profit-sharing plan that I'd like to roll over into an IRA. I already have one IRA. Can I set up a separate one for the rollover money?*
A: Yes, you can start a new IRA with your rollover. In fact, you can split the rollover and start several new IRAs. To avoid a 20% withholding tax applied to rollovers from company plans, have the company transfer the money directly to your IRA sponsor or sponsors. Also, it is advisable to keep your rollover IRA separate from other IRA funds if there is any chance that you will get another job that offers a retirement plan. You may be allowed to roll the money into the new employer's plan, a right you lose if you mix it with any other IRA money.

IRAs have had their ups and downs in the public's eye. They burst on the scene as "everybody's tax shelter" in 1981; suffered the indignity of losing tax-deductibility for higher-income individuals in 1986; and are now reclaiming acclaim thanks to the debut of a brand new kind of IRA—the Roth IRA, first available in 1998, with its promise of tax-free, not just tax-deferred, earnings.

If you gave up on IRAs during the years of confusion, now's the time to get back into the ball game. Although the law allows only $2,000 to go into an IRA each year, that seemingly modest amount can grow into a powerful part of your retirement fund. Imagine that you begin depositing $2,000 a year into an IRA starting in the year you are 35 and keep it up until you're 65. If the account earns an average of 10% a year, it will hold more than $360,000. If your spouse kicks in $2,000 a year, too, your combined IRAs will hold nearly $750,000 after 30 years. Assuming you use the Roth IRA, every dime will be tax-free when withdrawn in retirement. Which variety is best for you—traditional or Roth? And should you take Congress up on its offer to let you convert an old-style IRA to a Roth? We'll get to that in a discussion beginning on page 276, but, first, a review of the rules:

WHAT COMPENSATION IS REQUIRED?

To have any kind of IRA, you must have "compensation"— income from a job, self-employment or alimony. Investment income doesn't count, nor does income from pensions or annuities. The most you can put into an IRA each year is $2,000 or 100% of your compensation, whichever is less. Thus, if you earn just $1,000, your maximum IRA contribution for the year is $1,000. The government is serious about the annual limit. Excess contributions are hit with a 6% penalty tax every year until the extra money is removed from the account.

SPOUSAL ACCOUNTS. There is an important exception to the rule that you must have compensation to have an IRA. If you have a job but your spouse does not, you can contribute up to $2,000 of your income to a spousal IRA—either traditional or Roth—for him or her. If you choose a traditional IRA and are permitted to deduct contributions to your own account, you may write off deposits to the spousal IRA, too. In fact, even if you can't deduct traditional IRA contributions—because of the restrictions explained next—you can probably still write off spousal IRA contributions.

YOU'RE NEVER TOO YOUNG. There is no minimum age for IRA participation. If your 10-year-old has compensation—from a paper route, say, or from working in a family business—he or she can stash up to $2,000 of that pay in an IRA.

BUT YOU CAN BE TOO OLD. Although you're never too young to have an IRA, the law forbids contributions to traditional IRAs starting with the year you reach age 70½. There is no age limit for deposits to Roth IRAs, though.

WHO GETS THE DEDUCTION?

What made the original IRA a "no brainer" investment was a simple, indisputable fact: Contributions were deductible. Put $2,000 into an IRA, write off $2,000 on your tax return. In the 28% bracket, you saved $560 and received instant gratification. That was too simple, though, so Congress introduced restrictions to prevent some higher-income earners from getting that deduction.

INCOME TEST FOR A TRADITIONAL IRA. There are two tests that deter-

mine whether you can deduct deposits to a traditional IRA, and
tens of millions of taxpayers still qualify for the write-off:

Company plan test. First, are you an "active participant" in a company retirement plan? You are, as far as the law is concerned, if
you are eligible during any part of the year to participate in a
pension, profit-sharing, 401(k) or similar plan. (If you are in a
profit-sharing plan but no contribution is made to your account
for the year, however, you are not considered covered for that
year.) The Form W-2 you receive from your employer should
indicate to you—and to the IRS—whether you're covered.

If you're not tripped up by the company-plan test, you can
deduct IRA contributions no matter how high your income is.

Income test. If you are covered by a plan, however, you may lose
your right to the deduction. The write-off is phased out for active
participants in company plans whose "modified" adjusted gross
income (AGI)—which is basically AGI before subtracting IRA
contributions—exceeds certain levels.

For 1999, the phase-out started when AGI exceeded $31,000
on an individual return and $51,000 on a joint return ($32,000
and $52,000 for 2000). (The trigger points increase in the
future.) The IRA maximum deduction is reduced by $10 for each
$50 of AGI over the limit. AGI of $5,000 over the threshold,
then, would cut the maximum annual deduction by $1,000
($5,000 ÷ $50 x $10) to $1,000. You could still contribute up to
$2,000, but whether you deposited $1,000, $2,000 or any
amount in between, only $1,000 would be deductible. On a joint
return reporting AGI of $56,000, each spouse could write off up
to $1,000 of IRA contributions.

A higher trigger point is used to figure whether spousal IRA
contributions for the nonworking husband or wife of someone
who is covered by a retirement plan are deductible. In that case,
the right to the deduction is phased out as AGI rises between
$150,000 and $160,000.

INCOME TEST FOR ROTH IRAS. Although no one gets to deduct contributions to Roth IRAs, there is an income test to determine whether
you can use this tax shelter at all. The right to stash retirement cash
in a Roth disappears as AGI rises between $150,000 and $160,000

on a joint return and between $95,000 and $110,000 on the return of a single person, whether filing as an individual, a head of household or a surviving spouse. Married taxpayers who file separate returns may not contribute to Roth IRAs, regardless of their income.

If your AGI on a joint return is $155,000, for example, that's halfway through the phaseout zone, so that your maximum contribution would be cut in half: to $1,000. If you report $105,000 AGI on a single return—two-thirds of the way through the phaseout zone—your top Roth pay-in for the year would be $660, one-third of the $2,000 maximum. When AGI passes the top of the phaseout zone, you may not contribute to a Roth at all.

Note that the Roth phaseout zones apply regardless of whether you are covered by a retirement plan at work.

Do Nondeductible Contributions Make Sense?

Before Congress created the Roth IRA, nondeductible contributions to a regular IRA made good financial sense, because—deductible or not—money inside an IRA grows without annual interruption from the IRS. Now, however, it would be a serious blunder for anyone who qualifies to use a Roth (and that's almost everyone) to make nondeductible contributions to a regular IRA. Sure, Roth contributions are nondeductible, too, but the Roth has many advantages over the regular, nondeductible variety. In rejecting the traditional nondeductible IRA, however, you need to consider just one major advantage: Earnings inside a regular nondeductible IRA will be taxed when withdrawn; earnings inside a Roth can be completely tax-free.

What Deadlines Apply?

Regardless of what kind of IRA you use, the deadline for making your IRA contribution each year is the day your tax return is due for that year. That's usually April 15, of course, but it can be a day or two later if the 15th falls on a weekend. The deadline for making 1999 contributions, then, is April 17, 2000 (for 2000, April 16). The earlier you make your contribution, the sooner your money begins earning in the supercharged environment of the tax shelter.

How About Getting Your Money Out Before Retirement?

To make the right choice between a traditional and a Roth IRA, you need to know how the rules differ when it comes to getting at your money early. There are big differences on this point, and in nearly every case the advantage goes to the Roth.

A TRADITIONAL IRA. With a traditional IRA, if you dip into the account early—as far as the law is concerned, generally anytime before you're 59½ is early—you may be hit with a 10% penalty for premature distribution. Take $5,000 out at age 50, for example, and you probably will be slapped with a $500 penalty. In addition, the full $5,000 will be included in your income for the year and taxed in your top tax bracket. (If you've ever made nondeductible contributions, part of the withdrawal would be both tax- and penalty-free.)

We say you may be hit with a penalty because there's an ever-growing list of exceptions to the penalty: It's waived if you become permanently disabled, for example, or if you use the IRA money to pay medical bills that exceed 7.5% of your adjusted gross income. Also penalty-free is money you withdraw to pay for medical insurance during an extensive period of unemployment. Another little-known exemption is that at any age you can tap your IRA penalty-free, if you withdraw substantially equal amounts each year based on your life expectancy. Such withdrawals must last for at least five years or until you are 59½, whichever is longer. Even though qualifying withdrawals escape the 10% penalty, they would be taxed.

Here are two additional exceptions:

One allows you to withdraw up to $10,000 penalty-free from your traditional IRAs at any age to help pay to buy or build a first home for yourself, your spouse, your kids, your grandchildren or even your parents. That $10,000 is a lifetime limit, not an annual one. Sounds great, but there's a serious downside. Although the 10% penalty is waived, the money would still be taxed in your top bracket (except to the extent it was attributable to nondeductible contributions). That means as much as 40% or more of the $10,000 would go to federal and state tax collectors rather than toward a down payment.

The other exception allows penalty-free withdrawals (with no dollar limit) of money used to pay higher-education expenses for yourself, your spouse, a child or grandchild. Qualified expenses include tuition, fees, and room and board for postsecondary education, including graduate work. This break has the same drawback as the one for first-time home buyers. Although the 10% penalty doesn't apply, the regular federal and state tax bills do. So, a big chunk of your IRA money will wind up at the IRS rather than at the bursar's office.

EARLY OUT OF A ROTH. At first blush, Roth IRAs also threaten you with a 10% penalty if you cash in before age 59½. And any withdrawal that is penalized loses tax-free status, too, to deliver a painful double whammy.

To understand the early-withdrawal penalty, you must begin with the definition of a "qualified distribution" from a Roth, which is what the law calls a withdrawal that is tax- and penalty-free. To qualify, these tests must be met:

First, there's the five-year rule. It holds that a Roth must have been open for at least four calendar years after the year of your first contribution to it for you to qualify for tax- and penalty-free withdrawals. Say, for example, that you made your first contribution to a Roth sometime in 1999. The earliest you could make a tax- or penalty-free withdrawal would be in 2004. Note that a Roth doesn't have to have been open for five full years to pass this five-year test. Say that you opened a Roth for 1999 on April 15, 2000, for example, under the rule that allows you to make contributions up to the due date of the tax return for the year involved. That would start the clock ticking in 1999, so once four calendar years passed (2000, 2001, 2002 and 2003) payouts beginning in 2004—less than 45 months after the account was opened—could be tax- and penalty-free.

They could be, that is, if the payout also meets one of the following conditions:

It is made after you reach age 59½;

It is made after your death;

It is made after you become disabled; or

It is used to help buy a first home for you, your spouse, your kids, your grandchildren or your parents.

It seems your money is locked up tighter in a Roth than in a regular IRA, because tapping the account early generally not only incurs a 10% penalty, but also triggers a tax bill on earnings that would otherwise be avoided. But not necessarily...

Roth IRA investors can reclaim contributions at any time and at any age, without tax or penalty. And the first money coming out of Roth IRAs will be considered contributions. Only after you have withdrawn an amount equal to all of your annual contributions tax- and penalty-free do you have to begin to worry about the early-withdrawal penalty.

Say, for example, that you contribute $2,000 a year for five years and, at the end of the fifth year, the account is worth $13,500. Regardless of your age, you could withdraw $10,000 (the total of your contributions) tax- and penalty-free.

Note this: The exception to the early-withdrawal penalty for traditional IRA money used for college bills applies to Roth IRAs, too, but because such withdrawals wouldn't be "qualified distributions," any amount that represents earnings would not be tax-free.

How Do You Tap Your IRA in Retirement?

Finally, the day arrives when you can start withdrawing money from your IRA. You have choices to make no matter what kind of IRA you have.

A TRADITIONAL IRA. Once you reach age 59½, the threat of the 10% penalty disappears. You can withdraw as much from your regular IRAs as you want, penalty-free. Cash coming out of the account is taxable in your top tax bracket, except to the extent that it represents a return of nondeductible contributions.

You can cash in your IRA all at once, but doing so could sub-

Closing Out An IRA

Q: *I am approaching age 70 and would like to convert my mandatory IRA withdrawals directly into securities or another non-IRA account—in other words, I don't want to convert them to cash to satisfy the withdrawal requirements, but I want to reinvest them. Is this allowable and can a brokerage firm do this for me?*

A: Yes on both accounts. You do not have to take physical possession of your IRA withdrawals in order to satisfy the requirement that you withdrew a minimum amount starting at age 70½, and your broker can direct the funds into securities or another non-IRA account. The money from your IRA is taxed as ordinary income regardless of whether the withdrawals are liquidated, converted into securities or deposited into other accounts.

ject you to an enormous tax bill. You'll probably do better tax-wise by taking out as little as necessary each year. Not only does that hold down the tax bill you owe each year, but it also leaves more money in the tax shelter to enjoy continued tax-deferred growth. But this tax shelter doesn't last forever.

Regular IRAs were created to help you accumulate money for your retirement—not build to up a pile of money for your heirs. Thus, the law demands that you begin pulling money out by April 1 of the year following the year you reach age 70½. The minimum withdrawal schedule is designed to get all your money out (and taxed) by the time you die, or at least by the time your designated IRA beneficiary dies. If you don't take out the minimum required each year, the IRS will claim 50% of the amount you fail to withdraw.

ROTH IRAS. Things are a lot easier with Roth IRAs. Once you reach age 59½ and the account has been open for at least five years, you can take as much or as little from your account as you need—all tax- and penalty-free.

What if you open a Roth in 2000 and you're already older than 59½? You can pull out your contributions at any time tax- and penalty-free, but you need to wait until at least 2005 to take tax- and penalty-free withdrawals of earnings. Remember, you have to wait until four calendar years have passed after the year in which you made your first contribution.

You don't have to worry about a minimum distribution because you don't have to take a dime out of your Roth IRA, at age 70½ or any other age.

How Does Death Affect Your IRA?

What if you die while there's still money in your IRA? This is another area where the Roth comes out head and shoulders ahead of the traditional IRA. With either type of account, there's no early-withdrawal penalty for your beneficiary, regardless of your age when you die or the beneficiary's age when he or she withdraws the money.

The potential problem, however, is that the money pulled out of a traditional IRA is taxable to the beneficiary (except to the extent that it represents nondeductible contributions) in his or her top tax bracket. That could create a substantial tax bill if the IRA is cashed in all at once. The heir may be better off leaving the money in the IRA. But the IRS has something to say about that. It sets a minimum pace at which the money must be withdrawn and taxes paid.

With a Roth IRA, money goes to your beneficiary tax-free. Still, even though the government has no stake in the account, Congress doesn't want the heir to perpetuate the tax shelter forever. There is a minimum withdrawal schedule for heirs—but again, withdrawals are tax-free.

With both traditional and Roth IRAs, there's a special rule if a widow or widower is the beneficiary. In that case, the surviving spouse can claim the account as his or her own. If it's a traditional IRA, no withdrawals would be required until the new owner is 70½; if it's a Roth, the heir would never have to tap the account.

How Do You Choose Between a Roth IRA and a Regular IRA?

Which set of tax advantages is best for you? Which tax shelter will help you build the bigger nest egg? Does it make sense to convert an old IRA to a Roth? Good questions, and tough to answer.

First, if your income is too high to deduct regular IRA contributions, the Roth IRA is a great addition to your retirement-savings arsenal. Fund it to the max—$2,000 a year—if you can afford to.

Smile when you reflect that withdrawals will be tax-free.

But what if you can deduct your regular IRA contributions? The Roth still has clear advantages, primarily the facts that there's no mandatory withdrawal and that Roth money can go to your heirs tax-free. And if you need money before retirement, you can get at your contributions tax- and penalty-free. Another plus is that your tax-free withdrawals won't trigger extra tax on your social security benefits. (As taxable income—including regular IRA withdrawals—rises above certain levels, up to 85% of otherwise tax-free social security benefits can be taxed.)

What about the advantage of tax-free versus taxable withdrawals? Well, there's no guarantee that, when all else is equal, the Roth will beat the regular IRA. You need a crystal ball as much as a financial calculator to know whether it makes sense to give up tax deductions today in exchange for tax-free income tomorrow. It really depends on what your tax bracket will be when you retire. If you're in a lower tax bracket in retirement, the regular IRA will turn out to have been a better choice; if you're in a higher tax bracket then, the Roth will win.

For an apples-to-apples comparison, assume that you deposit $2,000 a year in a regular IRA and just $1,440 in a Roth—because that's all the regular IRA really costs you if you're deducting contributions in the 28% bracket. Assuming the money in the accounts earns at the same rate, at the end of any period, the "spendable" amount in the accounts will be identical. Sure, the traditional, deductible IRA will hold more money. But you'll owe tax on withdrawals. Assuming a 28% rate, the after-tax amount will be the same as the tax-free amount coming out of the Roth IRA.

As noted, however, there is a way to give the Roth a big advantage. Put a full $2,000 into the account each year rather than a stunted $1,440. That costs you more than a regular IRA contribution, and you'll come out way ahead in the end. So, if you can afford a $2,000 contribution without the help of a tax deduction, the Roth will help your nest egg grow bigger.

Assuming there will still be an income tax when you retire (which is a pretty good bet), how can you know whether you'll be in a higher or lower bracket? You can't. In the past, it was generally assumed that retirees would fall into a lower tax bracket because they'd have less taxable income. Now, however, it's increasingly likely that retirees will maintain their income levels. Ironically, because opting for a Roth will reduce taxable income in retirement, it's more likely that you'll be in a lower bracket (which is a minus for the Roth); conversely, using a regular IRA will boost taxable income in retirement, possibly pushing you into a higher bracket (which is a minus for the regular IRA).

Should You Convert an Old-Style IRA to a Roth?

If your AGI is $100,000 or less, you can convert your old-style IRA to a Roth, so that all future earnings inside the account would be tax-free. That $100,000 trigger point applies to all kinds of returns except married filing separately. If you are married and file a separate return, you are forbidden to covert an old IRA to a Roth.

Although rolling old IRA money into a Roth sounds great, there's a catch: You have to pay tax on the amount rolled over—except to the extent, if any, that you have made nondeductible contributions to the old IRA. Say, for example, that your IRA now holds $100,000, all of it from deductible contributions and tax-deferred earnings. To convert that IRA to a Roth, you'd have to report and pay tax on that $100,000 in your top bracket. Ouch. If you wish to convert all or most of it but can't deal with the big tax bite, you can convert some of it each year over a period of several years. For example, if you switch one-fifth of the account each year for five years, you'll spread the tax bill over five years. *Note:* Traditional IRA money that's included in your income doesn't count when figuring whether your AGI is over $100,000 for purposes of whether you qualify to make the conversion.

This isn't an all-or-nothing deal. If you have several old IRAs, you can convert one or more to Roths and maintain the others.

But does it make sense to pay a big tax bill now to avoid taxes in retirement, which may be a decade or more away? The dollars-and-cents answer depends on your tax bracket now and what it will be when you retire:

If you'll be in a higher bracket in retirement, switching to a Roth will pay off. You'll be paying tax at today's rate to avoid tomorrow's higher rate. (When figuring today's rate, remember that adding the IRA amount to your income could push you into a higher bracket.)

If you stay in the same tax bracket, paying tax now or later makes no difference. Although using IRA money to pay the tax bill now would leave a lower balance when you retire, it would produce the same spendable income as a regular IRA.

If you wind up in a lower tax bracket in retirement, paying tax at today's rates to avoid tomorrow's more lenient rates would be a mistake.

That win-lose analysis assumes that you pay the tax on the conversion with money that's inside the regular IRA now. If you can pay the tax bill without tapping your IRA, switching to a Roth account can put you far ahead because it lets you keep more money in the tax shelter, where it will grow faster than it would on the outside.

There's a big catch to using IRA money to pay the tax on a Roth conversion, anyway. If you're under age 59½, you'll have to pay a 10% penalty on the amount that's not rolled over into the Roth, or rolled into a Roth and then pulled out to pay the tax. Adding 10% to your tax rate makes it more likely that you'll face a lower rate in retirement—and therefore you'd be better off skipping the conversion.

HOW POWERFUL IS THE IRA—TRADITIONAL OR ROTH?

Don't let the new choice in IRAs distract you from the real attraction of this tax shelter. Whether you choose a traditional IRA or a Roth, remember that earnings inside the account grow minus the drag of taxes.

Consider a 45-year-old, shooting for retirement at 65, who contributes the $2,000 maximum to an IRA for 20 years. He or she will have kicked in $40,000 to the IRA over that time. If the money grows at an average rate of 8% per year, the total value of the account will be about $98,800—an extra $58,800 on top of what was contributed to the account.

But if that $2,000 a year was invested where the 8% interest earned would be taxed each year—that is, outside an IRA—the $40,000 in savings would grow to only $75,800 over 20 years, assuming earnings were taxed in the 28% bracket. That's $23,000 shy of where that nest egg would be with the power of tax-free compounding on its side. (There'd be even less if state income taxes take a bite out of each year's earnings.)

Now look what happens if the rate of return is higher, say, 12%. A $2,000 annual retirement set-aside would skyrocket to over $160,000—more than four times the $40,000 invested over those 20 years. The $120,000 of earnings generated inside the IRA is the result of tax-free compounding.

If the earnings were taxed every year at 28%, the account would reach just $106,800 after 20 years, trailing the untaxed sum by over $50,000.

A two-income couple can supplement their retirement savings to an even greater extent with dual IRAs. Even if a couple are late starters, if each spouse puts $2,000 into an IRA annually starting at age 50 and the money earns an average 10% per year, their combined IRA retirement pool will be almost $140,000 in 15 years—the $60,000 they contributed plus $80,000 generated by tax-free growth.

That's the power of tax-deferred growth. The opportunity for completely tax-free withdrawals offered by the new Roth IRA is icing on the cake.

How About Moving Your IRA Money?

Another important IRA feature is flexibility. With a vast array of investment choices available, it's comforting to know that you have the ability to exploit new opportunities as they arise by moving your IRA money. The ability to react to changing conditions is a key weapon in your worry-free retirement arsenal. Not only does your own situation change as you and your family grow older, but market conditions change, too.

You might, for example, decide to add a type of mutual fund to your IRA that isn't offered by your current sponsor. You could switch your account to a different sponsor with a wider selection or simply shift a portion of your IRA money elsewhere by setting up an additional account.

What if it turns out that the IRA investment you thought would soar like an eagle flails like a turkey? The ability to adapt is built right into an IRA, letting you move your money into more promising investments.

Another reason to make a move would be to bring some or all

of your IRA into a self-directed IRA account at a brokerage firm. This becomes an option if you want to invest in individual stocks or real estate and have enough money in the account—say, $40,000 or so—to justify the move because commissions and fees will be involved in a self-directed IRA.

No matter why you want to move your IRA money, you have two ways to do it—a direct transfer or a rollover. *Note this:* Unless you are converting a traditional IRA to a Roth IRA—which, as noted earlier, triggers a tax bill on the amount converted—you can't move money between the two varieties of accounts. The discussion here assumes that you are moving from traditional to traditional or from Roth to Roth.

DIRECT TRANSFER. In most cases, a direct transfer will be the best way to move your IRA money. It's simple: You instruct your current IRA sponsor to pass the money directly to another sponsor of your choosing—from a bank to a mutual fund, for example. The money in the account never actually passes through your hands. All you need to do is issue the orders, usually relayed through the new sponsor once you've set up your account there.

You can transfer all the funds in your IRA or only a portion. And you can make as many moves as you want. You could, for example, order $30,000 in a bank IRA transferred in $10,000 chunks to three separate mutual funds.

Although this method is the easiest, it's not necessarily the fastest. The new sponsor you are switching to should be willing and able to offer tips on how to expedite the move. Sponsors giving up an account are sometimes less than swift.

First, open an account with the new sponsor you've selected. You needn't deposit any money right away. Instead, you'll fill out a form with instructions to the old sponsor for transferring your funds to the new account.

Unfortunately, things don't always run smoothly. Some transfers take weeks or, in the most horrific cases, months. Snags can occur for several reasons. The paperwork might be forgotten, misinterpreted, misdirected or buried on someone's desk. The information it contains could be incomplete or incorrect, causing further delay.

Barring any hitches, though, three weeks should be ample

time to complete a direct transfer. If you haven't gotten confirmation within that time, call both the new and old IRA sponsors and make it clear that you're concerned. Request a definite answer about what is causing the delay and when it will be resolved. Ask whether you can do anything to expedite the process. If nothing happens, talk to a supervisor and follow up in writing.

ROLLOVER. The second way to move your IRA is with a rollover. In this case you're the go-between. The current sponsor closes the account and sends you the money. You're then responsible for sending it on (rolling it over) to a new IRA sponsor. For example, you close an IRA bank account, receive a check and send the money on to a newly opened mutual fund IRA account.

This method has two advantages that can be useful strategic moves. One is speed. Because you take control, you can personally push things along. Thus, if you spot an investment opportunity—an attractive stock you want to buy through a self-directed IRA brokerage account, for example—you can quickly shift money where needed by using this rollover method.

The other advantage is flexibility. Because the rules grant you 60 days to complete your rollover, you can, in effect, tap this money for a 60-day loan to meet a short-term financial emergency.

But it's crucial not to breach the 60-day limit. If you miss the deadline, the IRA tax shelter dissolves, the money withdrawn from a traditional account is taxed (except for already-taxed contributions) and, if you're under age 59½, you'll be hit with a 10% early-withdrawal penalty as well. If you miss the deadline on a Roth rollover, you can be taxed and penalized on any amount that exceeds your contribution to your Roth accounts.

To make sure you're not penalized, you must get the assets into the new account by the 60th day. Also make sure the old sponsor knows you're rolling over your IRA so that no money will be withheld for taxes. Otherwise the sponsor may nab 10% of the amount involved and send it to the IRS. Ask whether any documents must be signed to prevent the 10% withholding. Also note that rollovers are permitted just once every 12 months for each IRA that you have.

Deferred Annuities

D EFERRED ANNUITIES ARE USUALLY SOLD BY INSURANCE COM- panies, which would like you to think of annuities as per- sonal pension plans with lifetime income protection. That they are, but the price you pay the insurance company for that pension is often more than you'd pay for a do-it-yourself plan. Taxes are the reason, which we'll describe later on. First, though it's important to understand how annuities work.

You make one big payment or a series of regular payments to the company. After deducting its fee, the company puts your money in an investment vehicle you choose, which grows as the years go by. When the annuity matures, instead of paying you a lump sum, the company pays you a steady income—for life or for some other period you select.

Annuities come in two basic varieties, the first of which sounds a lot like a defined-benefit pension plan (see page 262):

A fixed annuity earns interest at a rate declared by the company each month or quarter. You might have some money earning 5%, some 6% and some 7%, just as if you owned a bond portfo- lio of various maturities. At this low rate of earnings, fixed annu- ities aren't worth the expense. You can almost certainly do bet- ter investing the money yourself to provide for yourself, and that's why insurance companies are selling fewer fixed annuities these days.

A variable annuity, the other type, gives you a choice of invest- ment options—mainly different kinds of mutual funds. Probably the most heavily promoted plan is called the flexible- premium variable annuity. It gives you a range of investment choices and the freedom to invest your money at your own pace. You may have a choice of more than a dozen funds or only a few. A number of mutual fund companies, including USAA, Vanguard and Scudder, manage special funds open to holders of variable annuities. Because all variable annuities depend on mutual funds, they are legally securities and must be sold by prospectus.

Deferred annuities work a lot like nondeductible IRAs, and in that sense they seem to have a tax advantage: Your contributions are not tax-exempt, but your money grows tax-deferred until you withdraw it, at which time your earnings are taxed at regular rates in your top tax bracket. There are important differences, however. Annuities impose no annual limit on contributions, for instance. Like IRAs, annuities charge penalties if you withdraw the money before age 59½. But not only will you owe the 10% tax penalty on early withdrawals, but you may face additional early-withdrawal charges imposed by the insurance company.

WHAT DO YOU PAY TO GET IN?

Variable annuities usually charge a variety of fees. Here's what you'd pay for one widely sold plan:

An annual contract maintenance fee between $20 and $40 per year.

A 1.25% annual deduction from the assets of the annuity for mortality and expense risk and administration.

Asset management fees ranging from about 0.3% for the company's own common stock fund to 2.5% for a portfolio managed by an outside mutual fund company.

A "back-end" load, or surrender charge, that starts as high as 9% if you withdraw money in the first year and diminishes to zero over a number of years.

Because investors tend to divide their assets among both inside- and outside-managed funds, an average management fee in this plan would work out to about 1%, making the annual expense around 2.24% plus $30 on a $25,000 investment. That's a typical expense ratio for a deferred variable annuity. Terms vary and will be spelled out in the prospectus, so check it carefully.

HOW DO YOU GET THE MONEY OUT?

Both fixed and variable annuities work about the same when it comes time to take the money out. The insurance company pays you a monthly income, usually for the rest of your life, based on three factors: the amount of money in your account, your life expectancy, and the interest the company figures it can earn on the unpaid portion of your account while you're alive. If the company miscalculates and the investment account expires before you do, the company is on the hook to continue the payments until you die. (Actually, you can choose from a variety of payout plans, including some that pay a guaranteed income for your life and that of your spouse as well.)

What if you die before you start collecting payments from your annuity? Most companies will pay to your designated beneficiary a death benefit equal to the account value at the time of your death. If your investments were running at a loss, some companies will pay the full amount of your contributions.

WHAT ABOUT TAXES, FEES AND OTHER DRAWBACKS?

Consider the following before you purchase a variable annuity:

HIGHER TAXES. Investors who buy annuities to stave off the tax bill on earnings pay a heavy price: They forfeit the chance to use the lower capital-gains rates for those earnings. Although the top rate on capital gains is now 20%, earnings from an annuity are always taxed in your top bracket, which could be as high as 39.6%. That difference means that it takes longer for the benefit of tax deferral inside the annuity to overcome the loss of capital-gains treatment.

HIGHER FEES. Fees are much higher than for mutual funds. A few companies, including Fidelity and Vanguard, have cut fees, but the average variable annuity still charges 2.09%, according to Morningstar. That's $2,090 each year on a $100,000 account. The average mutual fund claims 1.4%, or $1, 400 per year on the same account.

THE DEATH BENEFIT IS EXPENSIVE. A large of chunk of the fees pays for the death benefit, which typically pays off only if you die when your account has fallen below the minimum guarantee. But few purchasers ever benefit, because, fortunately, few long-term investors lose in the stock market. Even if you die within a few years of investing, the odds are good that your annuity will be worth more than you paid for it.

You could probably do better by purchasing a term life insurance policy. The average annuity charges $1,110 per year to cover the death benefit on a $100,000 account. Yet a healthy 60-year-old man would pay about the same amount—$1,100 a year—for a $200,000, twenty-year, level-term (payments remain the same over the course of the policy) policy. That's twice as much coverage for his heirs—protection that would in no way be dependent upon what happened in the stock market.

YOU DON'T NEED TO BUY AN ANNUITY TO GUARANTEE INCOME FOR LIFE. If lifetime payments are important to you, realize that you don't need a variable annuity to get them. You can invest in stocks or mutual funds until you're ready to start tapping your nest egg, then sell them and use the proceeds to buy an immediate annuity. Yes, you'll have to pay tax on capital gains at that time, leaving you less to invest in the annuity. But because only after-tax money goes into the annuity, less of each payment you receive will be taxed than would be the case if you had built up your account inside a tax-deferred annuity.

Alternatively, you could "annuitize" your investments on your own—drawing down a certain amount each month on a schedule of your choice. You don't get the lifetime-payments guarantee, but neither do you guarantee that payments end with your death (or the death of a survivor, if you choose a joint annuity). With systematic withdrawals, your heirs get what's left in the account when you die. A drawback is that with systematic withdrawals, 100% of all withdrawals are taxable until you have depleted all earnings; then withdrawals are tax-free. When you annuitize, part of each payment can be tax-free.

YOU NEED TO HOLD AN ANNUITY FOR AT LEAST 15 YEARS. It takes at least that long for the benefits of tax deferral to make up for the higher taxes and fees. The breakeven point depends on what your tax bracket is, what the fees are, whether you withdraw the money in a lump sum or gradually over the years, and what you're comparing the annuity with—particularly, how often you trade taxable mutual funds outside an annuity and how well they perform.

Sales pitches that show a closer breakeven point are probably

A Variable Annuity Mistake

Q. *I think that I made a mistake when I bought a variable annuity. What should I do?*

A. It's rarely worth paying the 10% penalty to get out before age 59½. But that doesn't mean you're locked into the same policy until then. It does mean that you'll have to do more shopping in the variable-annuity marketplace. Once most of the surrender period is over–so that you don't forfeit as much as 5% to 9% of your principal–you can make a tax-free exchange (called a 1035 exchange) to another variable annuity that has lower fees and better performance. As with an IRA rollover, the money must move directly frrom one annuity to the other to avoid the penalty.

If you're older than 59½, you need to get a fix on the tax liability you would face if you cashed in the policy. Remember, the difference between what you invested and the current value will be taxed in your top bracket. It's possible that the high tax cost of cashing in will make the ongoing annuity fees seem a small price to pay to keep all your money working for you.

You may want to begin tapping the annuity rather than other sources–such as an IRA–as your income needs require. Although traditional IRA withdrawals, like annuity payouts, are generally full taxable, those accounts don't carry the extra fees associated with annuities.

based on an assumption that you'll trade frequently outside the account and invest in funds that make significant capital-gains distributions each year. The taxes incurred this way stack the deck in favor of annuities, which grow tax-deferred. The advantage of tax-deferred growth can be yours outside the annuity if you buy and hold funds that make relatively small, taxable year-end distributions. As gains build up inside a fund, though, you get the same tax-deferral benefit you would inside an annuity, and the benefit of a 20% capital-gains rate when you do sell.

Variable Annuity Analyzer software offered by T. Rowe Price (free; 800-469-5304) lets you compare the performance of low-fee variable annuities with no-load mutual funds. In most scenarios, you'll end up about even if you buy a variable annuity or a mutual fund, hold it for 15 years and withdraw a lump sum. Beyond 15 years, the variable annuity begins to pull ahead, particularly if you plan to withdraw some money each year and leave the rest inside the tax-deferred account.

WHEN CAN ANNUITIES WORK?

Even if you do have a long time horizon, variable annuities make sense only if you can answer yes to all of the following questions:

Are you contributing the maximum to your IRA, 401(k) or other retirement plans? These plans provide tax deferral without many of the fees. Some offer an employer match and let you invest pretax money. If you use a Roth IRA, earnings are tax-free in retirement, not just tax-deferred.

Note: Many variable annuities are held in accounts that are already tax-deferred, such as 401(k) or 403(b) plans. That redundancy—buying a tax-deferred investment inside a tax-deferred plan—just adds an extra layer of fees and gains you nothing.

CAN YOU LIVE WITHOUT THE MONEY UNTIL YOU REACH AGE 59½? If not, you'll be hit with the 10% tax penalty and may have to pay a surrender charge. Make sure you have enough money available for emergencies and preretirement needs, such as paying for your children's education, buying a house and supporting aging parents.

ARE YOU IN THE 28% TAX BRACKET OR HIGHER? If you're in the 15% bracket, the benefits of tax deferral may never make up for the fees. You'll do best if you defer taxes while you're in a high tax bracket and withdraw the money when you drop into a lower bracket in retirement.

ARE YOU SURE YOU NEED THE INCOME STREAM? Variable annuities are no way to pass along an inheritance. If unused in your lifetime, your heirs will owe income tax on earnings just as you would have. Mutual funds outside an annuity pass to heirs income-tax-free.

HAVE YOU FOUND A LOW-FEE VARIABLE ANNUITY? Annual insurance fees range from less than $400 to nearly $2,000 on a $100,000 account. The higher the fees, the more they eat into the annuity's performance. All other things being equal, why would you want to pay 1.5% insurance expenses to buy a fund within one policy if you could pay 0.75% in expenses to buy the same mutual fund in a different policy?

How Do You Find a Good One?

Variable Annuity Research & Data Service (VARDS), of Marietta, Ga., tracks the total returns of more than 6,000 annuity funds and publishes extensive information about variable annuity contracts and their issuers. Nearly every variable annuity that VARDS follows has some funds that consistently beat the mutual fund averages for the same class of investment and trail it for others. Ask your agent or broker or visit www.vards.com for the VARDS reports on the funds available to you in an annuity you're considering, and apply the kinds of considerations described in Chapter 6.

The monthly *S&P Stock Guide,* described in Chapter 4 and available in many public libraries, follows a number of annuity funds.

Morningstar Inc. (800-735-0700; www.morningstar.com), which also tracks mutual funds (see Chapter 6), publishes monthly performance reports on several hundred variable annuities. Its *Variable Annuity/Life Performance Report* costs $495 a year ($95 for one issue) but may be available at a local library.

Morningstar's Variable Annuity/Life Performance Report (monthly; 800-735-0700) is most detailed, but pricey: $95 for one issue, $295 for four and $495 for one year. The CD-ROM version, called *Principia Pro for Variable Annuities/Life,* costs $195 for quarterly updates, $395 for monthly.

The Insurance News Network Web site (www.insure.com) provides almost as much information free. Click on "Annuities," then "Morningstar variable annuity database," then search for information by policy name, insurance company, subaccount (the policy's investment options) or other criteria.

What If the Insurance Company Goes Broke?

From time to time an insurance company may declare a conspicuously high rate on a fixed annuity, such as 10% when the average is 8%, in an effort to attract business. Banks do the same thing when they offer to pay an unusually high rate on a certifi-

Variable Life Insurance

Q: *I am 38 years old and am considering investing via variable life insurance. Should I do it?*
A: If you need the insurance and have the discipline to stick with the plan, variable life could make sense. It lets you invest part of your cash value in stocks and other securities, offering the possibility of higher tax-deferred yields than whole life, which pays a set rate based on fixed-income securities. Both the total death benefit and the cash value of a variable policy rise and fall with the results of the investment accounts. A minimum death benefit generally is guaranteed, but the cash value is not—so you take some risk.

Variable life is sold by prospectus, which will tell you how a company's investments have performed and give projected returns based on various investment options. Most insurers offer mutual funds in which to invest your premiums.

One major attraction of variable life is that, as in an IRA, the investment earnings are tax-deferred (as long as you keep them inside the policy). When you evaluate the performance of the investment earnings against investments outside a policy, remember that the first year's premium is largely consumed by administrative costs and the agent's commission. Thus, it will take some time to accumulate much cash value.

cate of deposit. The difference is that bank accounts are insured but the assets of insurance companies issuing annuities are not.

Mutual funds sold through variable annuities must sequester their holdings in accounts separate from those of the insurance company, a requirement that provides some measure of protection. But the guarantees of fixed annuities depend on the health of the insurance company. Thus, a supposedly conservative fixed annuity can actually be dicier than a variable annuity if the company isn't rock-solid.

In sizing up an annuity, bear in mind that it's the soundness of the company, not the last half-point of interest, that matters most. Do business only with insurers whose claims-paying abilities are rated high by the rating services:

The A.M. Best Co. ranks insurers on a scale of A+ to C– and considers A+ and A the top two ratings. For a charge of $4.95, you can receive information by phone on a specific insurance company. The "Bestline" number is 908-439-2200, ext. 5742. Or you can contact the company online at www.ambest.com.

Weiss Research is a Florida-based rating company that for $15 each will give you oral reports over the phone on companies it follows. Call 800-289-9222.

Three other companies follow the insurance industry and will give you ratings over the phone at no cost.

Moody's Investors Service (99 Church St., New York, NY 10007; 212-553-0377) will provide ratings for up to three companies.

Standard & Poor's (25 Broadway, New York, NY 10004; 212-438-2400) will provide ratings for up to five companies.

Duff & Phelps (55 East Monroe St., 35th Floor, Chicago, IL 60603; 312-368-3157; www.dcrco.com) will provide ratings for up to five companies or you can search online.

Most larger libraries have Moody's or S&P ratings in their reference section. Insurance agents also should have one or more of these guides on hand.

Keogh Plans

I F YOU ARE SELF-EMPLOYED, EITHER FULL- OR PART-TIME, SOME OF your retirement investments belong in a Keogh plan. You're eligible even if you're already participating in a company pension plan and are actively contributing to an IRA.
You can invest your Keogh money in just about anything you like. Most people choose stocks, bonds and mutual funds. Contributions to a Keogh plan are deductible from your taxable income in the year in which they're made. Earnings accumulate tax-free until you take them out at retirement.

A money-purchase defined-contribution plan—the most popular version of a Keogh—permits annual contributions of 25% of earned income, up to a maximum of $30,000. (To arrive at the definition of earned income for Keogh contributions, you must first deduct the contributions, which has the effect of lowering the limit to 20% of precontribution income.)

Differences in Keoghs

Q: *How does a profit-sharing Keogh differ from a plain Keogh, which has a higher contribution limit—25% of net self-employment income, or 20% of income before the contribution?*
A: The key difference between the profit-sharing Keogh (with its 15% of net income contribution cap) and the money-purchase defined-contribution plan (with the 25% cap) is that with the latter, you are required to make a fixed-percentage-of-income contribution each year. With the profit-sharing plan you can put in as much or as little profit as you like—up to the ceiling. Thus, although you get a lower ceiling, you also get more flexibility. Many people combine the two types of Keoghs to give themselves both flexibility and the maximum contribution.

A profit-sharing defined-contribution Keogh has smaller annual percentage limitations on contributions but is more flexible and thus favored by many part-timers whose self-employment income may be too sporadic to permit them to set up a regular schedule of contributions. The maximum deductible contribution is 15% of earnings per year, up to a maximum deduction of $24,000, which is reduced to an effective rate of only about 13% for the same reason that the effective limit on defined-contribution Keoghs works out to 20%.

A "defined-benefit" Keogh, which is designed to produce a predetermined amount of retirement income, permits you to exceed the $30,000 maximum. With a defined-benefit plan you decide, within certain limits, how much you would like to receive in annual retirement income. If you think this kind of plan might work for you, contact an accountant or financial planner with experience in retirement planning. You will need professional help to design a program that will accumulate enough money to pay that defined benefit when the time comes for you to retire.

As with an IRA, withdrawals from a Keogh before you turn 59½ will usually trigger a 10% penalty. As with an IRA, you can get around that penalty by scheduling payouts to deplete the fund over your expected lifetime. And, as with an IRA, you must start drawing down the fund shortly after you reach age 70½. You can take the money out in a lump sum, in installments or in annuity payments, and it is taxed accordingly. The payouts must be scheduled to deplete the fund over the period of your life expectancy at age 70½.

For an IRS guide to the intricacies of Keogh plans and related retirement tax shelters, call 800-TAX-FORM and ask for IRS Publication 560, Retirement Plans for the Self-Employed. It's free. Or contact the Web site at www.irs.ustreas.gov.

Simplified Employee Pensions

A RELATIVE OF BOTH THE KEOGH PLAN AND THE INDIVIDUAL retirement account, the simplified employee pension, or SEP, also lets you set aside self-employment income in a tax-sheltered account. The annual contribution limit is about 13% of income, up to $24,000—the same as for profit-sharing Keoghs. The rules are similar to those governing IRAs, but there are no income limits restricting the deductibility of contributions. What's more, the annual reporting requirements are less stringent than they are for Keoghs. Because of their similarity to IRAs, these plans are usually called SEP-IRAs or Super IRAs. The IRS publication mentioned earlier explains the rules.

The SIMPLE Plan

T HIS IS DESIGNED TO ENCOURAGE SELF-EMPLOYEDS TO SAVE for retirement. SIMPLE stands for "savings incentive match plans for employees," and these plans were really created by Congress as a simplified retirement plan for small companies. Only firms with fewer than 100 employees can use a SIMPLE. But the definition includes self-employed workers with no employees. Whether your business is full-time or you do free-lance or consulting work in addition to a full-time job, you can have a SIMPLE. And you can have one even if you have a job that offers a pension plan. You may not, however, have both a SIMPLE and a Keogh.

There are actually two kinds of SIMPLE plans—a SIMPLE IRA and a SIMPLE 401(k). It's likely that the IRA version will be best for a self-employed person with no employees. A real

Normal Limits on Employer 401(k) Contributions

Q: *Last year my husband contributed $10,000 to his 401(k) plan but in January his employer said that that was too much—that because he was paid more than $80,000, his contribution was limited to just $8,200. The extra $1,800 was returned to him as taxable income. I thought the law allowed contributions up to $10,000?*

A: One part of the law does allow 401(k) contributions of up to $10,000, but other provisions can squeeze that. Your husband is caught up in rules designed to prevent highly paid employees from reaping a disproportionate share of the tax benefits delivered by a 401(k). One definition of "highly compensated employees" are those who earn more than $80,000.

advantage: You can stash up to $6,000 a year into a SIMPLE IRA—and deduct every dime of it—even if that was 100% of your self-employment income.

401(k) Plans

I F YOUR EMPLOYER OFFERS ONE, A 401(K) SALARY REDUCTION option (or its cousin, the 403(b) plan offered to public school teachers and employees of nonprofit organizations) is an excellent vehicle for retirement savings. Money you earmark—usually 2% to 15% of your annual salary, depending on your employer's plan, up to an inflation-indexed annual maximum of $10,000 in 1999—goes into the account tax-free, and earnings are tax-deferred. You can get your money if you quit as early as age 55 without incurring a 10% tax penalty. A bonus: Many employers match employee contributions 50 cents on the dollar, or even dollar for dollar, up to a certain amount.

The employer may offer a variety of options for investing your salary set-asides, usually giving you a choice of stock in the company itself, a stock, bond or money-market fund, or something called a guaranteed investment contract (GIC). If you have such a choice, size up the company stock using the criteria described in Chapter 4. Be tough. After all, you already depend on the company for your livelihood. Do you want to depend on it for your investment results as well?

Stock and bond and money-market mutual funds offered by

CHAPTER 14 **Retirement: Investing for Yourself**

the company 401(k) plan can be evaluated according to the standards described in the appropriate chapters in this book.

Guaranteed Investment Contracts (GICs)

NEARLY THREE-FOURTHS OF ALL 401(K) PLANS OFFER GUARANteed investment contracts (GICs, also known as "stable value" funds or guaranteed-interest accounts) as an investment option. The plans buy GICs from insurance companies, which guarantee up front what the rate of return will be for the term of the GIC, which is between one and seven years. Probably attracted by the word "guaranteed," 401(k)-plan members have invested hundreds of billions of dollars in GICs and similar investment products.

How Do They Work?

Your plan manager takes the money designated for GICs and shops among insurance companies that offer them, looking for attractive interest rates and maturities. To spread risk, fund managers may sign contracts with as many as 20 issuers and blend the different rates of return at various maturities to arrive at the yield on your investment.

The insurance companies in turn invest GIC money in a variety of places—government bonds, corporate bonds, private placements of stock, high-yield junk bonds and mortgages. They keep a portion of the income from these investments as a fee and pass the rest on as your guaranteed yield. The yield is usually competitive with CDs, and amounts to between one-half and

The Safety of 401(k)s

Q: *If a company fails, would the money in a 401(k) plan be lost?*
A: It shouldn't be. Under the Employee Retirement Income Security Act (ERISA), employers and pension-plan trustees have a responsibility to safeguard employees' pension funds—and a company would be breaking the law if it tapped those funds. Generally, your account is as safe as your investments. You could run into trouble if you've selected company stock for your 401(k) and the company goes under.

295

one-and-a-half percentage points more than yields from Treasury notes of comparable maturities. When the term of the GIC contract is up, your pension fund gets back the principal and either reinvests it in another GIC or returns it to employees, who are retiring or cashing out of the plan.

ARE GICs SAFE?

GICs have delivered what their name implies: a guaranteed return. You know going in what you'll get coming out. The major risk is that a GIC is only as good as the insurance company that issues it. Concern for insurance companies' creditworthiness has prompted pension fund managers to take another look at their GIC investments. If you hold some, you should consider conducting your own investigation.

Ask your plan manager for the names of the insurance companies backing your GICs. As a member of a 401(k) plan you are legally entitled to at least annual reports from your plan manager on how your investments are performing. If you don't find the names there, ask a representative of your pension plan for a list of companies.

Check the firms' credit ratings. Most companies have begun including credit-rating information on the issuers of GICs they hold. If your company does not do this, you can find that information from the rating companies described in the section on deferred annuities in this chapter. Few pension plans buy GICs from companies with less than an A rating. If you find one rated lower than A on your company's list, request an explanation of why the company is taking that additional risk.

Look for diversification. Your pension manager should be buying GICs from at least three to five separate insurance companies— more, if your firm is large enough. That way the risk is spread, reducing the chance your plan will be affected by the failure of one insurance company.

Consider the plan's other investment options if you are uncomfortable with the GIC offered by your 401(k), and consider putting your money in one of them instead.

Because GICs in an individual company's plan are most likely drawn from a number of insurance companies, the failure of one would not ordinarily mean a significant drop in your 401(k) assets. And in most states, GIC contract holders would be covered by guaranty insurance plans under the same terms as holders of life insurance policies, which means that the state would make good on at least some of the loss. At any rate, the worry is probably overdone. Most of the major GIC sellers are holding only small amounts of non-investment-grade junk bonds.

HOW ABOUT MORE RISK FOR A BETTER— IF NOT GUARANTEED—RETURN?

A bigger worry for younger members of 401(k) plans should be whether too much of your money is tied up in relatively low-yielding GICs. If you are in your forties or younger, consider stepping up your risk a little by shifting a significant portion of your money—say, 70% or 80%, or even more—into a good stock mutual fund offered by the plan. But make sure the fund meets the standards described in Chapter 6. The further you are away from retirement, the more of your 401(k) money should be in stock-oriented funds because of their superior long-term results. (Buying their own company's stock through the 401(k) plan can be a good deal for employees of companies with a bright future, but for some of the potential drawbacks, see the following discussion.) You can diversify your funds among the plans' investment alternatives, and you should periodically assess how your account is performing.

Employee Stock Ownership Plans

EMPLOYEE STOCK OWNERSHIP PLANS (ESOPs) LET EMPLOYEES buy stock in their company through payroll withholding or some other way, or the corporation may contribute shares of its stock to funds that allocate the shares to employees based on their annual compensation. The advantage to employees is that they acquire stock of the company they work for at little or no cost. Employees must pay taxes on the value of the stock when they take possession of it when they leave the company, but in the meantime, the stock can appreciate tax-free. When employees receive it, they can continue the tax-favored treatment by rolling it over into an IRA.

An ESOP can be a great deal—if the company makes adequate contributions and the stock does well. But there are no guarantees. A recession, stock-market slump or downturn in business at your company could savage your account. Examples of each aren't hard to find.

What can you do to make sure your retirement dollars don't go down the drain with your company? Read on.

How Do ESOPs Work? The Promise

The company contributes a certain amount for each participating ESOP employee, based on salary. ESOP contributions average between 8% and 15% of annual pay. At 10%, for example, $5,000 (or $5,000 worth of company stock) would be contributed to the account of an employee earning $50,000. Company contributions and earnings on them are not taxed until the employee quits or retires and receives the money.

But unlike other retirement plans, in which the trustees are obligated to diversify investments prudently, an ESOP by its nature invests primarily—sometimes entirely—in company stock. As a result, an ESOP can be a high-stakes gamble.

The employer can contribute shares it owns to the ESOP, or it can give cash that the plan's trustees use to buy company stock. As a rule, though, the trustees get a company-backed loan to pay for the stock, and the employer's contributions go to repay the loan.

Once the shares are allocated to an employee's account, that employee has voting rights. In publicly traded companies, employees can vote on all issues put before the shareholders. In closely held firms—those in which the stock is owned by relatively few people and is not traded on an exchange—voting rights of ESOP shareholders can be limited to major issues, such as the sale or merger of the company.

In theory, a well-run ESOP can be good for everybody. Giving workers a direct financial stake in their company should make them more productive. If morale is high, the company is more likely to prosper, and if it does, so will its employees. And so will the other stockholders. Today, the plans are in place at dozens of blue-chip corporations, including Polaroid, Anheuser Busch, Lockheed and Procter & Gamble, as well as hundreds of smaller concerns.

HOW DO ESOPS WORK? THE WORRIES

There is some concern that companies may create ESOPs more to cut costs and block takeovers than to give workers a bigger stake in the enterprise. And ESOPs apparently have had little or no effect on productivity or profits. Indeed, ESOPs offer unique advantages to the corporate sponsors. For one thing, the company gets the right to deduct dividends paid on shares allocated to ESOP accounts. ESOPs can also be used as a source of low-cost financing. Setting up an ESOP to borrow money to buy newly issued shares, for example, can provide a cash infusion for the company.

WHAT SHOULD YOU DO ABOUT AN ESOP?

It's crucial that you know just where you stand if your employer has an ESOP or is considering starting one. Federal law requires disclosure of the major provisions of the plan and values of the stock, but you should also get a full explanation from key company officers and assess the plan in light of your long-term financial goals.

An ESOP is a defined-contribution benefit plan, like a deferred profit-sharing plan or a 401(k) plan with a company match. An ESOP is riskier than some of the other defined-contribution plans, though, because its success depends altogether on the sponsoring company's success. Although a few plans are somewhat diversified, most are funded entirely with the company's stock. If the stock rises in value, everybody gains. But if it performs poorly, contributions taper off. If the company fails, ESOP members may wind up with nothing.

How can you find out whether an ESOP is in your best interest?

First, take a critical look at any other long-term benefits your employer provides, such as a profit-sharing or pension plan. The principal disclosure document required by federal law is called a summary plan description. If your company has a good retirement-income plan with federally guaranteed benefits, much less will be riding on the ESOP.

The plan description for an ESOP must include information on the workings of the plan and the rights and obligations of employees. In addition, employers must furnish annual statements showing the balance of their accounts, the value of the stock and the extent to which each worker is vested—that is, how much you would get if you quit. The law requires that you be fully vested after no more than seven years in the plan.

The leading public companies are tracked by security analysts who forecast future performance. Sources of this kind of information are listed in Chapter 4. Unfortunately for your fact-gathering process, most ESOPs are not at public companies. They are at privately held concerns. Those firms are subject to the same benefit-disclosure rules but not the federal securities laws. Still, many do furnish workers with an abundance of financial and performance information, and you should be able to get what you need from the company benefits manager.

How Can You Protect Yourself?

Don't make the mistake of confusing an ESOP with a pension plan. An ESOP is really an investment in the company you work for and should be evaluated as such—in light of other investments you have, your stage in life and your tolerance for risk.

As a participant in an ESOP, you have the right to diversify your account as you near retirement age. A worker reaching age 55 who has been in an ESOP for ten years can direct that 25% of the assets in his or her account be invested outside of company securities. At age 60, you can shift 50% of your account to non-company investments.

The ability to diversify is a key point to study in the plan summary. What provisions does the ESOP make for diversification? Are alternative investments provided within the plan? Will the percentage you shift out of company stock be paid to you in cash so that you can roll it over into an IRA? The decision whether to diversify should turn on both your view of the company's prospects and the way the ESOP fits into the rest of your investment plan.

Employee Stock Options

THERE WAS A TIME WHEN ONLY TOP EXECUTIVES GOT STOCK options, but these juicy perks have now gone mainstream. Even the baristas at Starbucks and the burger flippers at Wendy's get stock options these days. In some industries, most notably high-tech ones, stock options are the norm.

Employee stock options give the holder the right to buy company stock in the future at a "strike" price fixed when the option is granted. If the stock goes nowhere, neither does your net worth. But if the price takes off, you could get rich as you buy low, sell high in a simultaneous transaction.

Options come in two flavors: nonqualified stock options and incentive stock options (ISOs). Nonmanagerial employees generally get the nonqualified kind, meaning that they don't meet the government's rules for special tax treatment. ISOs pass those tests and are usually reserved for managers and key executives.

With both types, your strike price is generally the fair market value of the stock on the day you get the option. Most options have no cash value when you get them because you can't convert them to cash or stock until they vest, which usually happens gradually over three to five years. For example, if you have options to buy 100 shares and become 50% vested after two years, at that point you could exercise half your options and buy 50 shares.

You usually get ten years to exercise nonqualified stock options and somewhat less time before ISOs expire. At publicly traded companies, vested options can usually be exercised at will. But if your employer is a privately held company, your right to cash in your options may be tied to a future event, such as an initial public offering of stock or the sale of the company.

It's important to remember that stock-options plans are not a sure thing, but more like a defined-contribution pension, with no guarantee of future value. Even if your company's prospects are outstanding, you'll want to make sure that you haven't got too much of a good thing: Add up the market value of all your vested stock options. Then add the value of any company stock you already own, including shares purchased with contributions to your 401(k) plan or through a discount stock-purchase plan. Next, compute how much of your total net worth is made up of your company's stock. How much is too much? Consider that federal regulations prohibit employers from sinking any more than 10% of a pension plan into their own stock. If your exposure seems too high, set a target price for the exercise of some of your nonqualified options, then take the cash rather than the stock and use the money to diversify your investment portfolio. This action will help you lower your risk.

What if you cash in too early and miss a burst of growth? Use your knowledge of the company and its prospects to set a "no-looking-back number"—the price at which you won't second-guess your decision.

Review your options at least twice a year, especially as you near retirement or begin to think of leaving the company.

PART FOUR

Get Help When You Need It

Financial Planners & Other Helpers

 THIS CHAPTER STEPS BACK A BIT FROM THE TRANSAC- tion stage to the investigating and decision- making stages. Here we examine the kind of help you can get from financial planners, investment clubs, newsletters and other sources not described elsewhere.

What a Financial Planner Can Do for You

THE BUSINESS OF FINANCIAL PLANNERS ONCE CONSISTED largely of selling life insurance, mutual funds and lifetime "plans" in loose-leaf binders the size of dictionaries. So it seemed, anyway. If you want a plan like that, you can still get one, and it can be a valuable tool: a comprehensive overview of your current financial condition, along with recommendations for achieving your financial goals. Depending on its complexity, such a plan can cost you from several hundred to several thousand dollars.

These days, though, people are more likely to turn to a plan- ner for help with less sweeping problems. What to do with a lump sum received from an inheritance is a common dilemma, teeming with tax and investment decisions that need to be made in a hurry. As a result of the growing demand for this sort of ad hoc advice, many planners have begun charging for their services by the hour rather than by the plan. Their fees—often $100 to $150 an hour—put them in the same league as lawyers and psychiatrists. And, as with lawyers and psychiatrists, finding a good planner is the key to getting your money's worth.

A good planner can see to it that your investments are diversified and appropriate for your goals and stage in life: growth funds for an IRA, for example, or municipal bonds to generate tax-free income if your bracket warrants it. A good planner can also help you anticipate the tax consequences of your investment decisions.

Many planners are registered with the Securities and Exchange Commission as investment advisers, and that is what they like to be most of all because investment management provides an ongoing stream of revenue. Many offer what are known as wrap accounts. Usually you can open a wrap account only with a minimum of $100,000 or more. There are no sales fees or commissions on trades, and you receive a consolidated statement. The advisers serve as money managers, creating and managing investment portfolios and charging a management fee comparable to that charged by mutual funds.

More common are simple fee-based accounts. Like wrap accounts, they may include stocks, bonds, mutual funds and cash. The investment choices are worked out between you and your planner. You pay a fee that is a fixed percentage of assets, usually from 0.75% to 2.5%. There may or may not be additional charges for transactions. Thus, these accounts can serve as money managers for their clients, creating and managing investment portfolios, and charging a fee comparable to that charged by mutual funds.

If you are going to turn your investment decisions over to a planner, it is especially important that you choose an able one, that the planner keep you informed about what's happening to your investment account, and that you not hesitate to disagree when you become uneasy about what's being done with your money. Even then, it is up to you to make sure that the planner stays in tune with your goals and risk tolerance.

How Do You Pick a Planner?

A planner's credentials are the most obvious clue to his or her preparation for the job. The best-known credential is the Certified Financial Planner (CFP) designation from the Certified Financial

Planner Board of Standards, Inc. To earn the CFP, planners have to pass a ten-hour comprehensive exam administered by the International Board of Standards and Practices for Certified Financial Planners. The vast majority of practicing CFPs prepare for the exams by taking home-study courses from the College for Financial Planning, which usually take a couple of years to complete. Graduate courses are available for advanced planners who have already earned the CFP.

The College's fiercest competitors for status in the business are the 30 or so colleges and universities that offer undergraduate or graduate degrees in planning or that prepare students to take the CFP exam. Among them are Baylor, Georgia State, San Diego State, and Clemson universities.

In addition to academic degrees and the CFP, other leading planning credentials indicating extensive training include the ChFC (Chartered Financial Consultant), which is awarded by the American College, in Bryn Mawr, Pa., and the CPA/PFS (Certified Public Accountant, Personal Financial Specialist), awarded by the American Institute of CPAs.

WHERE CAN YOU FIND A PLANNER?

The Yellow Pages are full of the names of planners, but you should start your search with a reference of some kind. Lawyers, accountants and insurance agents are good people to ask.

The International Association for Financial Planning (5775 Glenridge Dr., N.E., Suite B-300, Atlanta, GA 30328-5364; 888-806-7526, 404-845-0011; www.iafp.org), to which more than 17,000 planners belong, has a registry service you can use to get names of members in your area, as well as a searchable data base online.

The Institute of Certified Financial Planners (3801 E. Florida Ave., Suite 708, Denver, CO 80210-2544; www.icfp.org/cpfsearch; 800-282-7526) will give you names of qualified planners nearby, or you may search its Web site.

The National Association of Personal Financial Advisors (355 W. Dundee Road, Buffalo Grove, IL 60089; 800-366-2732; www.napfa.org)

will provide a list of fee-only practitioners in your area. Or you may search for a planner online. A fee-only planner earns no commissions for the mutual funds, insurance or other financial products he or she may recommend that you buy.

The American Institute of CPAs (Personal Financial Planning Division, Harborside Financial Center, 201 Plaza III, Jersey City, NJ 07311-3881; 888-777-7707) will provide the names of certified public accountants with the CPA/PFS credential.

The American Society of CLU and ChFC (www.financialpro.org; 800-392-6900) will send you the names of ChFCs and CLUs (see above) who are planners or you can request the names of planners via its Web site.

What Do You Ask a Planner?

Once you've got a list of planners with recognized credentials, call or visit two or three, comparing their fee structures and their competence as investment advisers.

FEE STRUCTURE. Planners earn their keep in one or more of three ways. Some work on a fee-only basis, charging you by the hour or by the specific task. Others collect commissions on the products they sell you, such as stocks, bonds, mutual funds and insurance policies. Many planners charge a mixture of fees and commissions.

A planner's fee structure is no indicator of competence, although fee-only planners insist that commission-based planners have a built-in conflict of interest because they have a stake in selling you something whether you need it or not. That's something to think about. If you want to invest in a mutual fund, you can be certain that commission-based planners are going to pick a fund with a sales load; otherwise, they receive no compensation for their work. A fee-only planner would probably choose a no-load fund. In the end, you might not pay the commissioned planner any more in the end than you pay the fee-based planner, but in the case of that fund load, the fee is coming out of your investment, leaving less working for you in the market. (See the discussion of loads in Chapter 6.)

INVESTMENT RECORD. A planner you're considering as an invest-ment adviser should be willing to give you information on how other clients' portfolios have performed under his or her man-agement. Compare all those records with one another and the performance of the financial markets as a whole before making a choice. Often the planner will provide you with comparable performance benchmarks that will give you an idea of where to look on your own. Pay special attention to how well the planner has done in achieving the objective you'll be pursuing, whether it be investing for growth, income or a combination. Ask the planner to sketch out for you how he or she would deploy your financial resources, and decide whether you like the result.

Secrets of Successful Investment Clubs

INVESTMENT CLUBS ARE SMALL GROUPS OF PEOPLE—15 IS A TYPICAL number—who get together once a month, pool their ideas and money, and invest regularly in stocks and bonds they choose. Members may be friends, neighbors or co-workers who divide up the responsibility for researching potential invest-ments using methods very much like those described in this book. Along the way they may be aided by material provided by the National Association of Investors Corp. (P.O. Box 220, Royal Oak, MI 48068; toll-free 877-275-6242, or 248-583-6242; www.better-investing.org), a nonprofit alliance of more than 37,000 clubs across the U.S. Clubs pay $40 per year plus $14 per member to belong to the NAIC. Individual membership is $39 a year. For an additional fee, NAIC also sponsors a Computer Group membership, which features advice on using computer programs and Internet sources.

Over the years, more than half of clubs affiliated with the NAIC have regularly outperformed the Standard & Poor's 500-stock index—a record that's about as good as that of profession-al money managers. (Nobody knows how investment clubs have fared as a whole. NAIC members account for only about a third of all clubs.)

Forming a club that lasts isn't easy. About half of all newly formed NAIC affiliates disband within 18 months, usually because of incompatibility or policy disagreements. Still, most of the clubs that make it through the start-up phase do quite well.

HOW DO SUCCESSFUL CLUBS OPERATE?

An examination of successful investment clubs reveals common elements in their operating methods:

They invest all or nearly all of their money in stocks. Comparatively few clubs get into bonds, real estate, mutual funds, precious metals or limited partnerships.

They research new investment ideas extensively and debate the possible risks and rewards of each before committing their money.

They invest regularly, regardless of what the market is doing, and for the long term, keeping close watch on all the businesses they invest in.

They buy mostly high-quality stocks with good business records and some growth potential. Diversification among different industries is a high priority.

They reinvest all dividends.

They keep up with economic news and other developments that could affect the value of their portfolios.

In a typical investment club, each member invests $50 or so per month. At meetings, members who were assigned the previous month to check into specific stocks report their findings. If they recommend buying the stock, members vote on it and the majority rules, just as it does when stocks are sold. The clubs hold their stocks for an average of seven-and-a-half years. Nearly all members have personal portfolios in addition to their stake in their club's portfolio, and use the club as a source of investment ideas.

A chance to make money is only one of the benefits of investment club membership. Novice investors learn by doing, while experienced ones add to their store of knowledge.

In addition, the clubs provide a forum for discussion and debate of investment topics in general.

How Do You Join a Club?

Finding an investment club to join may be difficult. There is no known public list of clubs: The NAIC doesn't publish one; in fact, the Securities and Exchange Commissions prohibits the NAIC from helping individuals find investment clubs to join or vice versa.

In addition, clubs limit their size, and there isn't much turnover. Many clubs have waiting lists. When openings do occur, they're often filled by friends of members. And joining an older club may require a substantial investment to get your stake in the venture on a par with that of members who have been at it for a while.

(There are also online investment club sites. Model OnLine Investment Club (MOLIC) is an online investment club that was founded by a group of NAIC members. The club invests real money based on the club's investment decisions. MOLIC operates from NAIC's site at www.better-investing.org/molic. It's an open club that anyone can observe to learn how an online club might work.)

There are two possible alternatives if you can't get into an existing club:

FIRST, YOU COULD START ONE YOURSELF. For $20 for nonmembers, the NAIC provides step-by-step guidelines, including a sample partnership agreement and explanatory material that can be given to prospective members. It may not be necessary to recruit all the members yourself. People who you know are interested may be able to recruit others. When you get enough prospects, schedule a meeting to talk over the details.

SECOND, YOU COULD CONSIDER JOINING THE NAIC AS AN INDIVIDUAL. For $39 a year you get the organization's investment-oriented magazine, a helpful investment manual and other materials, plus free access to the association's information reports.

A Club for Do-It-Yourselfers

I F YOU'RE NOT THE GREGARIOUS SORT AND WOULD JUST AS SOON ponder your investment picks on your own, the American Association of Individual Investors may be to your liking. The credo of this organization is simple: As an individual, you can enjoy investment results better than those of most professionals—if you are willing to spend the necessary time and exert the necessary effort. The AAII has more than 60 local chapters, which meet several times a year to exchange investment ideas or listen to an expert discuss an aspect of investing.

The AAII preaches that individuals have an important edge over large institutions such as mutual and pension funds. Individuals, goes the theory, can move more quickly and have more choices than institutions trading big blocks of securities. Similarly, it's easier for an individual to change the mix of investments in a portfolio when the investment climate changes. A mutual fund, by contrast, is often locked into a specific investment strategy.

The AAII's followers are certainly individual investors, but not necessarily small ones. The average AAII member has a six-figure income and a half-million-dollar-plus investment portfolio, not including home equity. The great majority have a college degree.

AAII members are asked for as much or as little as they want to give of their time and concentration. You can choose to spend time only reading the articles in the somewhat academic *AAII Journal*, a 36-page monthly (except March and December) publication devoted to the development of overall investment strategies, not to specific investment recommendations. Or you can become involved in meetings of local chapters, attend seminars, buy home-study courses or tapes, or join various subgroups, such as one on computers and investing. The common thread is education—you're not told where to put your money, but how to become an intelligent investor and make up your own mind.

SHOULD YOU JOIN?

The AAII approach is not to everyone's liking. A lot of new members drop out at the end of the first year. But after that, most of those who are left stick with it. Among those who leave, the main gripe is that the material is too demanding and takes too much time. The AAII's road to riches involves hard work and persistence. Members spend an average of several hours a week tending to their portfolios. You needn't fit that profile, of course, but a novice might have a tough time keeping up.

WHAT YOU GET. Membership in the AAII (625 N. Michigan Ave., Chicago, IL 60611; 800-428-2244, 312-280-0170; www.aaii.com) costs $49 per year. That gets you, among other things, the *AAII Journal,* which, in addition to hard-core stock and mutual fund analysis, typically contains articles on portfolio management, retirement planning, tax angles of investing, and brief summaries of new books. Other features of membership include:

The *Individual Investor's Guide to Low-Load Mutual Funds* (annual; $24.95 to nonmembers; see Chapter 6).

Membership in one of the AAII's local chapters in 34 states, which typically meet monthly. Specialized subgroups also exist, including one on computerized investing that has its own AAII newsletter.

Access to many online features at www.aaii.com, including searchable archives of articles from its publications and lists of financial Web sites.

At extra cost, members are offered home-study courses, investment videos, newsletters and books devoted to using a home computer as an investment tool, plus beginning and advanced investment seminars.

Do You Need an Investment Newsletter?

I NVESTMENT NEWSLETTERS HAVE OCCASIONALLY BEEN THE STUFF of legend. In the past, one editor's instructions to his subscribers to buy something, or sell everything, could set off a chain reaction in the market, driving prices up or down as the herd instinct took hold. These days newsletters are quieter, just another voice among many. With high-quality investment information so widely available, it's fair to wonder which of the dozens of relatively expensive investment newsletters are worth the price.

Fortunately, the cost of testing the waters isn't steep. Most newsletter publishers will send you a free sample copy or sell you a trial subscription for $25 to $50 or so.

How Good Are They?

For nearly 20 years, Mark Hulbert, editor of *Hulbert Financial Digest* (free sample available online, $135 per year, introductory offer $59; 5051B Backlick Rd., Annandale, VA 22003; 800-485-2378; www.hulbertdigest.com), has been the arbiter of success among newsletters. Hulbert tracks and ranks the results of more than 160 letters on the basis of their buy and sell signals, model portfolios or specific recommendations.

Hulbert believes that there is a connection between a letter's performance over the past 10 or 15 years and its prospects for future accuracy. He finds virtually no correlation between one year's performance and the next year's. Even less encouraging is his discovery that the letters that beat the Standard & Poor's 500-stock index from 1980 to 1985 tended to lag behind it in the second half of the decade. If you were to keep score on any newsletter's ability to forecast accurately, you'd find that, at any given time, some are right, some wrong and others too early or too late in predicting the next turn of events.

The value of a newsletter often rests as much in its clarity, educational value and common sense as it does in its stock-picking prowess (provided that its prowess isn't simply awful). Newsletters can help you by providing good explanations of investment alternatives, well-supported recommendations, unusual ideas and guidance on asset allocation. A couple of general market letters with years of solid performance to recommend them are *The Outlook* and *Babson United Investment Report:*

The Outlook, by Standard & Poor's (26 Broadway, New York, NY 10004; 800-852-1641; www.personalwealth.com; weekly, $298). A conservative voice of Wall Street, this S&P publication uses good charts and graphs to present both a strategic overview and specific investment ideas. It grades stocks (five stars means it's a buy, one star a sell). and offers a straightforward and centrist view of the investment climate. No model portfolio is included, but a list of recommended five-star stocks is. Bonds get coverage, too. A typical issue delivers an investment commentary, updates of stocks on the recommended list, an in-depth look at one favored stock, a survey of an entire industry, and a list of stocks that meet certain criteria, such as financial strength or earnings growth.

Babson United Investment Report (101 Prescott St., Wellesley Hills, MA 02481; 888-223-7412 or 781-235-0900; www.babson.com; weekly, $268). This letter, first published by an old-line advisory firm founded by the legendary Roger W. Babson, is aimed at the educated masses. You get a little of everything. For example, an issue may touch on the federal budget, the strategic petroleum reserve, the Fed, the Japanese, and state tax revenues, as well as the stock and bond markets. Investment ideas can be both general and specific. If you're seeking a fast overview, complete with buy and sell recommendations, this letter will do nicely.

CHAPTER 16

Choosing & Using a Broker

EFORE YOU'RE READY TO CHOOSE A STOCK BROKER, you'll have to do a little thinking about what kind of investor you are and how you like to operate. This chapter will describe the three choices available to you: full-service, discount and online brokers. It's convenient to think of them as distinct choices, but in fact the lines separating these different categories are getting fuzzier and fuzzier, as you'll see.

But first, consider your investing style. Which of these statements best describes you?

You like to talk things over, weigh all the angles, check every source of information you can before you make a decision. You are a good candidate for a full-service broker.

You have no trouble making decisions on your own, you prefer to do your own research and don't want to pay someone to do it for you. A discount broker is definitely in your future.

You fit the second description, and you use the Internet a lot to shop and track down information. You'd probably be happiest with an online broker.

Full-Service Brokers

MOST OF THESE ARE THE HIGH-PROFILE NATIONAL FIRMS with armies of analysts who crank out buy and sell recommendations for a long list of stocks, bonds and mutual funds. Their fee structures reflect the expense of maintaining those research departments. Commissions vary according to the number of shares, type of shares and dollar amount involved, but on average you can expect to pay about 2% or so of the value of the shares each time you buy or sell. In general, the bigger the transaction, the smaller the bite taken out of it by the broker's commission.

Full-service firms also pride themselves on their comprehensive asset management services, the granddaddy of which is the Merrill Lynch Cash Management Account, or CMA. Other firms have followed suit, calling their comprehensive accounts by different names but offering the same kind of services under one roof. All include a money-market account into which the firm automatically "sweeps" idle funds (from dividend payments, for example); check-writing privileges; a substantial line of credit; a debit card or credit card tied to the account; and a comprehensive monthly statement that makes investment record-keeping a breeze. Minimum account size that qualifies for such deluxe service ranges from $5,000 to $25,000, depending on the broker.

You know the names of most of the full-service brokers because most have offices all over the country: A. G. Edwards & Sons, Edward D. Jones Co., Everen Securities, Morgan Stanley Dean Witter, Merrill Lynch, PaineWebber, Prudential Securities, Raymond James Financial, Salomon Smith Barney and others. Depending on where you live, you may also be familiar with some of the full-service regional firms, which have offices in certain parts of the country—for instance, U.S. Bancorp Piper Jaffray, which is based in Minneapolis; J.C. Bradford in Nashville; BT Alex. Brown in Baltimore (BT stands for Bankers Trust); Scott & Stringfellow in Richmond. (Some of these firms have been acquired by banks hoping to keep the brokerage business of their well-heeled customers.)

A LITTLE HELP FROM YOUR FRIENDS

The best way to start your search for a broker who's right for you at a full-service firm is to ask friends who are investors whom they use. Then quiz your friends as closely as you comfortably can about their investment goals and styles. Are they buy-and-hold types or do they trade frequently? Do they favor stocks or bonds? Small companies or large? Are they in contact with their broker frequently, or only once in a while? Are their phone calls returned? What do they think of the firm's account statements? Are they easy to understand or are they confusing? What about research reports—does the broker provide them and other backup for investment recommendations? Finally, knowing what they do about you, would your friends recommend their broker to be your broker?

This process will produce a few names for you to pursue. Call the most promising of the recommended brokers and tell them where you got their names. Briefly outline your investment goals and make an appointment to meet at the brokers' offices. At the meetings, inquire into the brokers' experience and educational background, both academic and professional. Ask about their approach to investments in general: Do they specialize in any particular area, or do they generalize?

Note what kinds of questions each broker asks about you and your financial situation. A broker should know your goals, your resources and your risk tolerance before he or she is in a position to advise you. Your interests and the broker's interests should be the same: to lay the seeds for a long-term, mutually beneficial relationship. If a broker shows little interest in finding out your financial position and goals, and instead presses you with a sales pitch on getting rich, scratch that one off your list and make plans to interview the next one.

COMMISSIONS

All of that is not to say that you should ignore commission rates. Deciding on a full-service broker means deciding that money isn't everything, but costs do matter. You're not out to throw money away. Ideally, you'll find the best combination of good service (quality of advice, chiefly) and lowest price. When we checked commissions and fees in late 1999, we found Edward Jones, A.G. Edwards, Raymond James and Merrill Lynch clumped together in that order near the bottom of the cost range for a representative collection of trades.

ASSET-BASED FEES. Most full-service brokers offer premium services at a savings to investors who sign up for what's called asset-based fees, or for a related service, the "wrap" account. For years, Merrill Lynch has allowed clients to pay a fee based on the percentage of assets under management instead of paying commissions for each trade. But these programs tended to be pretty pricey.

These days, asset-based fees are a much more reasonable alternative to commissions. At Merrill, the program costs 1% annually for stocks and stock mutual funds and 0.3% for bonds and money-market instruments such as Treasury bills. As a result, the program is less expensive than the annual costs on most no-load mutual funds.

Asset-based fees eliminate the conflict of interest inherent in a commission-based relationship, in which the more trades you make, the more the broker earns. But you have to think carefully about whether such an arrangement would save you money. If you don't trade much, it probably won't.

At any rate, the minimum account size may be barrier enough. Merrill Lynch's program has a $1,500 minimum annual fee, meaning that to take advantage of the 1% rate, you must have at least $150,000 to invest. Prudential and Salomon Smith Barney have similar programs, for which they charge 1.5% annually.

WRAP ACCOUNTS. With a wrap account, you pay the same way as with asset-based pricing: a percentage of assets under management annually, rather than commissions. But with wrap programs you get an independent, outside money manager instead of a stockbroker. The problem with wrap programs is that they are usually more expensive, and you may not get a lot of individual attention from your money manager.

E. F. Hutton was the pioneer in this field. That firm was purchased by Salomon Smith Barney, which is still a leader in wrap accounts. You can choose from among 300 money managers, and the fees vary from 0.6% to 3.0%, depending on the size of your account.

Whichever account you choose, as it grows, be sure ask about discounts. Most full-service brokers will shave their rates for especially good customers.

QUALITY OF ADVICE. This is what you pay for, of course—the whole reason for turning to a full-service broker in the first place. It's a moving target, of course, but be sure to ask for information about how various kinds of stocks picked by the firm's analysts have performed for investors with goals, assets and risk tolerance similar to yours. You can't predict the future, but you can draw some conclusions from the past.

Discount Brokers

ISCOUNTERS DON'T MAKE SPECIFIC BUY AND SELL RECOMmendations for your account. What you get is fulfillment of your order, period (although some discounters offer a range of investor services, which will be described later). Because they don't have to support research departments and because most of their business is done over the phone or on the Internet, discounters can charge considerably less than full-service brokers to accomplish your transactions. Discounts, depending on the size of the transaction, can amount to as much as 80% of what you'd pay a full-service broker, although 20% to 30% is a more representative range.

Despite their common devotion to bare-bones order-taking, it would be a mistake to think that discount brokers are interchangeable. Some offer a limited amount of research, some have investment-oriented libraries open to their customers, and some even offer all-in-one accounts that rival those of the full-service firms. Fidelity, Schwab and Quick & Reilly, for example, will set up accounts that automatically sweep idle cash into a money-market account. Fidelity's Ultra Service Account and the Schwab One asset management account provide comprehensive, consolidated monthly statements that help you keep track of all investment transactions conducted there.

Still, it is cut-rate commissions that put discounters on the map, and it is largely on that basis that they must be evaluated. Some very small trades are often cheaper at a full-service firm because discounters typically charge minimum commissions of at least $25, more often $35 or more for broker-assisted trades. Thus, buying or selling a few shares of a low-cost stock—ten shares of a $5 issue, for example—could actually cost you less at Merrill Lynch, where the minimum commission is $29.95, than it would at Charles Schwab, where the minimum is $39 for a broker-assisted trade (although if you trade using Schwab's online service, your commission is cut to $29.95).

Because it's savings you're after, it's important to know that commissions aren't necessarily the only charges you'll pay at a discount broker. Compare brokers on the following items, too.

NUISANCE FEES. Commissions may be the most important part of the equation, but charges for postage or for issuance and delivery of stock certificates can mount up.

PRODUCTS AND SERVICES. Some discounters are distinguishing themselves by adding frills such as credit or debit cards, variable annuities, touch-tone trading and other goodies. For these, you'll pay in some cases, save in others. In general, discounters charge less for a trade you complete yourself, either via touch-tone phone or online.

MUTUAL FUND PROGRAMS. One big attraction of discount firms is the opportunity to buy and sell no-load mutual funds, often with no transaction fees. Many firms offer hundreds of no-load funds, but some discounters are just dipping a toe into these waters.

INVESTOR TOOLS. You should be able to read your statement and find information you need without getting a headache. And forays online should not leave you frustrated.

Online Brokers

BECAUSE MANY DISCOUNTERS AND A FEW FULL-SERVICE BROKERS offer online trading these days, the lines between them aren't so clearly drawn. But there are important differences. Your choice of an online broker should depend mostly on how fast you turn over your portfolio—that is, how often you buy and sell.

If you're a frequent trader, you'll probably be happiest with a firm like Suretrade or Datek (see listing on page 326), whose commissions are less than $10 per trade.

If you want responsive, knowledgeable brokers available to talk to on the phone and Web sites loaded with solid research and financial calculators, you might prefer Fidelity Brokerage or Charles Schwab.

The Real Cost of Service

TO ASSESS the service you've received from your full-service broker, try the quiz, "Is Your Full-Service Broker Worth the Big Bucks?" at www.kiplinger.com/worksheet /brokquiz.htm. You'll learn whether you've chosen a winner or it's time to find a more compatible broker.

To see how much brokerage fees affect your investment rate of return, check the financial calculator at: www. calcbuilder.com/cgi-bin/calcs/STO6. cgi/Kiplinger.

To test responsiveness to investor inquiries, we called 21 brokers six times each over the course of two trading days. When we got brokers on the phone, we asked them questions intended to test their knowledge. We also examined numerous other attributes, such as the quantity and quality of research and other financial resources provided to investors.

Discover Brokerage Direct and Muriel Siebert & Co., the top scorers on this test, are not only responsive but both offer market orders for a reasonable (though not rock-bottom) price of $14.95. (These rates were in effect in the fall of 1999 and are subject to change.) Siebert charges the same price for a limit order (an order to buy or sell a security at a specific price; see Glossary), while Discover charges $5 more. Discover offers handy investment tools and a Web site that's easier to navigate than any other we've seen. Siebert boasts responsive brokers and good executions. You won't go wrong choosing either of these.

Next in line is Mr. Stock, a little-known firm whose knowledgeable brokers answer the phone quickly and provide good executions. Mr. Stock charges $14.95 for a market order and $19.95 for a limit order.

Mydiscountbroker.com finished fourth in our survey, despite being virtually unknown to most investors. It offers $12 trades.

Both Mr. Stock and Mydiscountbroker.com fail, however, to provide year-end, cost-basis information to clients.

Wall Street Access, ranked fifth, charges $25 for stock trades.

LOW, LOW RATES. The cheapest online broker, Brown & Co., charges $5 for a market order. The most expensive, Schwab, charges $29.95. All things being equal, you'll want to use a lower-priced broker—even though the differences in cost are not nearly so great as they once were. But the cheapest, Brown, offers little in the way of research and other materials on its Web site. For this reason, even some very active traders prefer Schwab.

As with discount brokers, commissions aren't the whole story when it comes to assessing cost. The "spread" between the price to buy and the price to sell a stock is important, and it's something you might not notice. A stock may be offered to buyers at $12.25 and simultaneously priced at $12 to sellers. If you place an order to sell, you may get a share price of $12, or you may get $11.875, or maybe $12.125, depending at least in part on which brokerage you use. On a 200-share sale, losing 12.5 cents per share will cost you $25—more than the commission in most cases.

HIDDEN COSTS. Many investors are unaware of the hidden costs of executing a stock trade, or of the ways that brokers and other market participants can jack up the costs of trading. Most important is payment for order flow. This is money a broker receives for routing stock orders to a particular market participant (the market participant is the firm that actually executes the trades).

Many brokers are paid an average of $2 per trade in payment for order flow, and some get more. Market participants, of course, must make enough money from a trade to pay the $2 and to turn a profit. This situation can encourage brokers to

A Walk on the Wild Side

MOST PEOPLE who use online brokerages are investing for the long term, much as they would if they were using a full-service broker. These investors are likely to attain the best result. Rapid trading—going in and out of stocks based on short-term hopes and hunches rather than any appreciation for a company's long-term potential—may not be good for most investors' bottom lines. But if you want the thrill of day trading without the risk, check out E*Trade's The Game (http://game.etrade.com/). You're "given" $100,000 in play money to trade. The best trader at the end of the month wins $1,000 in real money. The game teaches the mechanics of trading—and it encourages big bets on volatile stocks. But it's just virtual money.

Is Online Trading Safe?

NOTHING'S 100% GUARANTEED, but most online brokers are using one or more of the following strategies to safeguard your online transactions:

Encryption. The information you send and receive is encoded. Currently the online security standard is encryption using a secure browser such as Netscape Navigator version 3.0 or higher or Microsoft Internet Explorer version 4.0 or higher.

Time-out. After a specific amount of time during which users been inactive in the trading area, the system automatically logs them out.

"Three strikes." If a user incorrectly enters your PIN number three times, your account will be blocked. To reactivate your account, you will have to call the broker directly and answer several verification questions.

Cash controls. Many firms won't allow your cash balance to be withdrawn over the Internet. They may require that checks be transferred to a bank account or be made payable to the account holder.

lower their commissions and then send trades to wherever they get the biggest rebate.

How to tell what's going on? We looked at what percentage of trades in stocks listed on the New York Stock Exchange were actually executed on the NYSE, where investors typically receive first-rate executions, meaning fast and cheap. We also looked at how often investors got better prices on trades than they might have expected. Finally, we looked at how much brokers spread their orders around among different market participants—an indication they are shopping for a good price for investors—rather than using just one or two.

Several brokerages, such as Schwab and Fidelity, are the sole owners of market participants, to which they send all (or most, in Schwab's case) of their trades. That made it impossible to rank how well they execute trades. Schwab and Fidelity, however, have reputations for providing good executions.

If you think you've been the victim of a bad execution, call your broker and ask for the precise time of your trade. Then go to a Web site such as Bigcharts.com and punch up a one-minute intraday chart of the stock. If your order was filled at a much less favorable price than others that were executed about the same time, you may have a beef with your broker.

OTHER FEES. Fidelity, Net Investor, Schwab and WallStreet Electronica may impose inactivity fees if you don't trade, particu-

A Sample of Online Brokers

Before you choose an online broker, ask for descriptive literature about the firm. Examine it and note the differences in services offered by each firm. Then compare rates on a trade typical of your investment pattern.

BROKER	PHONE NUMBER	WEB SITE (WWW.)
Accutrade	800-882-4887	accutrade.com
Ameritrade	800-454-9272	ameritrade.com
Brown & Co.	800-822-2021	brownco.com
Datek	800-823-2835	datek.com
Discover Brokerage	800-688-6896	discoverbrokerage.com
DLJDirect	877-456-4355	dljdirect.com
E*Trade	800-786-2573	etrade.com
Fidelity Brokerage	800-544-7272	fidelity.com
Mr. Stock	800-470-1896	mrstock.com
Mydiscountbroker.com	888-882-5600	mydiscountbroker.com
National Discount Brokers	888-302-7764	ndb.com
The Net Investor	800-638-4250	netinvestor.com
Charles Schwab & Co.	800-435-4000	schwab.com
Scottrade	800-619-7283	scottrade.com
Muriel Siebert & Co.	800-872-0711	siebertnet.com
Suretrade	401-642-6900	suretrade.com
Wall Street Access	800-925-5781	wsaccess.com
Wall Street Electronica	888-925-5783	wallstreete.com
TD Waterhouse Group	800-934-4410	waterhouse.com
A. B. Watley	888-229-2853	abwatley.com
Web Street Securities	800-932-8723	webstreet.com

larly on small accounts. Datek charges $25 to open a traditional IRA, $40 annually to keep it open and $60 to close it. A. B Watley charges a $30 annual fee on IRAs. Discover, Net Investor, A. B. Watley and Web Street each charge $50 to close an IRA, Scottrade charges $60, and National Discount Brokers and Wall Street Access charge $85. These fees add up.

BELLS AND WHISTLES. Although online brokers seem to have stopped lowering their prices, they have increased their services. For instance, real-time stock price quotes, as opposed to quotes that are delayed 20 minutes or more, can be very helpful when you're about to place a trade. Almost all online brokers offer free quotes these days.

Many brokers now offer year-end cost-basis information on mutual funds and stocks you sell, which makes doing your taxes a lot simpler. And most brokers now trade funds as well as stocks. Many onliners even make initial public offerings available to their customers, although you'll typically need an account worth $100,000 to $500,000 or be an extremely active trader to have a chance of getting one.

If from time to time you would rather use your telephone keypad or an automated voice-recognition system, most online brokers can accommodate you, although you'll probably pay a little more.

Opening Your Account

WHEN YOU HAVE SELECTED A BROKER, YOU'LL BE ASKED TO fill out a new-account information form. On that form you'll have to make some choices about the kind of account you want.

A single account is one in which you, and only you, can authorize purchases, sales and other transactions.

A joint account works in much the same way as a joint bank account and is often the choice for married couples because of its flexibility.

A cash account is the most sensible choice for new customers. It requires that all trades be settled on a cash basis, meaning that if you want to buy $1,000 worth of stock, you've got to deliver the $1,000 to the broker within a few days of the transaction.

A margin account permits you to trade "on margin," meaning with money that you borrow from the brokerage firm. The size of the loan depends on the current "margin requirement," which for some years has been 50%. That means that you can borrow up to 50% of the cost of the purchase. If the cash (nonmargined) portion of the securities you buy on margin dips below a certain level (usually about 30%), you will have to come up with the difference, either by sending the broker more cash or by selling enough of the underlying securities to get your cash position back over the minimum. Meanwhile, you pay interest at a rate of 1% to 3% over the prime rate. Only experienced investors should consider trading on margin.

A discretionary account is one in which you authorize a full-service broker to buy and sell securities without getting your permission first. For most investors, this is a bad idea.

STREET NAME OR YOUR NAME?

When you open your brokerage account, you'll also be asked whether you want the broker to hold your stock and bond certificates at the firm in "street name" or send them to you, in which case the certificates will be sent to you, and you'll be responsible for their safekeeping. If you leave them at the firm, no certificates will actually be issued in your name. Instead, the firm keeps track of each customer's claim on the shares through a book-entry system. When dividends are paid by the company, they are sent to the brokerage, which parcels them out according to its records of who owns what.

The main advantages of keeping your shares in street name are liquidity and safety. If you want to sell, all you have to do is call your broker and direct the sale of as many shares as you wish. That's it. If the broker goes broke, your shares are protected by the Securities Investor Protection Corp., as explained later in the chapter.

If you have shares issued in your name and keep them yourself, you have to get the certificates delivered to the broker within three days in order to complete any transaction. Nevertheless, you are entitled to take possession of your shares, and many investors choose to do so. If you do, tell the broker so when you open your account, and arrange to rent a safe-deposit box in which to store the certificates.

Records You Should Keep

THE PAPERWORK GENERATED BY A BROKERAGE ACCOUNT CAN swamp you if you don't keep it sorted. Hang on to all purchase and sales slips, monthly account "activity" statements and annual 1099 forms that summarize the year's activity for tax purposes. Annual and quarterly reports from companies whose shares you own can also be kept in these files.

Set up a master file for each brokerage account, plus separate file folders within it for each stock, bond, mutual fund or other

investment bought or sold through that firm. This system will
make transaction slips, income statements and other pertinent
documents easy to find when you need them. After you get your
yearly 1099, you can get rid of some interim reports, but hang
on to the year-end account summary statements. If by chance
your broker does not supply a year-end statement, hang onto
the monthly account statements. Keep records of capital gains,
dividend distributions and other payouts because you'll need
them for tax purposes long after the transactions are completed.

It's especially important to keep records that show the cost of
investments, such as transaction slips and canceled checks.
Without them you may not be able to document profits and losses. It's also important to keep records showing amounts and
dates of reinvested dividends, and amounts and dates of principal payments from unit trusts.

How to Deal With Your Broker

IN THE BEST OF ALL POSSIBLE WORLDS, YOU AND YOUR BROKER
work out a good investment plan—a nice mix of stocks and
bonds and such—and the plan works beautifully. Your broker keeps you posted on the progress of your holdings, and you
chat amiably from time to time about the general direction of
the market.

In the real world, if you own stocks, bonds, unit trusts,
mortgage-backed securities or anything else sold by a broker, the
person or the company that sold it to you will eventually be calling you or sending your information to interest you in buying
something else. The broker may or may not be doing you a
favor. Individual investors have been known to snooze through
opportunities to enhance their yield, take their profits or make
other moves in their own interests.

A good full-service broker will keep you informed about market developments that may affect your portfolio. But that does
not mean you have to approve every suggestion, or even respond
right away. Nothing is so urgent that a decision can't wait until
you have time to investigate the broker's recommendation.
Here's how to deal with unsolicited investment suggestions from
a broker you know and trust. (If you get a call from a stranger
you know nothing about, the question of what to do is simple:

Tell the caller thanks very much but you already have a broker and you're quite satisfied with the service you're getting.)

GIVE THE TOPIC YOUR FULL ATTENTION. If you're distracted, tell the broker to call you back or arrange to return the call. Don't be tempted to mutter "Okay" and authorize the transaction just so you can get back to what you were doing.

CONSIDER WHETHER THE SUGGESTION FITS INTO YOUR INVESTMENT PLAN. The broker may be proposing that you leave a dividend-paying blue-chip stock in favor of a stock with more growth potential but less yield and more risk. A phone call out of the blue is not the time to change your plans. A broker with your interests in mind will know better than to push you in a direction you've said you don't want to go, but may genuinely feel that this is a superior opportunity. If it does seems appropriate, is fairly presented and you bite, you have no one to blame but yourself if things turn sour later on.

GET MORE INFORMATION. Ask the broker to send you written research on the recommendation. With so many kinds of investments to handle, no broker can be expert on everything. Most rely on written analysis by others, either within the firm or independent of the firm. Ask the broker to share this research with you. If you don't understand it, let this one pass.

How Brokers Foul Up

MOST BROKERS MAKE AN HONEST EFFORT TO SERVE THEIR customers well. They don't "churn" customers' accounts by engaging in excessive trading just to generate commissions. They don't misrepresent the risks involved in the investments they recommend. They don't initiate transactions without the customer's authorization.

But all those things and worse do happen. If they happen to you, you have the right to strike back. If you feel you've been cheated, it's possible to battle your broker and win. The most common customers' complaints fall into these categories:

INAPPROPRIATE INVESTMENT RECOMMENDATIONS. A broker should know your financial situation and investment objectives, and recommend only investments that fit them. Your retirement nest egg, for instance, doesn't belong in commodity futures contracts.

MISREPRESENTATION OF RISK. This happens when a broker fails to inform you of the risks involved in an investment or misleads you about the nature of those risks.

CHURNING YOUR ACCOUNT. It's illegal for brokers to trade excessively in order to run up commissions. You're probably being churned if you find yourself paying 10% to 12% or more in stock commissions and the stocks in your portfolio are turning over several times a year at the broker's recommendation.

UNAUTHORIZED TRADING. Unless you sign a contract giving your broker discretionary authority over your account (which you shouldn't do), the broker can make no trades without your permission. If your broker makes an authorized trade, don't waste any time before complaining. In the past, brokers' attorneys have argued successfully that a customer's failure to complain right away constitutes evidence that the customer "ratified" the broker's action.

FAILURE TO EXECUTE. "Failure to obey" is how the industry describes a broker's failure to execute a trade you called in or a lengthy delay that caused you to miss an opportunity. Even if it's a mistake, you have grounds for a complaint.

What to Do If You're Wronged

If you suspect that something illegal or unethical is going on with your account, the first step is to notify the broker. There may be an explanation or a way to resolve the matter to your satisfaction right away.

If you don't get satisfaction, the next step is to complain to the broker's boss: the branch manager. Call and ask for an appointment and take along a written account of what happened. Take notes on what happens at that meeting.

The next level up is the firm's headquarters office. Address your complaint to the compliance director and send it by certified mail. Your success at this level will depend on how well you have documented your case. Determine ahead of time how much money it will take to make you whole again, and be prepared to discuss a reasonable offer of settlement from the firm.

If the brokerage firm's compliance director can't or won't settle the matter to your satisfaction, your choice may well be predetermined. The agreement you signed when you opened your account at the firm probably restricts your avenue of complaint to the arbitration process set up by the industry to resolve such disputes. You can't sue in court if your agreement bars it—a legal restriction that has been upheld by the Supreme Court. Nearly all brokerages include a mandatory arbitration clause in their customer contracts, whether you read it or not. Consumers have been complaining about this and the American Arbitration Association (AAA) has been listening (www.adr.org). The AAA is named in many contracts as the organization responsible for overseeing arbitration. It has adopted a 15-point "Consumer Due Process Protocol" and will no longer participate in arbitration programs that "substantially and materially" deviate from them. In contracts that meet the AAA standards, you must be given the following:

Clear and adequate notice of what you are signing, and a statement indicating whether arbitration is mandatory or optional under the contract.

The right to sue in small-claims court. When the dollar amount of a claim is within the small-claims-court jurisdiction, you retain the right to go to court.

For information and details on the 15 points, go to www.adr.org/press/consumr_protocol_release.html.

Despite problems, the deck isn't necessarily stacked against you. Thousands of small investors have turned to arbitrators to settle disputes with the giants of the financial world, and many have come away winners.

Most contracts require you to take your case before one of the industry's ten self-regulatory organizations, or SROs. They are sponsored by the New York Stock Exchange (NYSE), the American Stock Exchange, several regional exchanges, the

Chicago Board Options Exchange, the Municipal Securities Rulemaking Board and the National Association of Securities Dealers (NASD; www.nasdr.com). Most investors wind up in the arbitration programs set up by the NYSE or the NASD. A few are heard by representatives of the American Arbitration Association (AAA), which has the advantage of having no direct affiliation with the securities industry.

The rules governing these procedures are similar, although filing fees for AAA cases, starting at $500, are considerably higher than for SROs, which are subsidized by the industry and start as low as $15. Both hold hearings in most major cities, and both have streamlined procedures for small claims. To get information about the process, along with the forms you need to file a claim, write or call:

The National Association of Securities Dealers (1735 K Street, N.W., Washington, DC 20006-1500; 800-289-9999; www.nasdr.com)

The New York Stock Exchange (New York Stock Exchange, Inc., 11 Wall St., New York, NY 10005; 212-656-5608; www.nyse.com)

The American Stock Exchange (86 Trinity Place, 7th Floor, New York, NY 10006-1881; 212-306-1442; www.amex.com)

What are your prospects for success? Quite good, actually. Small investors who bring arbitration actions against brokers win, on average, more than half the time.

WHAT IF YOUR BROKER GOES BROKE?

What would happen if the brokerage firm where you do your business went out of business? Your account should be protected by the Securities Investor Protection Corp. (SIPC), a federally chartered but private, nonprofit corporation that levies assessments on its members to protect brokerage customers in the event a member becomes insolvent.

Be sure to check that your broker is a member. Broker-dealers who sell securities are required by law to be members of SIPC. Some SIPC members have affiliated or related companies or persons who conduct financial or investment businesses but are not members of SIPC themselves. You can check by calling or writing the SIPC Membership Department or checking its Web site at www.sipc.org. (Securities Investor Protection Corp., 805 15th Street, N.W., Suite 800, Washington, DC, 20005-2215; 202-371-8300; www.sipc.org).

SIPC provides insurance for securities accounts of up to $500,000 per customer, with a limit of $100,000 per customer on cash being held by the firm. Many brokerages purchase additional coverage, often up to a couple of million dollars. It's important to know that the SIPC coverage applies only in the case of financial insolvency. It doesn't cover market-related losses from ill-advised or ill-timed investment decisions; those are considered part of the game. Nor does the SIPC cover you in case of broker theft or fraud; you must turn to the courts for redress in such cases.

Because it takes a lot of time to sort through a brokerage firm's records to determine who owns what, which securities are in customers' names and which in street name, which were in the process of being bought and sold but were not yet settled on the day the doors closed, it may be weeks, even months, after a shutdown before the firm completes its business and gets the proper securities distributed to the proper customers. In the meantime, the markets keep moving up and down but customers' assets are frozen. If the delay costs you money because the market moves against you, you're out of luck. SIPC protection is better than none, but it isn't perfect.

Useful Numbers for Every Investor

NVESTING IS A QUEST TO MAKE DOLLARS GROW, AND AN important tool for achieving such a goal is the ability to anticipate what will happen to those dollars as the years go by, given different assumptions about how much you can invest and on what schedule. On the pages that follow, you'll find a collection of tables and formulas you can use to do just that.

How Regular Investments Will Grow

THE TABLE ON PAGE 336 SHOWS HOW A SPECIFIC AMOUNT OF money invested on a monthly schedule at various rates of return will grow as the years pass. The table uses $10 as the sum because multiples of $10 convert easily to actual amounts you might put aside. For instance, say you can invest $150 a month. How much would you have after ten years if your investment earned an average annual return of 12%? The intersection of 10 years and 12% on the table shows that $10 would grow to $2,323. You'll be investing 15 times $10, so you multiply the result by 15. Answer: You'd have $34,845.

The table can also be used to determine how much you will need to invest in order to have a specific amount on hand at some future date. For example, suppose you want to accumulate $50,000 by the time your daughter starts college in 15 years. Assuming you could earn 14% on your investments, how much should you be socking into your investment account? Find the place in the table where 15 years intersects with 14%. Divide that

How $10 a Month Will Grow

ANNUAL RATES OF RETURN

YEAR	5%	6%	7%	8%	9%	10%	11%	12%	13%	14%	15%
				Amount Accumulated at End of Period							
1	$123	$124	$125	$125	$126	$127	$127	$128	$129	$130	$130
2	253	256	258	261	264	267	270	272	275	278	281
3	389	395	402	408	415	421	428	435	442	449	457
4	532	544	555	567	580	592	605	618	632	646	660
5	683	701	720	740	760	781	802	825	848	872	897
6	841	868	897	926	957	989	1,023	1,058	1,094	1,132	1,171
7	1,008	1,046	1,086	1,129	1,173	1,220	1,268	1,320	1,374	1,430	1,490
8	1,182	1,234	1,289	1,348	1,409	1,474	1,543	1,615	1,692	1,773	1,859
9	1,366	1,435	1,507	1,585	1,667	1,755	1,849	1,948	2,054	2,168	2,288
10	1,559	1,647	1,741	1,842	1,950	2,066	2,190	2,323	2,467	2,621	2,787
15	2,684	2,923	3,188	3,483	3,812	4,179	4,589	5,046	5,557	6,129	6,769
20	4,128	4,644	5,240	5,929	6,729	7,657	8,736	9,991	11,455	13,163	15,160
25	5,980	6,965	8,148	9,574	11,295	13,379	15,906	18,976	22,714	27,273	32,841
30	8,357	10,095	12,271	15,003	18,445	22,793	28,302	35,299	44,206	55,571	70,098

number—$6,129—into your goal of $50,000. That tells you that your goal is 8.16 times the total generated by $10 monthly deposits, meaning you'll have to set aside $81.60 each month to reach your goal on time, assuming a 14% return.

How Compounding Affects Your Return

WHEN YOU'RE SHOPPING AROUND FOR A CERTIFICATE OF DEPOSIT or a similar savings instrument, comparing "nominal" (stated) rates of return is a waste of time. What you need to know is the real yield, usually called the effective yield, which takes into account the effects of compounding.

The difference between the nominal yield and the effective yield depends on the frequency of compounding, as shown in the table at right. For example, an 8% nominal interest rate produces an 8.45% effective yield if interest is compounded daily, but only 8.24% if interest is compounded quarterly. For an account containing $5,000 the difference amounts to only about $10 per year, but over a span of several years, it can have a substantial impact.

Warning: How often your compounded return is credited to

What's the Real Yield?

NOMINAL ANNUAL PERCENTAGE RATE	EFFECTIVE YIELD IF COMPOUNDED QUARTERLY	IF COMPOUNDED DAILY
5.00%	5.0945%	5.1997%
5.50	5.6145	5.7343
6.00	6.1364	6.2716
6.50	6.6602	6.8116
7.00	7.1859	7.3543
7.50	7.7136	7.8998
8.00	8.2432	8.4481
8.50	8.7748	8.9992
9.00	9.3083	9.5530
9.50	9.8438	10.1096
10.00	10.3813	10.6691
10.50	10.9207	11.2314
11.00	11.4621	11.7966
11.50	12.0055	12.3646
12.00	12.5509	12.9355

your account has an effect on your yield, too. For example, if the interest isn't credited to your daily-compounded account until the end of the quarter and you withdraw $1,000 five days before the quarter ends, you usually lose all of the interest earned on that amount up to that point. The ideal account is one that pays the highest rate, compounds interest daily (or "continuously," a formula that yields a little more) and credits interest daily.

How Much Money You'll Need

IN DETERMINING HOW MUCH YOU'LL HAVE TO ACCUMULATE FOR A goal such as retirement, you need to figure how long the money will last when you start drawing it down for living expenses or some other purpose. The table on the next page lets you do just that.

Your nest egg won't stop earning money when you start to deplete it, so the first step is to estimate how much you think it can earn. In retirement, you'll probably pull back a bit (but not completely) from the kinds of investments that can produce handsome returns over the long run but may be a bit risky for your current

How Much You'll Need to Get $100 a Month

YEAR	5%	6%	7%	8%	9%	10%	11%	12%	13%	14%	15%
				Amount Needed to Yield $100 a Month							
5	$5,299	$5,173	$5,050	$4,932	$4,817	$4,706	$4,559	$4,496	$4,395	$4,298	$4,203
10	9,428	9,007	8,613	8,242	7,894	7,567	7,260	6,970	6,697	6,441	6,198
15	12,646	11,850	11,125	10,464	9,860	9,306	8,798	8,332	7,904	7,509	7,145
20	15,153	13,958	12,898	11,955	11,114	10,362	9,688	9,082	8,536	8,042	7,594
25	17,106	15,521	14,149	12,956	11,916	11,005	10,203	9,495	8,867	8,307	7,807
30	18,628	16,679	15,030	13,628	12,428	11,395	10,501	9,722	9,040	8,440	7,909

ANNUAL RATES OF RETURN

circumstances. Thus, it's best to assume a more modest rate of return than you have reason to expect during the wealth-accumulation phase of your life. Here's how to use the table:

Find the number of years you plan to draw on your savings in the left-hand column and choose an estimated annual rate of return from the row across the top. The point at which the two figures intersect is the amount you'll need to draw $100 a month for the number of years selected. (At the end of the period, the $100 will be exhausted.) Divide your actual nest egg by the amount shown there, then multiply it by 100 to see how much you'll be able to draw per month before you deplete your savings.

For example, assume you've accumulated $200,000 and you plan to draw it down over a 25-year period. How much can you take out each month? Assume you can earn 9% on the money. Where the 25-year column intersects with the 9% column, you see $11,916. That would yield you $100 a month. Dividing $11,916 into $200,000 gives you a multiplier of 16.78. Because your fund is 16.78 times larger than $100, you can draw out $1,678 a month for 25 years before your nest egg is gone.

The same table can also be used to figure things the other way around: to calculate how much capital you'd need to yield $100 a month for various periods. For example, say you want to be able to have $1,000 a month for 20 years and you think that you can earn 9% on the money during the draw-down phase. The 9% and 20-year columns intersect at $11,114. That means you'd need ten times that amount, or $111,140, to draw $1,000 a month for 20 years.

What Your Money Will Be Worth in the Future

YEAR	5%	6%	7%	8%	9%	10%	11%	12%	13%	14%	15%
					ANNUAL RATES OF RETURN Future-Value Multiplier						
1	1.05	1.06	1.07	1.08	1.09	1.10	1.11	1.12	1.13	1.14	1.15
2	1.10	1.12	1.14	1.17	1.19	1.21	1.23	1.25	1.28	1.30	1.32
3	1.16	1.19	1.22	1.26	1.29	1.33	1.37	1.40	1.44	1.48	1.52
4	1.22	1.26	1.31	1.36	1.41	1.46	1.52	1.57	1.63	1.69	1.75
5	1.28	1.34	1.40	1.47	1.54	1.61	1.69	1.76	1.84	1.93	2.01
6	1.34	1.42	1.50	1.59	1.68	1.77	1.87	1.97	2.08	2.19	2.31
7	1.41	1.50	1.61	1.71	1.83	1.95	2.08	2.21	2.35	2.50	2.66
8	1.48	1.59	1.72	1.85	1.99	2.14	2.30	2.48	2.66	2.85	3.06
9	1.55	1.69	1.84	2.00	2.17	2.36	2.56	2.77	3.00	3.25	3.52
10	1.63	1.79	1.97	2.16	2.37	2.59	2.84	3.11	3.39	3.71	4.05
15	2.08	2.40	2.76	3.17	3.64	4.18	4.78	5.40	6.25	7.14	8.14
20	2.65	3.21	3.87	4.66	5.60	6.73	8.06	9.65	11.52	13.74	16.37
25	3.39	4.29	5.43	6.85	8.62	10.83	13.59	17.00	21.23	26.46	32.92
30	4.32	5.74	7.61	10.06	13.27	17.45	22.89	29.96	39.12	50.95	66.21

How a Lump Sum Will Grow

THE TABLE ABOVE IS USEFUL FOR ANTICIPATING HOW MONEY you've already accumulated will grow over various lengths of time at various rates of return, compounded annually. Simply read down the left-hand column to the number of years and across the top for the assumed rate of return, and multiply the starting amount by the factor that's shown at the intersection of the two columns. For example, say you have $4,000 in a mutual fund that you expect will pay 15% per year. How much will you have after ten years? Where the 15% and 10-year columns intersect, the factor is 4.05. Multiplying that by $4,000 gives you $16,200.

How to Account for Inflation

THE SAME KIND OF COMPOUNDING HAS A NEGATIVE EFFECT AS well. To see how inflation could erode your investment results, choose a number of years in the future from the left-hand column in the table at right, above, and follow that row

339

What You'll Get After Inflation

					RATE OF INFLATION						
YEAR	3%	4%	5%	6%	7%	8%	9%	10%	11%	12%	13%
					Future Value Multiplier						
5	1.16	1.22	1.28	1.34	1.40	1.47	1.54	1.61	1.69	1.76	1.84
10	1.34	1.48	1.63	1.79	1.97	2.16	2.37	2.59	2.84	3.11	3.39
15	1.56	1.80	2.08	2.40	2.76	3.17	3.64	4.18	4.78	5.47	6.25
20	1.81	2.19	2.65	3.21	3.87	4.66	5.60	6.73	8.06	9.65	11.52
25	2.09	2.67	3.39	4.29	5.43	6.85	8.62	10.82	13.59	17.00	21.23
30	2.43	3.24	4.32	5.74	7.61	10.06	13.27	17.45	22.89	29.96	39.12

across to where it intersects with a rate of inflation listed across the top. Multiply your anticipated nest egg by the number to see how much you'll need to have the equivalent amount in the future. For instance, assuming 4% inflation (a reasonable assumption for the next decade or so), a $10,000 nest egg today would have to be $14,800 to have the equivalent purchasing power ten years from today.

How to Compare Tax-Free vs. Taxable Yields

MUNICIPAL BONDS AND OTHER INVESTMENTS THAT PAY TAX-free interest make sense for you only if their yields top what you could earn in after-tax interest from taxable investments. The table on the following page shows the taxable-equivalent yields of tax-exempt investments for various brackets. (The income levels that fall into each bracket are those in effect for 1999. Because they are indexed to inflation, the levels will rise a little each year.)

Here's how to use the table. Say you're in the 28% bracket and are considering investing in a municipal bond paying 6% interest. Find the column where your tax bracket and the tax-free yield intersect. It shows a taxable-equivalent yield of 8.33%. If you can find a taxable yield higher than that, then you're better off taking it and paying the taxes. Remember that if you also escape state income taxes, your taxable-equivalent yield would be higher.

If the tax-free yield falls in between the numbers on the table, you can get a pretty good idea of the taxable equivalent by esti-

Tax Free vs. Taxable Yields

1999 TAXABLE INCOME	TAX BRACKET	4%	5%	6%	TAX-FREE YIELD 7%	8%	9%	10%
SINGLE RETURN					Taxable-Equivalent Yield			
Up to $25,750	15%	4.71%	5.88%	7.06%	8.24%	9.41%	10.59%	11.76%
$25,751–$62,450	28	5.56	6.94	8.33	9.72	11.11	12.50	13.89
$62,451–$130,250	31	5.80	7.25	8.70	10.14	11.59	13.04	14.49
$130,251–$283,150	36	6.25	7.81	9.38	10.94	12.50	14.06	15.63
More than $283,150	39.6	6.62	8.28	9.93	11.59	13.25	14.90	16.56
JOINT RETURN								
Up to $43,050	15%	4.71	5.88	7.06	8.24	9.41	10.59	11.76
$43,051–$104,050	28	5.56	6.94	8.33	9.72	11.11	12.50	13.89
$104,051–$158,550	31	5.80	7.25	8.70	10.14	11.59	13.04	14.49
$158,551–$283,150	36	6.25	7.81	9.38	10.94	12.50	14.06	15.63
More than $283,150	39.6	6.62	8.28	9.93	11.59	13.25	14.90	16.56

mating. For instance, 6.5% falls halfway between 6% and 7%, so in the 28% bracket, the taxable equivalent would be halfway between 8.33% and 9.72%, or about 9.03%.

If you prefer a more precise answer, use the formula from Chapter 5:

$$\frac{\text{tax-free rate}}{1 - \text{federal tax bracket}} = \text{taxable-equivalent yield}$$

How to Figure Bond Yields

ENOUGH BOND-YIELD TABLES HAVE BEEN PUBLISHED OVER THE years to fill your living room, each volume the size of an unabridged dictionary. But in the age of handheld calculators, it's probably faster to apply the simple formulas for figuring yields yourself than to heft one of those weighty tomes.

To calculate the current yield of a bond, divide the annual interest payment of the bond by its purchase price and multiply the result by 100.

$$\text{Current yield} = \frac{\text{Annual interest payment}}{\text{Purchase price}} \times 100$$

Example: Say you pay $900 for a $1,000 bond issued to pay 5%. What's your current yield?

$$\text{Current yield} = \frac{50}{900} = .0556 \times 100 = 5.56\%$$

The yield to maturity, which takes into account the fact that you'll receive the full face value of a discounted bond at maturity even though you paid less than full value at purchase, is more complicated:

$$\text{Yield to maturity} = \frac{\text{Annual interest payment} + \text{annualized discount}}{\text{Average of face value and current price}} \times 100$$

That shorthand formula produces only an approximate answer, but when you're comparing alternatives, this will lead you in the right direction (see Chapter 5).

Example: You buy a $1,000 bond with six years to go until maturity. Its stated interest rate is 5% and it costs you $880. Thus, your discount is $120, or $20 per year on an annualized basis.

$$\text{Yield to maturity} = \frac{50 + 20}{\frac{1,000 + 880}{2}} = \frac{70}{940} \times 100 = 7.45\%$$

How to Keep Some Perspective

IN ADDITION TO PATIENCE, AN INVESTOR NEEDS PERSPECTIVE. Here are some important indicators of where the market has been and where it might be going.

Market Indicators

	HISTORIC HIGH	HISTORIC LOW
One-year total return of S&P 500	37.6% (1995)	−26.4% (1974)
Price-earnings ratio of S&P 500	32.2 (1998)	3.6 (1946)
Average yield, long-term (Moody's AAA) corporate bonds	14.2 (1981)	2.8 (1950)
Average yield, municipal bonds	11.6 (1982)	1.3 (1946)
Yield of U.S. savings bonds	11.1 (1983)	2.9 (1941)
Dividend yield, S&P 500	11.2 (1931)	1.2 (1999)

Investment Terms You Should Know

Account executive. The title given by some brokerage firms to their stockbrokers. Other variations on the title include **registered representative,** financial counselor and financial consultant.

Accrued interest. Interest that is due but hasn't yet been paid. It most often comes into play when you buy bonds in the secondary market. Bonds usually pay interest every six months, but it is earned (accrued) by bondholders every month. If you buy a bond halfway between interest payment dates, you must pay the seller for the three months' interest accrued but not yet received. You get the money back three months later when you receive the interest payment for the entire six-month period.

Alpha. A mathematical measure of price volatility that attempts to isolate the price movements of a stock from those of the market. A stock with a high alpha is expected to perform well regardless of what happens to the market as a whole. (See also **beta.**)

American depositary receipt. Certificates traded on U.S. stock exchanges or over the counter, representing ownership of a specific number of shares of a foreign stock.

Annuity. A series of regular payments, usually from an insurance company, guaranteed to continue for a specific time, usually the annuitant's lifetime, in exchange for a single payment or a series of payments to the company. With a deferred annuity, payments begin sometime in the future. With an immediate annuity, payments begin right away. A fixed annuity pays a fixed income stream for the life of the contract. With a variable annuity, the payments may change according to the relative investment success of the insurance company.

Arbitrage. An attempt to profit from momentary price differences that can develop when a security or commodity is traded on two different exchanges. To take advantage of such differences, an arbitrageur would buy in the market where the price is lower and simultaneously sell in the market where the price is higher.

At-the-market. When you buy or sell a security at-the-market, the broker will execute your trade at the next available price.

Back-end load. A fee charged by mutual funds to investors who sell their shares before owning them for a specified time.

Back office. The support operations of a brokerage firm that don't deal directly with customers. "Back office problems" usually refers to slow paperwork or other bottlenecks in the execution of customers' orders.

Bearer bond. Also called a coupon bond, it is not registered in anyone's name. Rather, whoever holds the bond (the "bearer") is entitled to collect interest payments merely by cutting off and mailing in the attached coupons at the proper time. Bearer bonds are no longer being issued.

Bearish. A bear thinks the market is going to go down. This makes bearish the opposite of **bullish.**

Beta. A measure of price volatility that relates the stock or mutual fund to the market as a whole. A stock or fund with a beta higher than 1 is expected to move up or down more than the market. A beta below 1 indicates a stock or fund that usually jumps up and down less than the market.

Bid/asked. Bid is the price a buyer is willing to pay; asked is the price the seller will take. The difference, known as the **spread,** is the broker's share of the transaction.

Blue chips. There is no set definition of a blue-chip stock, but most would agree it has at least three characteristics: It is issued by a well-known, respected company; has a good record of earnings and dividend payments; and is widely held by investors.

Boiler room. A blanket term used to describe the place of origin of high-pressure telephone sales techniques, usually involving **cold calls** to unsuspecting customers who would be better off without whatever is being offered to them.

Bond. An interest-bearing security that obligates the issuer to pay a specified amount of interest for a specified time, usually several years, and then repay the bondholder the face amount of the bond. Bonds issued by corporations are backed by corporate assets; in case of default, the bondholders have a legal claim on those assets. Bonds issued by government agencies may or may not be collateralized. Interest from corporate bonds is taxable; interest from municipal bonds, which are issued by state and local governments, is free of federal income taxes and, usually, income taxes of the issuing jurisdiction. Interest from Treasury bonds, issued by the federal government, is free of state and local income taxes but subject to federal taxes.

Bond rating. A judgment about the ability of the bond issuer to fulfill its obligation to pay interest and repay the principal when due. The best-known bond-rating companies are Standard & Poor's and Moody's. Their rating systems, although slightly different, both use a letter-grade system, with AAA the highest rating and C or D the lowest.

Book value. For investing purposes, this is the net asset value of a company, determined by subtracting its liabilities from its assets. Dividing the result by the number of shares of common stock issued by the company yields the book value per share, which can be used as a relative gauge of the stock's value.

Brokered CD. A large-denomination certificate of deposit sold by a bank to a brokerage, which slices it up into smaller pieces and sells the pieces to its customers.

Bullish. A bull is someone who thinks the market is going to go up, which makes bullish the opposite of **bearish.**

Call. See **options.**

Capital gain or loss. The difference between the price at which you buy an investment and the price at which you sell it. Adding the capital gain or loss to the income received from the investment yields the **total return.**

Certificate of deposit. Usually called a CD, a certificate of deposit is a short- to medium-term instrument (one month to five years) that is issued by a bank or savings and loan association to pay interest at a rate higher than that paid by a passbook account. CD rates move up and down with general market interest rates. There is usually a penalty for early withdrawal.

Charting. Another name for **technical analysis.**

Churning. Excessive buying and selling in a customer's account undertaken to generate commissions for the broker.

Closed-end investment company. Also called a closed-end fund, it is a pooled investment fund that issues a set number of shares and then no more. When the initial offering of shares is sold out, the closed-end fund trades on the secondary market at a price determined by investor supply and demand. For contrast, see the definition of **mutual fund.**

Cold calling. The practice of brokers making unsolicited calls to people they don't know in an attempt to drum up business.

Commercial paper. Short-term IOUs issued by corporations without collateral. They are bought in large quantities by money-market funds.

Common stock. A share of ownership in a corporation, which entitles its owner to all the risks and rewards that go with it. In case of bankruptcy, common stockholders' claims on company assets are inferior to those of bondholders. For contrast, see **preferred stock.**

Contrarian. An investor who thinks and acts in opposition to the conventional wisdom. When the majority of investors are bearish, a contrarian is bullish, and vice versa.

Convertible bond. A bond that is exchangeable for a predetermined number of shares of common stock in the same company. The appeal of a convertible is that it gives you a chance to cash in if the stock price of the company soars. Some preferred stock is also convertible to **common stock.**

Coupon rate. A way of expressing a bond **yield,** a coupon rate is the fixed annual interest payment expressed as a percentage of the face value of the bond. A 9% coupon bond, for instance, pays $90 interest a year on each $1,000 of face value. The payment is set when the bond is issued and doesn't change as the bond's price fluctuates.

Covered call. See Option.

Day trading. Buying and selling stocks by computer, typically in 1,000-share lots using real-time (or nearly real-time) market information. A single buy-sell transaction often takes just minutes. Click to buy a stock at $26, click again to sell at $26.50, and you've made $500, not counting brokerage and other fees. (Of course, if the price goes the other way, you lose money just as quickly.) Day traders rarely hold a position overnight.

Debenture. A corporate IOU that is not backed by the company's assets and is therefore somewhat riskier than a **bond.**

Derivative. Financial instrument whose value depends on changes in the value of some other security. Derivatives range from the tried and true, such as puts and calls and other options, to the exotic, or structured derivatives, which may be called inverse floaters, interest-only or principal-only securities. Structured derivatives are generally blamed for the carnage in some financial markets that took place in 1994 and 1995 and led to the bankruptcy of Orange County, Cal., for example.

Discount broker. A cut-rate firm that executes orders but provides little if anything in the way of research or other investment aids.

Discretionary account. A brokerage account in which the customer has given the broker the authority to buy and sell securities at his or her discretion—that is, without checking with the customer first.

Dividend. A share of company earnings paid out to stockholders. Dividends are declared by the board of directors and paid quarterly. Most are paid as cash, but they are sometimes paid in the form of additional shares of stock.

Dividend reinvestment plan. Also called a DRIP, this is a program under which the company automatically reinvests a shareholder's cash dividends in additional shares of common stock, often with no brokerage charge to the shareholder.

Dollar-cost averaging. A program of investing a set amount on a regular schedule regardless of the price of the shares at the time. In the long run, dollar-cost averaging results in your buying more shares at low prices than you do at high prices.

Dow Theory. A belief that a major trend in the stock market isn't signaled by one index alone but must be confirmed by two—specifically, a new high or low must be recorded by both the Dow Jones industrial average and the Dow Jones transportation average before it can safely be declared that the market is headed in one direction or the other.

Due diligence. The work performed by a broker or other representative in order to investigate and understand an investment thoroughly before recommending it to a customer.

Duration. When applied to bond mutual funds, duration is a measure of the sensitivity of the fund's portfolio to a change of one percentage point in interest rates. The portfolio of a bond fund with a duration of six years, for example, can be expected to lose 6% of its value if the interest rates on similar bonds rise by one percentage point. By the same token, the fund should gain 6% in value if rates on similar bonds decline by one point.

Earnings per share. A company's profits after taxes, bond interest and preferred-stock payments have been subtracted, divided by the number of shares of common stock outstanding.

Ex-dividend. The period between the declaration of a dividend by a company or a mutual fund and the actual payment of the dividend. On the ex-dividend date, the price of the fund will fall by the amount of the dividend; as a result, new investors don't get the benefit of it. Companies and funds that have "gone ex-dividend" are usually marked by an X in the newspaper listings.

Fannie Mae. Formerly known as the Federal National Mortgage Association, which buys mortgages on the **secondary market,** repackages them and sells off pieces to investors. The effect is to infuse the mortgage markets with fresh money.

Fixed-income investment. A catch-all description for investments in **bonds, certificates of deposit** and other debt-based instruments that pay a fixed amount of interest.

401(k) plan. An employer-sponsored retirement plan that permits employees to divert part of their pay into the plan and avoid current taxes on that income. Money directed to the plan may be partially matched by the employer, and investment earnings within the plan accumulate tax-free until they are withdrawn. The 401(k) is named for the section of the federal tax code that authorizes it.

403(b) plan. Similar to 401(k) plans, but set up for public employees and employees of nonprofit organizations.

Freddie Mac. Formerly known as the Federal Home Loan Mortgage Corporation; it operates much as Fannie Mae does.

Front-end load. The sales commission charged at the time of purchase of a **mutual fund,** insurance policy or other product.

Full-service broker. A brokerage firm that maintains a research department and other services designed to supply its individual and institutional customers with investment advice.

Fundamental analysis. Study of the balance sheet, earnings history, management, product lines and other elements of a company in an attempt to discern reasonable expectations for the price of its stock. For contrast, see **technical analysis.**

Futures contract. An agreement to buy or sell a certain amount of a commodity (such as wheat, soybeans or gold) or a financial instrument (such as Treasury bills or deutsche marks) at a stipulated price in a specified future month. As the actual price moves closer to or further away from the contract price, the price of the contract fluctuates up and down, thus creating profits and losses for its holders, who may never actually take or make delivery of the underlying commodity.

Ginnie Mae. The nickname for the Government National Mortgage Association, which buys up mortgages in the **secondary market** and sells them to investors via securities known as pass-through certificates.

Good-till-canceled order. An order to buy or sell a security at a specified price, which stays in effect until it is executed by the broker because that price was reached, or until it is canceled by the customer.

Individual retirement account (IRA). The regular IRA is a tax-favored account designed to encourage retirement saving. If your income is below a certain level or you're not covered by a retirement plan at work, IRA deposits can be deducted. The maximum annual contribution is $2,000. Tax on earnings is postponed until you withdraw funds. In most cases there is a penalty for withdrawing funds before you're 59½. (See also **Roth IRA.**)

Initial public offering. A corporation's first public offering of an issue of stock. Also called an IPO.

Institutional investors. Mutual funds, banks, insurance companies, pension plans and others that buy and sell stocks and bonds in large volumes. Institutional investors account for 70% or more of market volume on an average day.

Junk bond. A high-risk, high-yield bond rated BB or lower by Standard & Poor's, or Ba or lower by Moody's. Junk bonds are issued by relatively unknown or financially weak companies, or they have only limited backing from reasonably solvent companies.

Keogh plan. A tax-sheltered retirement plan into which self-employed individuals can deposit up to 20% of earnings and deduct the contributions from current income. Investments within the Keogh grow untaxed until they are withdrawn. Withdrawals from the plan are restricted before age 59½.

Leveraging. Investing with borrowed money in the hope of multiplying gains. If you buy $100,000 worth of stock and its price rises to $110,000, you've earned 10% on your investment. But if you leveraged the deal by putting up only $50,000 of your own money and borrowing the rest, the same $10,000 increase would represent a 20% return on your money, not counting interest on the loan. The flip side of leverage is that it also multiplies losses. If the price of the stock goes down by $5,000 on the all-cash deal, your loss would be 5% of your $100,000 investment. On the leveraged deal, your loss would be 10% of the money you put up, and you'd still have to pay back the $50,000 you borrowed.

Leveraged buyout. The use of borrowed money to finance the purchase of a firm. Often, an LBO is financed by raising money through the issuance and sale of **junk bonds.**

Limited partnership. A business arrangement put together and managed by a general partner (which may be a company or an individual) and financed by the investments of limited partners, so called because their liability is limited to the amount of money they invest in the venture. Limited partnerships can invest in virtually anything, but real estate is the most common choice. They have often been characterized by high fees for the general partners, complicated tax-reporting requirements and elusive payouts for the limited partners.

Limit order. An order to buy or sell a security if it reaches a specified price. A **stop-loss order** is a common variation.

Liquidity. The ability to quickly convert an investment portfolio to cash without suffering a noticeable loss in value. Stocks and bonds of widely traded companies are considered highly liquid. Real estate and **limited partnerships** are illiquid.

Load. See **back-end load** and **front-end load.**

Margin buying. The act of financing the purchase of securities partly with money borrowed from the brokerage firm. Regulations permit buying up to 50% "on margin," meaning an investor can borrow up to half the purchase price of an investment. See **leveraging.**

Margin buying. The act of financing the purchase of securities partly with money borrowed from the brokerage firm. Regulations permit buying up to 50% "on margin," meaning an investor can borrow up to half the purchase price of an investment. See **leveraging.**

Market order. An order to buy or sell a stock at the price available when the order is executed. This differs from a **limit order,** which sets a maximum buy or sell price.

Mutual fund. A professionally managed portfolio of stocks and bonds or other investments divided up into shares. Minimum purchase is often $500 or less, and mutual funds stand ready to buy back their shares at any time. The market price of the fund's shares, called the net asset value, fluctuates daily with the market price of the securities in its portfolio.

Nasdaq. Pronounced Naz-dak, it started out as the acronym for the National Association of Securities Dealers Automated Quotations

System, a computerized price-reporting system used by brokers to track over-the-counter securities as well as some exchange-listed issues.

Odd lot. A stock trade involving fewer than 100 shares. For contrast, see **round lot.**

Opportunity cost. The cost of passing up one investment in favor of another. For instance, if you pull money out of a money-market fund, where it is earning 5% interest, to invest it in a stock that has promise but yields just 3%, your opportunity cost while you're waiting is 2%.

Option. The right to buy or sell a security at a given price within a given time. The right to buy the security is referred to as a call. Calls are bought by investors who expect the price of the stock to rise. The right to sell a stock is called a put. Puts are purchased by investors who expect the price of the stock to fall. Investors use puts and calls to bet on the direction of price movements without actually having to buy or sell the stock. One option represents 100 shares and sells for a fraction of the price of the shares themselves. As the time approaches for the option to expire, its price will move up or down depending on the movement of the stock price. Options can also be used to wring a little income out of stock you own without selling it. By writing (selling) a "covered call," you collect the premium and, assuming the stock price stays under the call price, get to keep the stock. The risk, of course, is that the stock will get called away and you will miss out on the price rise.

Over the counter. The place where stocks and bonds that aren't listed on any exchange (such as the New York or American stock exchange) are bought and sold. Despite the small-stock, small-town image conjured up by its name, in reality the over-the-counter market (OTC) is a high-speed computerized network called **Nasdaq,** which is run by the National Association of Securities Dealers.

Par. The face value of a stock or bond. Also called par value.

Penny stock. Generally thought of as a recently issued stock selling for less than $5 a share and traded over the counter. Penny stocks are usually issued by small, relatively unknown companies and lightly traded, making them more prone to price manipulation than larger, better-established issues. They are, in short, a gamble.

Pink sheets. Pink sheets of paper listing the prices for **over-the-counter** stocks that aren't traded on **Nasdaq.** Some stocks appear only on pink sheets because they sell for pennies a share and don't meet any exchange's minimum price and asset requirements. Others have too few shares to be listed on an exchange. Some companies don't want to file the SEC documents or pay the exchange's fees and thus are content to be "pink sheeted."

Preferred stock. A class of stock that pays a specified dividend set when it is issued. Preferreds generally pay less income than bonds of the same company and don't have the price appreciation potential of common stock. They appeal mainly to corporations, which get a tax break on their dividend income.

Price-earnings ratio. Usually called the P/E, it is the price of a stock divided by either its latest annual earnings per share (a "trailing" P/E) or its predicted earnings (an "anticipated" P/E). Either way, the P/E is considered an important indicator of investor sentiment about a stock because it indicates how much investors are willing to pay for a dollar of earnings.

Price-sales ratio. The PSR is the stock's price divided by its company's latest annual sales per share. It is favored by some investors as a measure of a stock's relative value. The lower the PSR, according to this school of thought, the better the value.

Program trading. A complex computerized system designed to take advantage of temporary differences between the actual value of the stocks composing a popular index and the value represented by **futures contracts** on those stocks. To simplify, if the stocks' prices are higher than the futures contracts reflect, computer programs issue orders to sell stocks and buy futures contracts. If the stocks are lower than the futures contracts reflect, program traders buy stocks and sell the futures. The result is virtually risk-free profits for the program traders and more volatility for the market because of the vast numbers of shares needed to make the system work.

Prospectus. The document that describes a securities offering or the operations of a **mutual fund,** a **limited partnership** or other investment. The prospectus divulges financial data about the company, background of its officers and other information needed by investors to make an informed decision.

Proxy. The formal authorization by a stockholder that permits someone else (usually company management) to vote in his or her place at shareholder meetings or on matters put to the shareholders for a vote at other times.

Put. See options.

Real Estate Investment Trust (REIT). A **closed-end investment company** that buys real estate properties or mortgages and passes virtually all the profits on to its shareholders.

Registered representative. The formal name for a stockbroker, so called because he or she must be registered with the National Association of Securities Dealers as qualified to handle securities trades.

Return on equity. An important measure of investment results that is obtained by dividing the total value of shareholders' equity—that is, the market value of **common and preferred stock**—into the company's net income after taxes.

Roth IRA. First available in 1998, this is also known as a back-loaded IRA. Contributions are not deductible, but withdrawals can be completely tax-free in retirement.

Round lot. A hundred shares of stock, the preferred number for buying and selling and the most economical unit when commissions are calculated, except for online purchases.

Sallie Mae. Nickname for the Student Loan Marketing Association, which buys student loans from colleges, universities and other lenders and packages them into units to be sold to investors. Sallie Mae thus infuses the student-loan market with new money in much the same way that Ginnie Mae infuses the mortgage market with new money.

Secondary market. The general name given to stock exchanges, the **over-the-counter market** and other marketplaces in which stocks, bonds, mortgages and other investments are sold after they have been issued and sold initially. Original issues are sold in the primary market; subsequent sales take place in the secondary market. For example, the primary market for a new issue of stock is the team of underwriters; the secondary market is one of the stock exchanges or the over-the-counter market. The primary market for a mortgage is the lender, which may then sell it to Fannie Mae or Freddie Mac in the secondary mortgage market.

Short selling. A technique used to take advantage of an anticipated decline in the price of a stock or other security by reversing the usual order of buying and selling. In a short sale, the investor (1) borrows stock from the broker and (2) immediately sells it. Then, if the investor guessed right and the price of the stock does indeed decline, he can replace the borrowed shares by (3) buying them at the cheaper price. The profit is the difference between the price at which he sells the shares and the price at which he buys them later on. Of course, if the price of the shares rises, the investor will suffer a loss.

Sinking fund. Financial reserves set aside to be used exclusively to redeem a bond or **preferred-stock issue** and thus reassure investors that the company will be able to meet that obligation.

Specialist. A member of the stock exchange who serves as a market maker for a number of different stock issues. A specialist maintains an inventory of certain stocks and buys and sells shares as necessary to maintain an orderly market for those stocks.

Spread. The difference between the bid and asked prices of a security, which may also be called the broker's markup. In options and futures trading, a spread is the practice of simultaneously buying a contract for the delivery of a commodity in one month and selling a contract for delivery of the same commodity in another month. The aim is to offset possible losses in one contract with possible gains in the other.

Stop-loss order. Instructions to a broker to sell a particular stock if its price ever dips to a specified level.

Street name. The description given to securities held in the name of a brokerage firm but belonging to the firm's customers. Holding stocks in street name facilitates trading because there is no need for the customer to pick up or deliver the certificates.

Technical analysis. An approach to market analysis that attempts to forecast price movements by examining and charting the patterns formed by past movements in prices, trading volume, the ratio of advancing to declining stocks and other statistics. For contrast, see **fundamental analysis.**

Tender offer. An offer to shareholders to buy their shares of stock in a company. Tender offers are usually a key element of a strategy to take over, or buy out, a company and thus are usually made at a higher-than-market price to encourage shareholders to accept them.

10-K. A detailed financial report that must be filed by a firm each year with the Securities and Exchange Commission. It is much more detailed than a typical annual report that is published and sent to shareholders.

Total return. A measure of investment performance that starts with price changes, then adds in the results of reinvesting all earnings, such as interest or dividends, generated by the investment during the period being measured.

Triple witching hour. A phrase made popular by **program trading,** it is the last hour of stock market trading on the third Friday of March, June, September and December. That's when **options** and **futures** contracts expire on market indexes used by program traders to hedge their positions in stocks. The simultaneous expirations often set off heavy buying and selling of options, futures and the underlying stocks themselves, thus creating the "triple" witching hour.

12b-1 fees. An extra fee charged by some **mutual funds** to cover the costs of promotion and marketing. In practice, 12b-1 fees are often used to compensate brokers for selling low-load and no-load funds. The effect of the fee is reflected in the performance figures reported by the funds.

Yield. In general, the return earned by an investment. In discussing bonds, yield can be any of several kinds. "Coupon yield" is the interest rate paid on the face value of the bond, which is usually $1,000. "Current yield" is the interest rate based on the actual purchase price of the bond, which may be higher or lower than the face amount. "Yield to maturity" is the rate that takes into account the current yield and the difference between the purchase price and the face value, with the difference assumed to be paid in equal installments over the remaining life of the bond.

Zero-coupon bond. A bond that pays all its interest at maturity but none prior to maturity. These "zeros" sell at a deep discount to face value and are especially suitable for long-term investment goals with a definite time horizon, such as college tuition or retirement.

Index

H

Hammer, Armand, 60
Harbor mutual funds
   Bond, 253
Hearst, William Randolph, 202
Hewlett-Packard, 156
HH bonds. *See* U.S. savings
   bonds
Hirsch, Yale, 77
Hitachi, 154
H.J. Heinz Co., 156
Home equity loans, 244
Homestake, 195
Honda, 154
Hope scholarship credit,
   256-258
H&R Block, 69
Hybrid funds, 209

I

Ibbotson Associates, 49
IBM, 5, 156
Illinois Tool Works, 156
Income stocks, 53
Individual retirement accounts,
   259, 263
   age and, 269
   choosing between a Roth
IRA and a traditional IRA,
   268, 276-278
   closing out an IRA, 275
   college investment
      option, 274
   combining rollover
      accounts, 238
   converting to a Roth
      IRA, 278-279, 281
   deadlines for, 271-272
   direct transfer, 281-282
   early-withdrawal penal-
      ties, 272-274, 282
   education IRAs, 257-258
   effect of death on,
      276-277
   five-year rule, 273
   income tax when you
      retire, 277-278
   income test for a tradi-
      tional IRA, 269-270
   income test for Roth
      IRAs, 270-271

minimum withdrawal
   schedule, 275
moving your IRA money,
   280-282
mutual funds in, 120
profit-sharing money
   and, 268
required compensation,
   268-269
rollover, 282
Roth IRAs, 258, 268-269,
   273-276
self-directed accounts,
   281
spousal accounts, 269
surviving spouse, 276
tax issues, 257, 267,
   269-272, 275-280
using for retirement,
   274-276
withdrawals to pay
   college bills, 258
zero-coupon bonds and,
   113
Inflation factors, 9, 193-194
The Institute of Certified
   Financial Planners, 307
The Insurance News Network
   Web site, 289
Integrated Resources Inc., 100
Intel, 156
Interest rates
   bonds and, 187
   controlling risk for CDs,
      43
   moderation, 10
   mortgage-backed securi-
      ties and, 187
   spikes in, 40-41
   U.S. savings bonds, 246
Internal Revenue Service. *See*
   Tax issues
The International Association
   for Financial Planning,
   307
International Board of
   Standards and Practices
   for Certified Financial
   Planners, 307
Internet
   See also Online brokers;
      Online sources

auctioning of collectibles,
   200
buying U.S. Treasury
   securities, 103
cybersmears, 215
"spam," 215
stock scams, 215
Inverse floaters, 190
Invesco mutual funds
   European, 155
Investing in foreign markets
   closed-end funds, 152-153
   cross-border commerce,
      154
   the euro, 154-155
   foreign tax credit,
      236-237
   reasons, 149
   risks, 150-151
   single-country funds, 152
   via American depository
      receipts, 153-154
   via mutual funds, 151-152
   via U.S.-based companies,
      155-156
Investment clubs
   description, 309
   for do-it-yourselfers,
      312-313
   forming, 309-310
   joining, 311
   joining the NAIC as an
      individual, 311
   online clubs, 311
   operating, 310-311
   resources, 312-313
   starting one yourself, 311
Investment Company Institute,
   117, 124
Investment newsletters
   resources, 314-315
   value of, 314
Investment ups and downs
   (table), 27
Investors National, 326
IRAs. *See* Individual retirement accounts
IRS. *See* Tax issues

J

Janus mutual funds, 129